THAT SECOND BOTTLE

MANCHESTER
UNIVERSITY PRESS

1 Woodcut from *The Works of John Earl of Rochester* . . . 1714

THAT SECOND BOTTLE
Essays on John Wilmot, Earl of Rochester

EDITED BY

NICHOLAS FISHER

MANCHESTER
UNIVERSITY PRESS
Manchester and New York

distributed exclusively in the USA by St. Martin's Press

Copyright © Manchester University Press 2000

While copyright in the volume as a whole is vested in Manchester University Press,
copyright in individual chapters belongs to their respective authors, and no chapter
may be reproduced wholly or in part without the express permission in writing of both
author and publisher.

Published by Manchester University Press
Oxford Road, Manchester M13 9NR, UK

and Room 400, 175 Fifth Avenue, New York, NY 10010, USA
http://www.manchesteruniversitypress.co.uk

Distributed exclusively in the USA by
St. Martin's Press, Inc., 175 Fifth Avenue, New York, NY 10010, USA

Distributed exclusively in Canada by
UBC Press, University of British Columbia, 2029 West Mall,
Vancouver, BC, Canada V6T 1Z2

British Library Cataloguing-in-Publication Data
A catalogue record for this book is available from the British Library

Library of Congress Cataloging-in-Publication Data
That second bottle : essays on John Wilmot, Earl of Rochester / edited by Nicholas Fisher.
    p.   cm.
Incorporates the papers originally presented at a colloquium held at Wadham College,
Oxford, April 2–3, 1997.
Includes bibliographical references and index.
ISBN 0–7190–5683–7 (hardcover)
    1. Rochester, John Wilmot, Earl of, 1647–1680—Criticism and
interpretation—Congresses.   2. Verse satire, English—History and criticism—Congresses.
3. Love poetry, English—History and criticism—Congresses.   I. Fisher, Nicholas.

PR3669.R2 T43 2000
821'.4—dc21
                                                                                    00–021937

ISBN 0 7190 5683 7 *hardback*

FIRST PUBLISHED 2000

07   06   05   04   03   02   01   00   10   9   8   7   6   5   4   3   2   1

Designed by MaxNettleton, FCSD
Typeset in Minion by Graphicraft Limited, Hong Kong
Printed in Great Britain
by Bookcraft (Bath) Ltd, Midsomer Norton

FOR
KEN ROBINSON
magistro primo

oh that second bottle Harry
is the sincerest, wisest, & most impartiall
downwright freind wee have, tells us truth
of our selves, & forces us to speake truths of
others

Rochester – letter to Henry Savile

CONTENTS

ILLUSTRATIONS

FIGURES

PLATES

CONTRIBUTORS

WARREN CHERNAIK is Emeritus Professor of English at the University of London, Visiting Professor of English at the University of Southampton, and Senior Research Fellow of the Institute of English Studies, University of London. His publications include *The Poet's Time: Politics and Religion in the Work of Andrew Marvell* (1983), *Sexual Freedom in English Literature* (1995), in which Rochester is a central figure, and *The Art of Detective Fiction* (2000).

HOWARD ERSKINE-HILL is Professor of Literary History in the Faculty of English at Cambridge University. He is the author of *The Augustan Idea in English Literature* (1983), and *Poetry and the Realm of Politics* and *Poetry of Opposition and Revolution* (1996). His essay 'Rochester, Augustan or Explorer?' was published in *Renaissance and Modern Essays*, edited by G. R. Hibbard (1966).

DAVID FARLEY-HILLS is Professor Emeritus, University of Wales. His publications include *The Benevolence of Laughter: Comic Poetry of the Commonwealth and Restoration* (1974), *Shakespeare and the Rival Playwrights* (1990), and two books specifically on Rochester: *Rochester's Poetry* (1978), and *Rochester: The Critical Heritage* (1975, reprinted 1985).

JULIAN FERRARO is a lecturer in the Department of English Language and Literature at the University of Liverpool. His primary areas of interest lie in the eighteenth century and in literary modernism, particularly Pope and Conrad. He is the general editor of the new edition of Pope's poetry in the Longman Annotated English Poets series.

NICHOLAS FISHER is a doctoral student in the School of English, University of Leeds, and a police superintendent serving in Her Majesty's Inspectorate of Constabulary. The executive producer of *Charming Strephon*, a CD celebrating the Earl of Rochester recorded on the Etcetera label by The Consort of Musicke in 1997, he is also co-editor with Steven Devine of *Songs to Phillis* (1999), a performing edition of the early settings of Rochester's poems.

BREAN HAMMOND, formerly Rendel Professor of English and Pro Vice-Chancellor of the University of Wales, Aberystwyth, is now Professor of English at Nottingham University. He has written on seventeenth- and eighteenth-century topics, most recently as author of *Professional Imaginative Writing in England, 1670–1740* (1997), and he contributed to the collection *Reading Rochester* edited by Edward Burns (1995).

PAUL HAMMOND is Professor of Seventeenth-Century English Literature at the University of Leeds. He is the author of *Love between Men in English Literature* (1996) and *Dryden and the Traces of Classical Rome* (1999), and editor of the Longman Annotated English Poets edition of *The Poems of John Dryden: Volume I: 1649–1681* and *Volume II: 1682–1685* (1995).

SIMON HAMPTON teaches for the Open University and the Centre for Lifelong Learning at the University of Newcastle upon Tyne. He is also Head of Drama and Theatre Studies at Mowden Hall School, Northumberland, and he directed a reconstruction on stage of the opening night (2 September 1788) of the Theatre Royal, Richmond. A biography of the actor-manager Stephen Kemble is in preparation.

RICHARD HARRIES has been the Bishop of Oxford since 1987. He is the author of eighteen books, including *The Real God* (1994); *Questioning Belief* (1995); and *Art and the Beauty of God* (1993), which was selected by the late Anthony Burgess as a Book of the Year in *The Observer*. He was elected a Fellow of the Royal Society of Literature in 1996.

PAULINA KEWES is Lecturer in English at the University of Wales, Aberystwyth. Her publications include *Authorship and Appropriation: Writing for the Stage in England, 1660–1710* (1998) and articles on seventeenth- and eighteenth-century drama criticism, and publishing history. A book on representations of history on the early modern stage is in preparation.

HAROLD LOVE holds a personal Chair in English at Monash University, Melbourne. He is the author of *Scribal Publication in Seventeenth-century England* (1993). Oxford University Press published his edition of Rochester's works in 1999.

GILLIAN MANNING has taught for the Open University, and in the School of English at The Queen's University of Belfast. Her doctoral thesis was on Rochester's poetry, and her publications include articles on seventeenth-century writing. She is currently editing *Libertine Plays of the Restoration*, and Charles Blount's *Great is Diana* and *Anima Mundi*. A book on Rochester's poetry is in preparation.

DAVID QUENTIN read English at Pembroke College, Cambridge, and was subsequently awarded the degree of M.Phil. in English Renaissance Literature. His published work includes *Pembroke Poets* (1997), for which he edited the pre-1900 section. He is now a bookseller with the antiquarian book dealing firm of Bernard Quaritch Limited, London.

MARIANNE THORMÄHLEN is Professor of English Literature at Lund University, Sweden, and the author of books and articles on T. S. Eliot, among them *The Waste Land: A Fragmentary Wholeness* (1978) and *Eliot's Animals* (1984). Her publications also include *Rochester: The Poems in Context* (1993) and *The Brontës and Religion* (1999).

KEITH WALKER took early retirement from University College, London, after teaching English literature there for thirty-two years. He has edited a selection of the poems of Dryden (1987) and with Frank Kermode co-edited the poems of Marvell (1990). His edition *The Poems of John Wilmot Earl of Rochester* (1984) was the first to make extensive use of the manuscript material.

ACKNOWLEDGMENTS

The core of this volume comprises papers read at a colloquium held at Wadham College, Oxford, on 2 and 3 April 1997 in celebration of the 350th anniversary of the Earl of Rochester's birth. The model and stimulus were provided by Jeremy Treglown's tercentenary conference at Wadham in 1980 and the critical success of the ensuing *Spirit of Wit* collection; a silent recognition of my debt to that 'first bottle' is incorporated within the title of this book. The benefic presence of comet Hale Bopp in the Oxford night sky during the colloquium (recalling the comet seen in London shortly before Rochester presented himself at Court in 1664) was supplemented by a genuinely warm and hospitable welcome to Wadham by its Warden, John Flemming, and by the exemplary care and consideration of the Domestic Bursar, Mike Sauvage, in matters administrative (this extended to accommodating a barrel of 'John Wilmot Premium Ale' from the Butcombe Brewery, Bristol). My thanks go to them, to all who attended, and especially, of course, to those whose work appears in the following pages. Many of the authors enjoy exceptionally busy and distinguished lives, and none more so than Harold Love and Marianne Thormählen, who made special journeys to middle England from Australia and Sweden respectively; the collective willingness to help commemorate the anniversary was much appreciated, and the outcome was a relaxed, informed and memorable celebration that paid a proper tribute to the poet. I hope something of the agreeableness of the occasion can be sensed in this collection.

Three people deserve special mention. My prime obligation is to Ken Robinson, an inspirational and caring teacher who, as my undergraduate tutor at the University of Newcastle upon Tyne, first exposed me to the Earl of Rochester, and then as my postgraduate supervisor guided and developed the enthusiasm he had raised; in consequence, the time I spent at my 'mother university' well prepared me for both work and leisure. I owe, too, a special debt to Paul Spicer, composer, choir trainer and Artistic Director of the Lichfield International Arts Festival; some time in 1996, I approached him with the proposal that, by way of recognising the forthcoming Rochester anniversary, he should provide his Birmingham Bach Choir with a setting of some of Rochester's verse. He accepted the commission (the work *Man, Wretched Man* for choir and organ was the impressive result), but not before challenging me to organise a wider celebration of the anniversary: one of the consequences is the appearance of this volume. My third major obligation is to Paul Hammond of the University of Leeds, who, formally the supervisor of my present research, has been immensely tolerant of this extra-curricular activity of one of his students; I gratefully acknowledge his interest, encouragement and wise counsel.

There still remains considerable indebtedness. The support of my wife Pam, and teenaged children Francis, Rachel and Harriet has been constant and unstinting, even when the family computer has been occupied for long periods in the cause of Rochester; my debt to them is heartfelt and profound. Among the many individuals who helped me beyond the call of duty are Mike Brennan; Paul Cox and Tina Fiske of the National Portrait Gallery, London; John G. C. M. Fuller; Christopher Galloway of the Ditchley Foundation; Michael Gearin-Tosh; Pierantonio Gios, the librarian of the Seminario Maggiore in Padua; David Green; Frank Gresham; The Lord Hothfield; Arkadiusz Weremczuk; and Harvey Wilkinson of Abbot Hall Art Gallery, Kendal. I am most grateful too for the efficient service I received from staff at the British Library; the Government Art Collection; London Metropolitan Archives; Longleat House; the Museum of London;

the Pierpont Morgan Library, New York; and the Society of Antiquaries of London. Thanks also are owed to my commissioning editor, Matthew Frost, who not only regularly dispensed coffee and encouragement over the extensive period of the book's genesis but also took the pictures of the saloon at Ditchley Park (obtained, fortunately, before a genial lunch effectively discouraged thoughts of further work). The ultimate debt, of course, is (in John Oldham's apposite phrase) to 'our great witty bawdy Peer'.

Nicholas Fisher

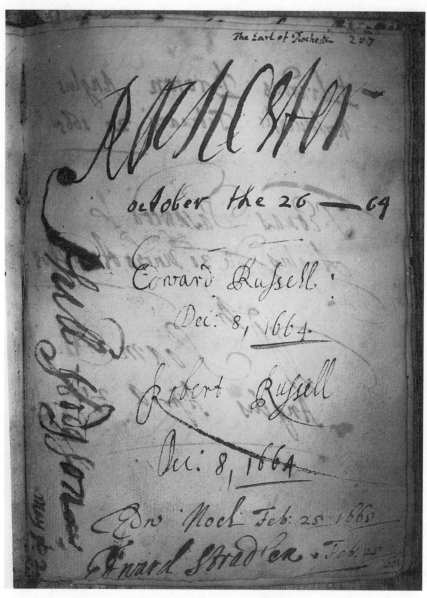

2 Rochester's entry in a register of the University of Padua

1

Introductory

NICHOLAS FISHER

ℭ

'No one doubts now the importance of Rochester's poetry.' Graham Greene's confident assertion conceals a heavy irony: it forms part of the preface to *Lord Rochester's Monkey*, a book he had written around 1931 to 1934, but which, in consequence of 'the almost Victorian atmosphere of the time', did not achieve publication, albeit in a sumptuously illustrated edition, until 1974.[1] I read this literate biography soon after it was published, and although recognising in the first part of Greene's statement a creative writer's gilding of the lily, I strongly supported his judgment in the second part. I had first encountered Rochester's work some four or five years earlier as a wide-eyed undergraduate, when the poet's coruscating wit, uninhibited humour and willingness to deal openly and directly with 'What oft was *Thought* but ne'er . . . *Exprest*'[2] had made a striking and lasting impression. Allied to this was the recognition of a supreme artistry in two distinctive verse forms: sensitive love lyrics and biting satire. Few poets, I sensed, could encompass in one *oeuvre* the tenderness of such verse as 'Absent from thee I languish still' and 'An Age in her Embraces pas'd' with the sustained and pointed satire of *A Satyre against Reason and Mankind* and *Artemiza to Chloe*, or the wry human observation in *Song. A Young Lady to her Antient Lover* and *The Disabled Debauchee* with the playfulness of the unexpected address to 'Phillis' in *Love and Life*.

Rochester's writing has consistently provoked a mixed, if not actually confused, response, which has largely resulted from the presence of what Mulgrave referred to as 'Bawdry barefac'd' and 'obscene words'.[3] Despite Robert Wolseley's extended attempt in his preface to Rochester's play *Valentinian* to defend this aspect of his friend's verse, generally it has not been felt 'nice', as Artemiza might say, that what was principally a manifestation of *comitas* and familiarity within the circle of the Court Wits, should have had a 'common' circulation.

In the November following the poet's death, Samuel Pepys confided to his friend Will Hewer, 'As he is past writing any more so bad in one sense, so I despair of any man surviving him to write so good in another'.[4] Despite his being hailed as a major poet not only by such influential fellow writers as Aphra Behn, Andrew Marvell and John Oldham, but also by a wide cross-section of the contemporary reading public, the 'bad' and the 'good' to which Pepys refers have regularly resulted in an objective assessment of his poetical achievement becoming entangled with a subjective consideration of his extra-curricular activity. Samuel Johnson, for example, declared that 'The glare of his general character diffused itself upon his writings', and the shadow of Rochester's non-poetical activities has continued to cloud critical judgment into modern times.[5]

Sidney Lee's entry on the 'poet and libertine' in *The Dictionary of National Biography*, still current despite dating from 1900, displays the influence of Johnson; although the essay extends across five pages, its period conflation of biography, bibliography and literary criticism is, at best, dated and over-blown and, at worst, salacious and inaccurate. The flavour of the piece may be judged by the summary assessment, 'His literary work was disfigured by his incorrigibly licentious temper',[6] and by its enthusiastic incorporation of a comment written some twenty years earlier by the scholar Edmund Gosse. In his brief introduction to a selection of Rochester's lyrics, Gosse had made reference to the quality of Rochester's 'exquisite lyrics' and the 'trenchant and vigorous' writing of the 'satires', before concluding:

> But the fact is that the muse of Rochester resembles nothing so much as a beautiful child which has wantonly rolled itself in the mud, and which has grown so dirty that the ordinary wayfarer would rather pass it hurriedly by, than do justice to its native charms.[7]

Lee made reference only to this conclusion, choosing to exclude Gosse's more balanced judgment, with the result that, for many readers during the last hundred years, his partial critique has shaped their response to Rochester's work.[8]

The essay by Charles Whibley on 'The Court Poets', published in *The Cambridge History of English Literature* in 1912, has been recognised as marking a watershed, in that, for the first time since Rochester's death, the legend was laid aside and the poet's true stature as 'one man of undisputed genius' and a major English poet began its journey of recovery.[9] Whibley's assessment is the more remarkable when it is considered that a further decade would pass before the publication of the first twentieth-century edition of the poet and over half a century before an accurate (although still not final) establishment of the Rochester *corpus* by David Vieth.

Following John Hayward's trail-blazing compilation of 1926, there have been in excess of twenty separate editions of Rochester's poetry, most notably those by Vivian de Sola Pinto (1953), David Vieth (1968), Keith Walker (1984), Frank Ellis (1994) and Harold Love (1999).[10] John Hayward's intendedly comprehensive edition contained much that was not by Rochester, and much that would have been censored had the volume not been published privately; Pinto's edition substantially refined the canon, but in order to avoid prosecution omitted at the request of the publishers two important poems (*The Imperfect Enjoyment*[11]) and *A Ramble in St. James's Park*); Vieth's edition provided the most accurate and complete text hitherto in a modern-spelling version, making it at last possible for Rochester's work to be properly assessed; and Walker's edition, while not differing substantially from Vieth's in its view of the canon, facilitated further scholarship through its substantial use of the manuscript material and its reproduction of the poetry using the spelling and punctuation of the Restoration Period. More recently, Ellis's edition, published in the Penguin Classics series, has not only made Rochester even more widely accessible, but has provided a symbolic acknowledgment of the general recognition of his true stature as a poet; and Love's scholarly Oxford English Texts edition, further confirming that stature, has provided the most extensive and thorough critical apparatus to date. Love's edition has been adopted as the standard text for this volume.

These texts have been accompanied by a vast range of articles, recorded by Vieth in 1984 as approaching four hundred, and subsequently continuing unabated.[12] The critical reception of Rochester from his lifetime until the turn of the twentieth century has been detailed, and during the last twenty years three separate collections of essays on the poet have been published.[13] A remarkable shared perception of the quality and radical uniqueness of Rochester's lyrics and satires has emerged.

David Brooks, editor of a selection of Rochester's poems published in Australia in 1980, is representative in his assertion: 'He is an original and striking lyrist, capable of registering moods of considerable complexity. He is also a witty and powerful satirist with a capacity for dramatic rendering.'[14] Johannes Prinz, the author in 1927 of the most detailed criticism of the poetry since Johnson's, sympathetically viewed Rochester as 'a representative *par excellence* of his period' and suggested that the best of his lyrics should be 'classed with the most exquisite in the English tongue'. Oliver Elton, in a 1933 survey of English poetry, described Rochester as 'the best singer between Herrick and Collins', an estimation echoed by the observations of Vieth that 'Rochester is one of the greatest of English song writers' and that some of the lyrics are 'the finest of the late seventeenth century and among the best in English literature'.[15] More precisely, Jeremy Treglown has suggested:

> he needs comparison with a number of major Renaissance and Augustan English poets. The emotional complexity of some of his lyrics is reminiscent of Shakespeare's sonnets, or of Donne, though in their ironic simplicity of surface they are closer to his near-contemporary Marvell.[16]

Rochester's satires have been similarly valued. His 'best known poem', *A Satyre against Reason and Mankind*, has been described by C. F. Main as 'Rochester's masterpiece that . . . heads the list of Augustan formal verse satires'; and Pinto, with even greater enthusiasm, has viewed it as the poet's 'most ambitious performance . . . The place of Rochester's poem is beside the great things in Swift.'[17]

Unexpectedly few critics in the twentieth century sought to argue against this critical mass. The most famous was F. R. Leavis, who, in as uncompromising a statement as Greene's, stated, 'Rochester is not a great poet of any kind'; as, however, this was a riposte to Pinto's enthusiastic accolade of Rochester as 'the great poet of unbelief', the rebutment has more the air of Touchstone's 'Countercheck Quarrelsome' than the conviction of a carefully thought position.[18] A more considered response, it would appear, is provided by Isobel Grundy, who admits, 'We have now mustered courage to admire the poetry of John Wilmot, earl of Rochester', which suggests that for many readers the poet's work continues to present something of a challenge.[19] The thrust none the less, particularly following the publication of Vieth's edition, has been to view Rochester as a *major* poet, as three representative statements indicate:

> The greatness of Rochester . . . is that he was able to transcend the limitations of polite learning, class and literary amateurism . . . He surpassed all noble poets of the age, and all professionals except Dryden, to make a major contribution to our literature . . .

> Rochester, though he wrote less than any other major poet, unquestionably deserves that rank . . .

> undoubtedly the wittiest and most brilliant poet and satirist of the Court of Charles II. Regarded today as a writer of considerable genius and complexity and one of the major English poets.[20]

And latterly in the wider artistic field, Rochester has been made the subject of two plays (*Restoration Comedy* by David Ambrose and Michael Gearin-Tosh, 1992, and *The Libertine* by Stephen Jeffreys, 1994), an anachronistic cameo portrait in a film about two eighteenth-century highwaymen (*Plunkett & Macleane*, directed by Jake Scott, 1999) and a chamber opera by the Dutch composer Hans Kox (in progress). This, then, is the background against which *That Second Bottle* appears.

The collection derives its title from a letter Rochester wrote to his closest friend, Henry Savile, in which he observed 'that second bottle . . . tells us truth of our selves, & forces us to speake truths of others'.[21] The studies cover the full range of Rochester's output, not only his songs and satires but also, profitably, his letters and *Valentinian*; three of the pieces focus upon music, art and religion, to create a multidisciplinary approach. None the less the common thread that either explicitly or implicitly runs through each critique is the essential truthfulness and honesty with which Rochester transmitted his unique vision of the exhilarating world in which he found himself. The book broadly divides into two sections, separated by two of the multidisciplinary papers. The first group of essays offers complementary but contrasting interpretations of love and friendship in Rochester: Warren Chernaik examines the treatment of these related terms across a representative selection of the poems and the letters, and then Howard Erskine-Hill casts a fresh light on Rochester's libertinism, largely by teasing out from Rochester's letters to his wife and Henry Savile evidence of the poet's awareness of Shakespeare's Falstaff. This is followed by Marianne Thormählen's examination of the nature, and importance, of love in Rochester's poetry, and this first section ends with a review by Paul Hammond of the homoerotic aspects of Rochester's writing, supported by reference to the poetry, the Rochester–Savile correspondence and *Valentinian*.

Two multidisciplinary papers form a bridge to the second group of papers. My survey of the extent to which Rochester's love lyrics continued to inspire composers more than a century after his death acts as a coda to the exploration of love and friendship, while Keith Walker's explanation of the satiric significance of the famous 'monkey portrait' serves as a prelude to the focus on the major satires and the theatre that follows. David Quentin, firstly, by reference to seventeenth-century poetics interprets *Upon Nothinge* in terms of its form and content, and Gill Manning explores the resonance of 'artemisa' to provide a richer understanding of *Artemiza to Chloe*. Julian Ferraro's examination of the impact of Rochester and Horace upon Pope illuminates, in particular, *An Allusion to Horace*, while Brean Hammond and Paulina Kewes use the perspective of the contemporary theatre to provide a valuable reading of *A Satyre against Reason and Mankind*. David Farley-Hills charts the elements of theatre in Rochester's satires as a group, an approach that is naturally followed by Simon Hampton's determination of Rochester's locus in the Restoration theatre. Harold Love, revealing in a scholarly piece of detective work how Rochester deliberately set his revision of Fletcher's tragedy *Valentinian* in Whitehall, discovers unexpected significances in Rochester's play, and the volume is brought to an appropriate end with the interpretation by the Bishop of Oxford of the final drama of Rochester's life as a genuine and sincere repentance.

Collectively, the multiple, even 'kaleidoscopic'[22], perspectives not only provide a convincing assessment of the poet 350 years after he was born, but also emphasise the increasingly powerful impact he makes on our culture. In this context, the point which Ernst Honigmann raises in his stimulating book *Myriad-minded Shakespeare* has a relevance here; asking how myriad-minded, or open-minded, the judicious spectator or reader of Shakespeare needs to be in order to respond to the dramatist's 'exceptional knowledge', he concludes:

The open-minded reader learns that Shakespeare criticism is a *jeu sans frontières* . . .
    We, too, must learn to look, with Hamlet, in all directions. Myriad-minded
Shakespeare deserves teachers – and actors, producers, readers – who willingly
follow wherever the plays may lead.[23]

While I do not suggest that Shakespeare's exceptional understanding of
humanity was matched by Rochester, the range of the criticism contained in
this volume suggests that Honigmann's question is one that can legitimately
be posed in relation to the later poet: for the open-minded reader, Rochester
criticism, too, is a *jeu sans frontières*. It is not extravagant to suggest that
the epithet 'myriad-minded', as interpreted by Honigmann, should also be
applied to the later poet; the weakness of Sidney Lee's *DNB* notice a century
ago was that it undervalued Rochester by looking in only one direction. It is
hoped that this collection will encourage readers to look in other directions
and willingly follow the poet's lead; by so doing, the open-minded reader will
better understand why Rochester amply deserves the accolade of 'one of the
most remarkable and most gifted men of his remarkable and gifted century'.[24]

2

'I loath the Rabble': friendship, love and hate in Rochester

WARREN CHERNAIK

> A Prostitute to all the Town
>   And yet with no man Freinds,
> She rails and scolds when she lyes down
>   And Curses when she spends.
>
> (*On Mrs Willis*, lines 13–16)

These vituperative lines by Rochester suggest a separation between the affectionate and sensual currents of a spectacular kind. The physical act of sex, as described here, is not exactly passionless, but the emotions Rochester attributes to the sexually promiscuous Sue Willis, even at the moment of orgasm, are angry and aggressive. Friendship, defined by Aristotle as 'wishing to another what one thinks good, for his sake and not for one's own',[1] hardly seems to be a word in Mrs Willis's vocabulary: the only relationship she appears to be capable of is a frustrating momentary contact of bodies. The opening lines of the poem present this disjunction between sex and affection in universal terms; the sexual impulse, indiscriminate in seeking an object, reduces man to the 'slave' of his untrustworthy body:

> Against the Charms our *Bollox* have
> How weak all human skill is
> Since they can make a Man a slave
> To such a Bitch as *Willis*.
>
> (lines 1–4)

Traditionally, love and friendship are closely related terms. The Greek word *philia* serves for both, and though Aristotle tends to emphasise reciprocity in friendship where Plato emphasises the instability of desire, both characterise friendship in terms of the flow of feeling between lover and beloved.

3 Letter from Rochester to Henry Savile, 22 June [?1671]

Rochester in writing to Henry Savile uses the two terms love and friendship interchangeably:

> Tis not the least of my happiness that I thinke you love mee, but the first of all my pretensions, is, to make itt appeare that I faithfully endeavour to deserve it, if there bee a reall good upon Earth 'tis in the Name of freind, without wch all others are meerly fantasticall, how few of us are fitt stuff to make that thing, wee have dayly the melancholy experience. (*Letters*, pp. 92–3)

In this letter, Rochester makes several traditional assertions and at least one untraditional one: that true friendship is rare; that friendship is conducive to happiness and is predicated on a love of virtue, the pursuit of 'a reall good upon Earth'; and that friendship is fundamentally a relationship among equals, the recognition of a spiritual kinship, where the current of affection flows in both directions. For Plato and for Aristotle, 'nothing can be worthy of love unless it is good', and Cicero in *De Amicitia* similarly associates the impulse toward affectionate friendship with the love of virtue: 'A compact of friendship is formed . . . when some indication of virtue shines forth; the heart fastens and yokes itself to this as to something like itself, and when this happens, love is bound to arise.'[2] What is untraditional, and characteristically Rochesterian, in this passage is the note of anxiety, the Hobbesian nominalism in the suggestion that there is no 'reall good' outside 'the Name of freind', and the 'melancholy' awareness that he may be deceived even in that ('I thinke you love mee'). A number of Rochester's poems express similar doubts:

> Fantastick fancys fondly move
> And in fraile joys believe,
> Taking false pleasure for true love,
> But pain can ne're deceive.
> (*Song* ('An Age in her Embraces pas'd'), lines 29–32)

These lines go beyond the hedonist ethic of the pursuit of pleasure and avoidance of pain, advanced in some of Rochester's poems, to propose that only pain provides a bedrock of certainty which can be trusted, as I have argued elsewhere: 'Sexual pleasure, taken here as the norm for all pleasures, is "false" because it does not last and because it is based on lies, the delusion of fidelity and stability.'[3]

In several poems as well as in letters, Rochester explicitly contrasts the companionship of an all-male society, convivially sharing several bottles of wine, with the more threatening and invasive pleasure sought in sexual pursuit. Cupid and Bacchus, wine and women, are sometimes seen by Rochester as compatible, different tastes for different moments ('whether wine or women I know not, according as my constitution serves me').[4] In one poem, Rochester justifies the 'Rivall bottle' to his jealous mistress by arguing that 'running after mirth and wine', rather than being indicative of a culpable inconstancy, acts as a spur to a lover's imagination, whetting the appetite:

> For wine (whose power alone can raise
>   Our thoughts soe farr above)
> Affords Idea's fitt to praise
>   What wee thinke fitt to Love.[5]

But more often, Rochester sees the pleasures of male friendship and the demands of sexual love as incompatible; on several occasions, he proposes a hedonist version of the choice of Hercules, arguing the need to choose the higher pleasure in preference to the lower, eschewing the company of women for the company of like-minded men:

> Farewell *Woman* – I entend
>   Henceforth every Night to sitt
> With my lewd well natur'd Freind
>   Drinking to engender witt.
>
> (*Love to a Woman*, lines 9–12)

In its final stanza, as we shall see, this poem extends the rejection of women to encompass the choice of males over females as sexual partners. The suggestion that men, or for that matter women, can 'Please themselves alone' sexually, so prominent in *Sodom* and in the fragmentary satire 'What vaine unnecessary things are men', is not present in Rochester's letter to Savile in praise of wine as cementing friendship: here again Rochester posits the need to choose to 'live & dye sheere drunkards, or intire Lovers', rather than trying to combine the two.[6]

This letter, dated by Treglown 22 June 1671, is Rochester's most extended definition of true and false friendship: though it refers in passing to 'freinds of both sexes' the letter generally accords with the poem *Love to a Woman* in banishing 'the whole sex' of women as potential impediments to male friendship. In praising the virtues of 'the second bottle' as 'the sincerest, wisest, & most impartiall downright freind we have', in that it 'tells us truth of our selves, & forces us to speake truths of others', Rochester draws on the traditional view, expressed by Cicero, Bacon and others, that 'an essential part of true friendship' is 'to offer and to receive admonition': 'For there is no such *flatterer*, as a man's self', Bacon says in his essay 'Of Friendship', 'and there is no such remedy against *flattery* . . . as the liberty of a *friend*'.[7] In the letter to Savile, the reciprocal trust necessary for friendship is contrasted with the 'distrust' and dissimulation which characterise both sexual and political intrigue, the main 'Buisnisses of this Age'. Here as in other letters to Savile, praise of his friend's 'good Nature' is accompanied by expressions of fear that his boon companion, distracted by the temptations of life at Court, might have 'forgotten' him at a time when they were physically separated.[8] A later letter, indeed, strongly hints that Savile is fallible enough to need to be reminded that his friend still exists: 'owning that though you excel most men in friendship and good nature, you are not quite exempt from all human frailty, I send this to hinder you from forgetting a man who loves you very heartily' (*Letters*, p. 117).

In the 'second bottle' letter, the element of insecurity in the friendship is explicitly associated with the competitiveness of a Court world where sexual conquest means betrayal. Here Rochester refers to an intrigue Savile carried on simultaneously with two Court ladies, the Countess of Northumberland and the Countess of Falmouth, both of whom rejected his advances:

> good Nature wch waites about you . . . is my security that you are not unmindfull of y^r Absent freinds; to bee from you, & forgotten by you att once, is a misfortune I never was Criminall enough to merritt, since to the Black & faire Countesses, I villanously betray'd the dayly addresses of y^r divided Heart; you forgave that upon the first Bottle & upon the second on my Conscience would have renounc'd them and the whole sex. (*Letters*, pp. 66–7)

The momentary intoxication afforded by the shared bottle not only serves to 'wash away . . . cares', but, Rochester suggests, provides a temporary suspension of the rule of self-interest: 'before god I beleive the errantest villain breathing is honest as long as that bottle lives'.[9] The bonds of friendship thus allow a brief respite from the dominant values of a world akin to the Hobbesian state of nature, where 'if any two men desire the same thing, which nevertheless they cannot both enjoy, they become enemies; and in the way to their end . . . endeavour to destroy, or subdue one another'.[10] True friendship, dependent on mutual trust, Rochester suggests, implies an ethical standard against which 'the meane Pollicy of Court prudence' can be measured and found wanting: '[it] banishes flattery from our tongues and distrust from our Hearts, setts us above the meane Pollicy of Court prudence, wch makes us lye to one another all day, for feare of being betray'd by each other att night' (*Letters*, p. 67).

In *The Disabled Debauchee*, which presents a particularly destructive instance of false, self-interested friendship – what Aristotle characterises as friendship for utility or for pleasure, essentially exploitative in nature – the effects of wine are portrayed in less favourable terms. The irony in this satire consists largely in the narrator's attributing noble and disinterested motives to behaviour which on both moral and practical grounds can only be condemned:

> So, when my days of Impotence approach,
>   And I'm by Pox and Wine's unlucky chance
> Forc'd from the pleasing Billows of Debauch
>   On the Dull Shore of lazy Temperance;
>
> My pains at least some respite shall afford
>   While I behold the Battels you maintain,
> When Fleets of Glasses Sail about the Board,
>   From whose broad sides Volleys of Wit shall Rain.

(lines 13–20)

By the mock-heroic imagery of battle, Rochester exposes the persistence of self-delusion in the superannuated rake who, his health ruined, seeks 'respite' from pain in reliving his own folly in his younger friends, encouraging them along the same path to destruction. Cupid and Bacchus in this poem operate in harmony, with equally disastrous results, as drink, loosening inhibitions, provides an inroad for violence and the pox. Standards of judgment are implied by the inversions in the rake's moral vocabulary.

> Should hopeful youths, worth being drunk, prove nice,
>   And from their fair Inviters meanly shrink;
> 'Twill please the Ghost of my departed Vice
>   If, at my counsel, they repent, and Drink.
>   . . .
> With Tales like these, I will such thoughts inspire
> As to important mischief shall incline;
> I'll make him long some Ancient Church to fire,
> And fear no lewdness he's call'd to by Wine.
>
> (lines 25–8, 41–4)

For Francis Bacon, friendship and sexual love are two very different things: one is a rational, reciprocal attachment, 'healthful and sovereign for the understanding' as well as the affections, where the other is a 'weakness', an 'excess', which 'men ought to beware of' because it 'doth much mischief': 'they do best who, if they cannot but admit love, make it keep quarter'.[11] Rochester's song *Love to a Woman* suggests a means for keeping the sexual impulses in their place, satisfying one's physical cravings with any available object, while protecting the higher pleasures of friendship against contamination:

> Love a Woman! Th'rt an Ass:
>   Tis a most insipid passion
> To Chuse out for thy Happiness
>   The dullest part of Gods Creation.
>
> Let the Porter and the Groom,
>   Things design'd for dirty slaves,
> Drudg in fair *Aurelias* womb
>   To gett supplies for Age and Graves.
>
> (lines 1–8)

As Harold Weber points out in his excellent commentary, the poem depends throughout on invoking an implicit hierarchy, in which the female body, stigmatised as an object of revulsion, is associated both with 'a world of physical corruption', 'the degrading movement from birth to death', and with social inferiors.[12] Here, as in *A Ramble in St. James's Park*, sexual desire is presented as a threat, an eruption from below creating disequilibrium. '*Porters Backs*, and *Foot-mens Brawn*', a 'stiff-Prick'd *Clown*' who does not need to worry about the adequacy of his sexual performance, a roomful of 'Porters, and Car-men' sitting around a fire drinking ale – these, Rochester or his personae in several poems suggest, all provide appropriate food for the 'devouring Cunt', indiscriminate in its appetites.[13] Rochester's song offers counsel to a friend, foolish enough to think he is in love, reminding him that a gentleman ought to rise above such considerations and choose the higher pleasures, ease rather than discomfort:

> Then give me health, wealth, Mirth, and wine,
>   And if buizy Love intrenches
> There's a sweet soft Page of mine
>   Can doe the Trick worth Forty wenches.

> (lines 13–16)

The catamite, here as in the ironic Song ('I Rise at Eleven'), is not simply an inferior but a dependant: in no sense sharing in pleasures or admitted to the equal status of a friend, he is there entirely to provide physical relief. In 'I Rise at Eleven', indeed, as I have argued elsewhere, 'lust becomes indistinguishable from rage', and ejaculation is presented as equivalent to vomiting. Here the physical act of sex, with whore or boy, is entirely devalued:

> I send for my Whore, when for fear of a Clap,
> I Spend in her hand, and I Spew in her Lap:
> . . .
> I storm, and I roar, and I fall in a rage,
> And missing my Whore, I bugger my Page.[14]

In some letters, Rochester allows for the possibility of a selfless friendship between a man and a woman. His correspondence with Elizabeth Barry suggests a highly volatile relationship, with considerable elements of 'jealousy or fear' on both sides:

> Anger, spleen, revenge and shame are not yet so powerful with me as to make me disown this great truth, that I love you above all things in the world. But I thank God I can distinguish, I can see very woman in you, and from yourself am convinced I have never been in the wrong in my opinion of women. 'Tis impossible for me to curse you, but give me leave to pity myself, which is more than ever you will do for me. (Letters, pp. 148, 180–1)

Yet a number of his letters to the actress purport to offer the 'faithful counsel' which, Cicero and Bacon claim, only a friend can give:

> since I must love you, allow me the liberty of telling you sometimes unmannerly truths when my zeal for your service causes, and your own interest requires it. These inconveniences you must bear with from those that love you with greater regard to you than themselves . . . I know by woeful experience what comes of dealing

with knaves . . . Therefore look well about you and take it for granted that unless you can deceive them, they will certainly cozen you. If I am not so wise as they and therefore less fit to advise you, I am at least more concerned for you and for that reason the likelier to prove honest and the rather to be trusted.[15]

An exchange of letters with Savile suggests a complex network of friendship, service and obligation involving Nell Gwyn. One letter outlines the 'advice' Rochester has consistently offered to the royal mistress, in keeping with the poet's Epicurean principles – to 'live in peace with all the world and easily with the King; never be so ill-natured [as] to stir up his anger against others' – where in another Savile relays to Rochester, as an act of friendship, a piece of Court gossip which 'may one day turne to her infinite disadvantage'. Both letters assume a Court world of ceaseless intrigue and jockeying for power: since Nell Gwyn is his friend's friend, Savile feels he must act to protect her interest, as long as this does not endanger his own precarious position at Court:

This I thaught it good for you to know, for though y^r L[ordshi]p and I have different friends in the Court yet the friendship betwixt us ought to make mee have an observing eye upon any accident that may wound any friend of yours as this may in the end possibly doe her, who is so much your friend and who speaks obliging and charitable things of mee in my present disgrace.[16]

A theme which recurs constantly in Rochester's poems and letters is that true friends are necessarily few. As we have seen, this is a traditional view: Montaigne sees the perfect friendship as 'indivisible', since 'each one gives himself so wholly to his friend that he has nothing else to distribute elsewhere', and Aristotle comments that to be everyone's friend is to be a friend to no one.[17] But in Rochester, the contrast between the private compact of friendship ('To value you in my thoughts, to prefer you in my wishes, to serve you in my words, to observe, study and obey you in all my actions') and the corrupt values of 'the pretending part of the proud World, . . . swoln with selfish Vanity' is particularly marked.[18] Again and again, he presents himself as one of an embattled minority, almost in Miltonic terms, as one who speaks the truth in a world of liars:

> On evil days though fallen, and evil tongues,
> In darkness, and with dangers compassed round,
> And solitude.[19]

Plain Dealings Downfall, excluded from the Vieth and Walker editions and included by Ellis and Love, is a poem of dubious authenticity, but the presentation of the honest, outspoken satirist rejecting the values of the 'Hauty Town' and treated by the fashionable world as a pariah accords well with the stance of martyr to truth in several of the letters to Savile:

> Long time plain dealing in the Hauty Town,
> Wandring about, though in thread-bare Gown,
> At last unanimously was cry'd down.
>
> (lines 1–3)

In expressing his gratitude to Savile for the services of friendship – 'I am now sensible that it is natural for you to be kind to me, and can never more despair of it' – Rochester presents himself not only as scorning the values of 'the Rabble and the Court', but as the object of hatred and scorn:

> If it were the sign of an honest man to be happy in his friends, sure I were marked out for the worst of men, since no-one e'er lost so many as I have done or knew how to make so few.

> I ever thought you an extraordinary man and must now think you such a friend who, being a courtier as you are, can love a man whom it is the great mode to hate.[20]

The world of the Court, as Rochester presents it in poems and letters, has little room for the disinterested 'kindness and care' of one friend for another: 'Misery makes all men less or more dishonest'.[21] Ingratitude and the naked pursuit of self-interest are presented in Rochester's satires as the ruling principles governing the Court world and humanity in general. Professions of friendship are rarely to be trusted:

> The Greate mans Gratitude to his best friend,
> Kings promises, whoores vowes, towards thee they bend,
> Flow swiftly into thee and in thee ever end.
>
> (*Upon Nothinge*, lines 49–51)

> But Man with smiles, embraces, friendship, praise,
> Inhumanly his fellows life betrayes;
> . . .
> And Honesty's against all common sense;
> Men must be Knaves, tis in their own defence.
> . . .
> Nor can weak Truth your Reputation save;
> The Knaves will all agree to call you Knave.
> Wrong'd shall he live, insulted o're, opprest,
> Who dares be less a Villain than the rest.
> (*A Satyre against Reason and Mankind*, lines 135–6, 159–60, 164–7)

And yet, for all the fierceness of Rochester's attacks on the dominant values of the Restoration Court, his poems and letters are consistently those of an insider, irresistibly drawn to a world he despises. He fills his letters and poems with the news and gossip of 'the Towne' ('I perceive you have no opinion of a letter that is not almost a gazette', he says to Savile[22]), treating Whitehall as the centre of the universe, like his character Artemiza:

> Y'expect att least, to heare, what Loves have past
> In this lewd Towne, synce you, and I mett last.
> What change has happen'd of Intrigues, and whether
> The Old ones last, and who, and who's togeather.
> But how, my dearest Chloe, shall I sett
> My pen to write, what I would faine forgett [?]
>
> (*Artemiza to Chloe*, lines 32–7)

There is never in Rochester's poetry the sense, so common in Milton or Bunyan, of a secure ethical perspective by which the vice and folly of the world can be judged, a clear, unambiguous guide to conduct set forth for readers to follow:

> Yet some there be that by due steps aspire
> To lay their just hands on that golden key
> That opes the palace of eternity.
>
> (*Comus*, lines 12–14)

Neither 'that lost thing (Love)', identified in *Artemiza to Chloe* as 'debauch'd' as soon as it is named, nor the hedonist ethic invoked in *A Satyre against Reason and Mankind* claiming that instinct alone can serve 'for Actions government' can be considered reliable as an ethical standard. In neither case, indeed, is there any readily recognisable way of distinguishing the true from the specious: if love is 'the most gen'rous Passion of the mynde', that very generosity makes it the more subject to abuse. The materialism and nominalism Rochester learned from Hobbes excluded the possibility of transcendent ideals; thus the 'Rules of Good and Ill' which, according to *Against Reason and Mankind*, 'Sense' can distinguish, can be in hedonist terms only 'the appetites, and aversions' of a particular individual at a given moment:

> But whatsoever is the object of any man's appetite or desire, that is it which he for his part calleth *good*: and the object of his hate and aversion, *evil*; and of his contempt, *vile* and *inconsiderable*. For these words of good, evil, and contemptible, are ever used with relation to the person that useth them: there being nothing simply and absolutely so; nor any common rule of good or evil, to be taken from the nature of the objects themselves.[23]

In *Tunbridge Wells*, the narrator, never characterised in any detail, other than as a competent horseman and a gentleman by birth (presumably the reference to 'Citizens' in line 5 indicates a higher social status, as does the scornful dismissal of the pretended 'young Gentleman' in line 177), bears witness to a number of scenes which, he consistently protests, he would rather not see. The reluctant, disenchanted narrator, dragged unwillingly from his comfortable seclusion to accompany one or more bores, is a standard motif in satire: we find it in Horace's *Satires*, I.ix, Donne's *Satires* I and IV, Marvell's *Fleckno*, and elsewhere. But in almost all the satires which provide a precedent (and in Rochester's *Satyr.* [*Timon*] as well), there is some inter-change between the narrator and those being satirised. In this poem the narrator simply sees and hears, without participating, moving restlessly from place to place, bemoaning his 'Cursed luck' in finding such 'Irksom' com-panions. At one point, he deliberately places himself so he cannot hear a conversation: 'The things did talk but th' hearing what they said / I did my selfe the kindnesse to Evade'. Marianne Thormählen has plausibly remarked that all the fops, would-be wits and knaves the narrator meets are upwardly mobile, sharing 'social ambitions'.[24] Yet the narrator's reaction at the outset of the poem, as soon as he catches sight of the crowds on their way to Tunbridge Wells, is not based on the individual characteristics of those he encounters, but is violently physical, as the instinct of aversion causes acute nausea:

> But turning head a suddain Cursed View
> That Innocent provision overthrew
> And without drinking, made me purge and spew.

> (lines 8–10)

One reason the narrator can confidently assert at the end of *Tunbridge Wells* that 'man . . . / In all his shapes . . . is rediculous' (lines 178–9) is that he meets no one he could remotely consider a friend. And yet there is an implicit discourse of friendship in the poem, since a substantial proportion of the characters turn out to be versions of figures in literary works circulating in the Court, written by close associates of Rochester: Sir Nicholas Cully from Etherege's *The Comical Revenge*, Fribble, Mrs Fribble, Cuffe and Kick from Shadwell's *Epsom-Wells*, and Bayes in Marvell's *The Rehearsal Transpros'd*, an identifiable historical figure (Samuel Parker) presented entirely in the terms of Marvell's satire. Recognisable, self-conscious allusions to each of these works presuppose an immediate audience for the poem who share the author's values and inhabit the same closed society.

A small group of friends is named explicitly at the end of Rochester's *An Allusion to Horace* as providing the ideal audience for his poetry. The lines imitate the conclusion of Horace's *Satires*, I.x, which lists a considerably larger number of learned men and friends (fifteen altogether, some of them poets but most of them men of wealth and position in Augustan Rome) as the readers of taste for whom he writes. Here are Rochester's concluding lines:

> I loath the Rabble, 'tis enough for me
> If Sydley, Shadwell, Shepheard, Wicherley,
> Godolphin, Butler, Buckhurst, Buckinghame
> And some few more, whome I omitt to name
> Approve my sence, I count their Censure Fame.

> (lines 120–4)

Standards of judgment, aesthetic if not moral, are more explicit in this poem than in any other by Rochester, and these artistic principles can readily be identified as neoclassical, set forth in lines closely adapted from Horace and anticipating Pope in their balance and precision, imitating what they advise:

> Compare each Phrase, Examine every Line,
> Weigh every word, and every thought refine;
> Scorne all applause the Vile Rout can bestow
> And be content to pleas those few who know.[25]

Aside from the updating of references, in a substitution of English for Roman names, allowing Rochester to include capsule judgments on a substantial number of his contemporaries, there are two main deviations from the Horatian model: Rochester's principal satiric victim is not a writer from an earlier generation, like Horace's Lucilius, but his formidable contemporary Dryden; and the focus of attention throughout *An Allusion to Horace* is not on verse satire, a genre in which Horace sought to surpass his predecessor, but on drama performed before a paying audience. The contrast between public and private, between works designed to 'divert the Rabble and the Court' (seen here as sharing in an uneducated taste, though divided by class and economic background) and works intended to be circulated to a limited audience, is central to Rochester's poem, far more than in the Horatian original:

> 'Tis therfore not enough when your false sence
> Hitts the false Judgment of an Audience
> Of clapping fools, assembling a vast Crowd
> Till the throng'd Playhous crack with the dull load.

(lines 12–15)

Truth hears and speaks to truth, false authors to false hearers, crowding the playhouse benches; in the last line quoted, I detect an allusion to Samson in the temple of the Philistines. One writes for friends, knowing that anyone beyond the circle of reciprocal affection is likely to be an enemy.

In the *Satyr. [Timon]*, Rochester's narrator, foolishly consenting to come to dinner with an acquaintance, hopes to find 'Sidley, Buckhurst, Savile', but instead finds another, less desirable set of drinking companions, whose names sufficiently indicate their characters:

> Noe; but there were above, Half-Witt, and Huffe,
> Kickum, and Ding-Boy; Oh tis well enough,
> They're all brave Fellows, crys mine Host; lets dine,
> I long to have my Belly full of Wine:
> . . .
> I saw my Errour, but 'twas now too late,
> Noe meanes, nor hopes, appeare of a Retreate.
> Well, wee salute, and each Man takes his Seate.

(lines 35–8, 41–3)

On the face of it, little distinguishes this *répas ridicule* from the conviviality which, according to Rochester and tradition, seals and reinforces friendship. 'Y'are all my Friends' (line 70), claims the host, and the wine flows freely, with literary and political conversation around the dinner table ('Some Regulate the Stage, and some the State' (line 112)), along with discourse of love and honour. Of course, Rochester is at pains throughout the poem to indicate to the reader that those attending the dinner fall short of the ideal of wit and suitable aristocratic conduct: they quote the 'Rumbling words' of bad poetry, taking it for good, and they end up in an undignified physical brawl:

> And at that word, at t'others head let fly,
> A greasy Plate, when suddenly they all,
> Together by the Eares, in Parties fall.
> Half-Witt, with Dingboy, joynes, Kickum with Huffe.
>
> (lines 127, 168–71)

And yet what this poem, like *Tunbridge Wells*, most strikingly suggests is that in a Court society one cannot choose one's companions or regulate one's conduct by any consistent principle. In a world where each man or woman is a potential enemy, where 'Six fresh Bottles' can buy a temporary 'Peace', where (as in the concluding lines of *A Ramble in St. James's Park*) the hope of fulfilment in love is turned in a moment to hate – 'In that most lamentable State, / I'll make her feel my scorn, and hate; / Pelt her with Scandals, Truth, or Lies' – then one faces the constant danger of hoping to find Buckhurst and Savile but having to be content with Kickum and Huffe.[26]

4 *Before* by William Hogarth, 1736. Detail shows Rochester's *Poems*

3

Dissolver of reason: Rochester and the nature of love

MARIANNE THORMÄHLEN

When I wrote a book about Rochester's poetry, one of the structural problems I had to face was the question of how to organise those poems that deal with the province of love, as distinct from the philosophical, social and personal satires and from *An Allusion to Horace*, in which the craft of writing is the chief subject. I ended up with a section which, borrowing a title from Browning, I called 'Men and Women'. Within that section, I set up three subdivisions: one dealt with *A Letter from Artemiza in the Towne to Chloe in the Countrey*, a poem with a strong satirical flavour which is nevertheless fundamentally concerned with what love is, and is not. Another subdivision covered the two long poems in which disaster hits the relationship between a man and a woman: *The Imperfect Enjoyment* and *A Ramble in St. James's Park*. And finally, the love lyrics were classified according to their approach to sexual union.

It seemed a reasonable system of categorisation at the time; but it is the aspect of the book which appears least satisfactory to me today. Of course, some sort of organising principle had to obtain: at the most basic level, for instance, anyone who works with a considerable number of texts should make it as easy as possible for readers to locate coherent discussions of individual items. It looked fairly neat, too, suggesting some sort of progression from the simple and derivative to the complex and mature; and after all, it is not as though the issue of sexual fulfilment is unimportant in Rochester's poetry. But it created the impression that this part of Rochester's output is overwhelmingly focused on the matter of physical consummation, and that impression is at least in part fallacious.

I did realise – and said so – that there is something paradoxical about poems which dwell so insistently on erotic activity while saying so little about what it is really like and why it matters in the first place. The subsection on the love lyrics ends with the statement, 'At the centre of Rochester's poems on love, there is an empty space',[1] a view I still subscribe to, but it was misleading the reader to imply that love in the sense of strong feeling is barely present in Rochester's poetry. There is love there, a raw, irrational force; and it is that force I now want to pursue.

Ten years ago, testing various designations of the passion of love on Rochester's texts, I came to the conclusion that the taxonomies adopted by seventeenth-century theorists on love did not apply. Terms such as *amour-désir*, *amour-tendresse* and *amour galant* were plainly inadequate: the fact that love is notoriously difficult to define at any time and in any context did not help. Recently, when I set myself the task of demonstrating that Rochester's verse comprises an emotional element that may be called love, I looked at what twentieth-century experts have had to say about this phenomenon, without finding much assistance. Although a reciprocal commitment was certainly present in some of Rochester's poems, it did not fit in with the definitions of love supplied by the connoisseurs. Concepts such as *eros* ('need-love') and *agape* ('gift-love'), employed by Milton as well as by present-day writers on love, were applicable to one or two individual contexts but unable to serve as general terms of classification.[2] Besides, the twentieth-century authorities insisted on the recognition of the loved one as a person in her own right, and Rochester's texts did not, on the whole, contain much awareness of the other as an 'other'. According to one modern expert on the psychology of love, 'Love is the power within us that affirms and values another human being as he or she is', 'the one power that awakens the ego to the existence of something outside itself', 'an *appreciation*, a recognition of another's value'.[3] Love conceived along those lines would truly be 'the most gen'rous passion of the mynde', in the words of Rochester's Artemiza. But Artemiza laments the loss of that feeling, and it cannot be said to be in evidence in any of the poems which have come across to me as genuinely concerned with love. Finally, repeated perusal of H. M. Richmond's classic study, *The School of Love*,[4] convinced me that the evolutionary patterns behind the Stuart love lyric would not help me set up a conceptual framework for my attempts to define the passion, the feeling, of love in Rochester's poetry. The upshot of all this casting about for a terminology was the decision to forgo one entirely, attempt to find out whether I had any sort of case and then see if it could be put in everyday language.

At this point I should try to explain how I distinguish between those poems which seem to me to be 'real' love poems and those which, in my view, chiefly constitute the results of a skilful craftsman's play with conventions. It is not an unproblematic distinction. Some of Rochester's lyrics, however, adhere so closely to traditional patterns in love poetry that one may safely speak of deliberate explorations *and* subversions of familiar attitudes

– amorous servitude in a Petrarchist mode, for instance, and the fruition-versus-anti-fruition antithesis. There may be a personal impetus in the form of an element of rhyming for one's pintle's sake in lyrics like *The Advice* ('All things submit themselves') and *Verses put into a Lady's Prayer-book*, but, finely wrought as they are, they do not deviate in any marked sense from the persuasion-to-enjoy mould in which so much Restoration lyric poetry was cast.

By contrast, the three lyrics 'Absent from thee', *The Fall* and 'An Age in her Embraces pas'd' do not conform to any seventeenth-century matrix, nor does *A Ramble in St. James's Park*, which I count among Rochester's poems on love. These love poems, of course, do not merely deviate from contemporary patterns: they differ markedly among themselves as well. Even so, they have one important characteristic in common: in the situations they proceed from, an amorous relationship exists before the 'action' begins. The lovers are past the stage of conquest, and there is no happy-ever-after. In fact, 'after' is all there is; and 'after' assumes various guises, none of them paralleled, as far as I am aware, in contemporaneous verse.

It has to be a tentative distinction, though, and usage and idiom in the texts do not constitute very firm ground either. Terms such as 'love' and 'heart' have a very wide range of applicability in Restoration poetry, including Rochester's. 'Love' can mean anything from an intrusive bout of sexual lust, most conveniently dealt with by a page-boy (*Love to a Woman*), to a vision of felicity with the perfect girl (*Song* ('To this Moment a Rebell')); similarly, 'heart' may be the seat of tender devotion (*The Fall*) or a despised sexual partner (*Song* ('Absent from thee')), depending on the context. In other words, the question of whether or not certain items of amorous vocabulary occur in the individual poem does not lead to any reliable conclusions.

A factor that further complicates attempts to isolate 'true' love in Rochester's poetry from 'false' protestations of adoration is that, in the words of *Upon Nothinge*, true and false are 'the subject of debate' as well. I would submit that the presence of love in Rochester's poetry is primarily sensed in the betrayal of it, that the strongest amorous passion is felt when falseness to love is either contemplated, feared or experienced. Such falseness is never simply a matter of sexual infidelity, a phenomenon to which Rochester's verse repeatedly and insistently attaches no significance *per se*. And yet there are poems – *Song* ('Absent from thee') is one example – where sexual relations with other people than one's regular partner are designated as 'false'.

Fortunately, however, there is a cluster of concepts that helps prevent the notion of real love in Rochester's poetry from utter submersion in doubt's boundless sea. I have drawn attention to them before, and so have other critics, but I do not think their implications have as yet been fully explored.[5] They make up an intriguing triad: safety, or security; rest, or quiet and peace; and truth, or sincerity. One of those Rochesterian contexts in which safety, rest and truth form the attributes and/or concomitants of love is the passage from *Artemiza to Chloe* to which I alluded earlier:

> *Love*, the most gen'rous Passion of the mynde,
> The softest refuge Innocence can fynde,
> The safe directour of unguided youth,
> Fraught with kind wishes, and secur'd by Trueth,
> That Cordiall dropp Heav'n in our Cup has throwne,
> To make the nauseous draught of life goe downe,
> On which one onely blessing God might rayse
> In lands of Atheists Subsidyes of Prayse
> (For none did e're soe dull, and stupid prove,
> But felt a God, and blest his pow'r in *Love*).
> This onely Joy, for which poore Wee were made,
> Is growne like play, to be an Arrant Trade;
> . . .
> But what yet more a Womans heart would vexe,
> 'Tis cheifely carry'd on by our owne Sexe,
> . . .
> They call whatever is not Common, nice,
> And deafe to Natures rule, or *Loves* advice,
> Forsake the Pleasure, to pursue the Vice.
> To an exact perfection they have wrought
> The Action *Love*, the Passion is forgott.

(lines 40–51, 54–5, 59–63)

For reasons I have explained elsewhere,[6] I do not regard this passage as satirical in the sense that Artemiza's stance is seen to be ridiculous. The irony here is directed against those – mainly women – who debase love against their own best interests. That irony hits hard, and the fixed point from which it lashes out is precisely those lines on 'the most gen'rous Passion of the mynde'.

The most striking aspect of that passion, partly because it is not necessarily what one would have expected to find, is the element of trust, of confidence: 'The softest refuge Innocence can fynde, / The safe directour of unguided youth' (lines 41–2). True love, in other words, is something one could have faith in, a power to which a young and vulnerable person might be entrusted, a reliable, even infallible, guide. That amounts to making a peculiarly exalted claim for love, and a striking contrast with the Hobbesian nominalism which one meets elsewhere in Rochester's work.[7] One would have to search long for a similar eulogy on any earthly phenomenon in the Age of Reason – even on Reason itself. But is it altogether an earthly phenomenon?

Part of the answer to that question may be supplied by Rochester's best-known, in the sense of most anthologised, poem, the song beginning 'Absent from thee':

Absent from thee I languish still
Then ask me not when I return,
The straying fool 'twill plainly kill
To wish all day, all night to mourn.

Dear from thine arms then let me fly
That my fantastick mind may prove
The torments it deservs to try,
That Tears my fixt heart from my love.

When weary'd with a world of woe
To thy safe bosome I retire
Where love and peace and truth doe flow,
May I contented there Expire

no satisfaction sought.

Least once more wandring from that heav'n
I fall on some Base heart unbles'd,
Faithless to thee, false, unforgiv'n
And loose my everlasting rest.

After the half-page of criticism which is still the unsurpassed general commentary on this lyric, Anne Barton (then Anne Righter) said, 'It both is and is not a secular poem'. Later, Warren Chernaik maintained that '[t]he primary emotion in this powerful, beautiful poem would appear to be a displacement of religious sentiment'. [8] These two statements touch the heart of the matter. *Song* ('Absent from thee') is a man's plea for permission to absent himself for as long as he likes from the woman who loves him, until he is weary of dissipation and hence ready to return to her. At that time, he hopes to die at her breast so as not to be physically able to stray again: a *Liebestod* for a particularly dismal reason. While it is not sensual appetite as such, but his restless mind, that pulls him away, his mind possesses no power to keep him off certain misery, and it is obviously unlikely ever to gain any such strength; in other words, only death can stop his straying and no responsibility can possibly attach to him. 'Absent from thee' is not a favourite with all Rochesterians,[9] but it remains the most remarkable love lyric I have ever read.

The preceding summary of 'Absent from thee' was 'secular' enough, but the poem has strong religious overtones. They are manifest at two levels: first, and most conspicuously, at the level of language, especially in the concluding stanza with words and expressions such as 'heav'n', 'unbles'd', 'Faithless', 'unforgiv'n' and 'everlasting rest'. Second, the relationship between the speaker and his addressee resembles the one between an errant sinner and God. It illustrates St Augustine's famous prayer in the *Confessions*, 'Give me chastity and continence, but not just now'.[10] A particularly grim feature in this poem is the lady's situation: her man is about to leave her to disport himself with other women; when he comes back he hopes to die in her embrace – never an enviable situation for the female partner – and she is asked to countenance proceedings which leave her with nothing. Worse still, she is exhorted not to vex his wretched conscience further by asking about the time of his return. It is difficult to imagine any 'normal' woman acceding to such requests, and only a saint would await the strayed reveller's homecoming quiescently under such circumstances.

Of course, if these stanzas are envisaged as a personal appeal directed at Lady Rochester, it might be countered that she had no choice but to stay where she was, having her family and estates to run. But there is much more to this poem than a husband's plea to his long-suffering and essentially captive wife not to sadden his leave-taking with remonstrances.

If the speaker disclaims any ability to desist from pursuing his own ruin, he likewise trusts the dispenser of forgiveness and eternal peace whom he abandons not to abandon him; that is to say, he places the same faith in her as the Christian does in God. To quote St Augustine again, 'No one can lose you, my God, unless he forsakes you' (*Confessions*, IV.9). By dying in the arms of the personage who bestows those Christian blessings of love, peace and truth, the speaker will, he hopes, avert that danger.

Read in this manner, 'Absent from thee' becomes a transposal to a man–woman relationship of a Christian's prayer, such as we might find in George Herbert's *The Temple*. If Rochester's editors are right, it would not have been the only time he did something along those lines. Such a transposal is exactly what took place when two of Francis Quarles's *Emblems* were turned into the poem beginning 'Why do'st thou shade thy lovely face?' Again, Anne Barton (Righter) has offered a commentary which is hard to improve on.[11] Assuming the minimalistic adaptation to have been made by Rochester,[12] she shows how he transformed Quarles's celebratory and supplicating stanzas directed to God into a wistful declaration of love for a woman. Barton's characterisation has often been quoted: 'The whole object of [Rochester's] exercise is to change as little as possible of the original while wresting it in a different direction, transforming it into its opposite'.[13]

So what designation should be put on the result? Is it a parody, as Ellis claims, or a creative pastiche, as Vivian de Sola Pinto said?[14] And what about the utilisation of religious concepts and imagery in 'Absent from thee' and other poems? Should it be taken to suggest that earthly and heavenly love are somehow equivalent? That would be blasphemous, of course, and so – only more so – would the notion that there is no such thing as divine love in the first place. Another, and also very grave, implication would be that humans are not capable of loving the Deity and that such love as they can muster must hence necessarily be restricted to their own kind.

Besides the classic critical turbulence around the notion of authorial intention, the chief danger of attempting to ascribe any one of these views to Rochester consists in forgetting that he is one of those rare poets who can be extremely funny even when exploring or touching on urgent and disturbing concerns. A recognition of the irreverent humour that is so attractive in Rochester's verse is mandatory, but it should not blind readers to the serious dimensions of his work. For the critic, striking a balance is not easy; the simultaneous perception of levity and gravity is a tall order at the best of times.

The centre of gravity where Rochester the love poet is concerned is located in the inversion of the qualities with which he invests true love: insecurity, unrest and falsehood (the opposites of safety, peace and truth). Restlessness is a pervasive feature in his work, as many scholars have observed.[15] The inability to achieve certainty and harmony infuses his poetry with that curious nervous mobility which is so characteristic of Rochester, and which has set up such massive challenges to critics trying to work out consistent points of view in his poems.

The fundamental paradox that confronts a student of Rochester's stances and values as expressed in his verse may be summed up in the following terms: on the one hand, the mind pursues satisfaction through the body; on the other, minds are particularly unreliable guides and bodies are lamentably fallible. The much-vaunted sensual pleasure may be the best that humans can strive for, but it is not good enough; it does not satisfy, in either the short term or the long run.

Rochester's poetry never portrays lasting satisfaction, but those texts which I regard as genuine love poems afford us an idea of what such satisfaction would entail: the harmonious union of the speaker with a giver and recipient of love who never fails, changes or deceives and who is, in other words, like God. It may seem curious that the quality most ardently desired in that lover is constancy, the very characteristic which is so thoroughly spurned in a number of Rochester's poems. Still, this constancy is not merely, or even predominantly, physical. In any case, poems such as *The Fall* and *Song* ('An Age in her Embraces pas'd') are informed by doubts of a loved one's reliability. The latter poem even suggests that, if it were not for the existence of that doubt, the couple's love would not be real:

> Nor censure us you who perceive
> My best belov'd and me
> Sigh and Lament, complaine and Grieve,
> You think we disagree –

> Alas! tis sacred Jealousy,
> Love rais'd to an extream,
> The only proof twixt her and me
> We love and doe not Dream.

> Fantastick fancys fondly move
> And in fraile joys believe,
> Taking false pleasure for true love,
> But pain can ne're deceive.

Kind Jealous doubt, tormenting fear
And Anxious cares (when past)
Prove our Hearts Treasure fixt and Dear
And makes us blest at last.

(lines 21–36)

The last stanza makes it clear that, while jealousy is a necessary goad, it is not itself the substance of true love. That can be realised only in a future state of peace, when the dark passions have served their quasi-purgatorial purpose.[16] The word 'fixt' is highly significant. In 'Absent from thee', the restless mind had the ability to tear away a fixed heart; but here a more sanguine speaker aspires to a state of ultimate bliss from which he will not be tempted to stray again.

The speaker of *The Fall* harbours no such hope:

How blest was the Created state
    Of Man and Woman er'e they fell
Compar'd to our unhappy Fate:
    Wee need not feare another Hell.

Naked beneath coole shades they lay:
    Enjoyment waited on desire.
Each member did their wills obey
    Nor could a wish sett pleasure higher.

But we poore slaves to hope and fear
    Are never of our Joyes secure:
They lessen still as they draw nere
    And none but dull delights endure.

Then *Cloris* while I Duly pay
    The nobler Tribute of a heart,
Be not you soe severe to say
    You Love me for a frayler part.

Perfect love, the total harmony of minds and bodies, was lost when Adam and Eve yielded to the temptation to know what it would have been much better for them to have remained ignorant of. The distressing outcome landed posterity in the hell of fear, anxiety and impermanence.[17] The quality of sensual pleasure was debased beyond recognition when mankind opted out of God's design. The 'unhappy Fate', however, does not entail an absence of the passion love. The final stanza adumbrates three levels in the couple's relationship: the lady, Cloris, occupies the highest position; her lover humbly pays her the vassal's tribute in the shape of his heart; and he begs her to be content with that rather than to perceive his worth in whatever sexual capacity he has – a capacity which he clearly does not rate very highly. The sovereign position of Cloris is to some extent undermined by the fear that she might fail to assign her priorities correctly. Her very pregnability in this regard heightens the apprehensive tone of the concluding stanza, where the possibility of a second 'fall' is suggested: like Adam and Eve, Cloris may succumb to the lure of an inferior object, much to the detriment of the couple's relationship (deficient as it already is in comparison to that of the prelapsarian lovers). That possibility underscores the gloominess of the poem's title and lends it a powerful ironic twist.[18]

The word 'blest' occurs in the first line of *The Fall* and the last of *The Mistress*. It is natural to think of it – and of 'unbles'd' in 'Absent from thee', line 14 – as an example of language with religious overtones; but Renaissance, Baroque and Restoration poetry had used the concept of 'bliss' so often in the sense of 'perfect erotic consummation on earth' that such connotations inevitably adhere to it as well.[19] Along with the apparent contradiction between wished-for constancy in love and rejected sexual fidelity, this duality makes it necessary to enquire further into the way in which Rochester's poetry positions sexual activity in relation to true love.

In none of the three lyrics held up as crucial in the present context is sexual pleasure regarded as the highest good. Indeed, so far as sexual pursuits are referred to at all, it is their inherent unsatisfactoriness that is emphasised: in the embraces of 'Base heart[s]', the fugitive from bliss will reap woes, not joys ('Absent from thee'); the stepping-stone to lasting happiness is pain, not 'false pleasure' (*Song* ('An Age in her Embraces pas'd')); and the sex is more fragile than the heart (*The Fall*). It would be tempting to postulate a division between love and sex, constructing one of those binary opposites so popular among some critics, but that would surely be too drastic a step. After all, there is a patent erotic dimension in those three troubled relationships, and it clearly matters: the joys of sex may be insecure and frail, but they are there. When Artemiza regrets that people devote so much attention to 'The Action Love', forgetting 'the Passion [Love]' (line 63), she is not saying that the 'Action' is worthless in itself, only that it is of little use or value without real inclination; and such an inclination is obviously present in these lyrics.

With regard to the issue of fidelity versus *fides* in Rochester's poetry, the central text is *A Ramble in St. James's Park*. The story is a simple one: the speaker, importuned by lust, goes out into the park for relief and accidentally runs into his mistress Corinna there. She will have none of him, however, having, one might say, her hands full with three young fools who conquer her by cheap flattery. Her lover bursts into a torrent of abuse, curses her and vows revenge.

Most commentators on this poem have concentrated on Corinna's sexual betrayal. Naturally, it must be galling to be cold-shouldered by one's favourite when in pursuit of gratification of which she would be the ideal purveyor, but her offence against her lover amounts to more than mere 'Jilting'. First, of course, it is the most gruesome aberration of taste: the three fops should be far beneath her notice, so her preference is doubly insulting. More importantly, as Barbara Everett expressed it, 'what maddens the poet to near screaming-point is that this semi-goddess has sold him *for nothing*':[20] not only does she go off with nonentities who are unlikely to be adept performers, but she betrays her true lover to these disgusting lackeys-on-the-make who are out for social status rather than sexual satisfaction.[21] To a Court Wit, aspirations of that sort do not constitute legitimate business anywhere, least of all in St James's Park, which is 'consecrate to *Prick* and *Cunt*' (line 10). What precisely does Corinna betray? The speaker wails over her 'Treachery / To humble fond, believing me / Who gave [her] priviledge above, / The nice allowances of Love' (lines 107–10). Reminding her that he had been content for her to have intercourse with anyone she pleased so long as she derived real physical pleasure from it (he flatters himself that it was he who originally aroused her appetite), he exclaims:

> You [. . .] cou'd make my Heart away,
> For Noise and Colours, and betray,
> The Secrets of my tender hours,
> To such *Knight Errant Paramours*;
> When leaning on your Faithless Breast,
> Wrapt in security, and rest,
> Soft kindness all my pow'rs did move,
> And Reason lay dissolv'd in Love.

(lines 125–32)

The situation recalled by the speaker is very like the one envisaged in stanza three of 'Absent from thee': in the arms of the loved one in whom he had total confidence, he was at peace, he knew no fear and felt no danger, and he told her things of which his heart was full. Those were hours of perfect trust, with bodies and feelings in harmonious union (or so he thought) and the mind, that continual rogue firework, neutralised and pacified at last: 'Reason lay dissolv'd in Love' (line 132). It is impossible to ignore the sexual implications of the verb 'dissolv'd' in a poem by Rochester who, like other Restoration writers, repeatedly uses it to denote ejaculation.[22] The quoted lines describe moments of post-coital repose when the only thing that moves is warm affection, all strenuous thought and all physical passion having been spent. It is this that Corinna's act of treason belies, for her conduct amounts to something other than mere infidelity: it constitutes a breach of faith. It is the more painful because her treachery is directed not against a hope, but against what the speaker believed to have been an achieved fact.

It is interesting that the furious rambler intends to concentrate his malevolent efforts on undermining Corinna's position after marriage. Such punishment fits the crime particularly well: Corinna betrayed her lover's trust, and now he anticipates destroying her future husband's trust in her.[23] This false goddess must never have another devotee; his revenge will take care of that.

Several scholars have noticed the frequent use of biblical and otherwise Christian expressions in *A Ramble in St. James's Park* and have drawn different conclusions from it.[24] As was the case with 'Absent from thee', the religious element operates on more than one level. There are the deliberately debased 'consecrate' and 'hallow'd' in lines about the Park itself (lines 10 and 33); the similarly blasphemous lines on the ambitious crab-louse and on the inability of doctors, doormen of life and death, to believe in the Incarnation (lines 147–9); and the representations of Corinna's vagina as a once-sacred vessel that has been '*prophane*[*d*]' (line 166). There is also the suggestion of human and divine love coalescing in the lines that end in 'And Reason lay dissolv'd in Love' (line 132). To seventeenth-century Anglican theologians, reason was certainly a precious guide towards the Godhead, but the agent of transcendence was love: God's for man and man's for God, and it was the stronger power.

While the religious analogies should not be pushed too far, it is worth remembering that the quality which Rochester's entire *oeuvre* so significantly lacks – peace, quiet, rest – was and is frequently held up as a priceless concomitant of Christian faith. If Gilbert Burnet's account of his talks with Rochester are to be credited as reliable biographical material, Rochester was perfectly aware of that; indeed, the wily prelate seems to have worked on this promising tack. According to Burnet, Rochester

> often confessed, that whether the business of Religion was true or not, he thought those who had the perswasions of it, and lived so that they had quiet in their Consciences, and believed God governed the World, and acquiesced in his Providence, and had the hope of an endless blessedness in another State, the happiest men in the World: And said, He would give all that he was Master of, to be under those Perswasions, and to have the Supports and Joys that must needs flow from them.[25]

Burnet made Rochester admit that 'the whole Systeme of Religion, if believed, was a greater foundation of quiet than any other thing whatsoever: for all the quiet he had in his mind, was, that he could not think so good a Being as the Deity would make him miserable'.[26] It is a distinctly pathetic hope which Burnet lost no time in quashing.

There is reason to review other religious analogies in the poems brought up here as exponents of Rochester the poet of genuine, if troubled and painful, love. Love in these poems is a matter of faith and trust; it is a thing beyond reason, and the truth with which it is associated is supra-rational, too. It is also, essentially, a reciprocal phenomenon; unlike nineteenth-century theorists on love such as Schopenhauer and Stendhal, the poet Rochester explores actual partnerships, however conscious of their flaws, biased towards the male perspective and obsessed with the lover's tribulations rather than with the loved one's intrinsic worth.[27] Similarly, divine love is always a two-way concern, encompassing both God's love and the love of God.

But before it all begins to sound too idyllic, it has to be said that the visions of what I have ventured to call 'true love' in Rochester's verse are either unrealised or have been shattered by experience. We do not know that the addressee in 'Absent from thee' will live up to those God-like qualities with which the speaker has invested her. In 'An Age in her Embraces pas'd', uncertainty is pronounced: will the lady brave the purgatory of jealousy with the man who loves her? It is, at best, an ardent wish. As for *The Fall*, the accent in that poem is on the imperfection of present-day amorous pursuits in relation to those of the perfect lovers, prelapsarian Adam and Eve, and the moment of truth in *A Ramble in St. James's Park* was dishonoured by subsequent perfidy. Whether or not one feels that the pulse of genuine emotion is at least occasionally felt in Rochester's love poetry, one thing is perfectly clear: it affords no scope for sentimentality.

And how could it be otherwise? Rochester's lovers live in a fallen world. The difference between Artemiza's outline of perfect love – a description in which love is expressly designated as a gift from God – and the everyday reality she sees everywhere around her is as radical as the shift from innocent wedded bliss to post-lapsarian concupiscence in *Paradise Lost*.[28] Rochester's verse illustrates the contemporary malaise and disillusionment that prevailed in the realm of love, the subject *par préférence* in the *salons* of Europe. Appropriately, the chapter on the seventeenth to the nineteenth century in Martin S. Bergmann's historical study *The Anatomy of Loving*[29] is headed 'Love in a Disenchanted World'. That decline in 'the Passion Love', and the exclusive concentration on 'the Action' which Rochester's Artemiza complained of, are expressed in another chapter heading by a modern historian of love: quoting Sébastien Chamfort, Morton M. Hunt called his review of love in the Age of Reason 'The contact of two epidermises'.[30]

As the preceding discussion has shown, Rochester's verse contains expressions of regret at this state of affairs, and those expressions are associated with religious concepts and conceptions. The connection simultaneously exalts and abases 'the Passion Love' and its exponents. To quote a single example: the restless and unhappy lover in 'Absent from thee' refuses to admit even the possibility that he might save himself by his own efforts; all his hopes for everlasting rest are centred in his lady's goodness. Similarly, the Protestant Christian (and Rochester was reared by a devout Puritan mother) knows that he has no prospect of salvation but in the grace of God. It is a similarity that extols the lady, but it inflicts savage humiliation on the man. There is evidence that Rochester always had what might be called a religious temperament; the things of this world were never enough for him. At the same time, he was an out-and-out sceptic, and such a man cannot, as Burnet found out, be reasoned into believing: it takes an act, a leap, of faith, dissolving reason.[31]

It is hardly a coincidence that the poems where Rochester's centre of gravity as a love poet is located contain allusions to Christianity. There are plenty of religious references in the other love poems, but they are characteristically pagan: 'The Gods no sooner give a Grace' (*A Pastoral Dialogue between Alexis and Strephon*, line 16); 'There the kinde Deity of Wine / Kis't the soft Wanton God of Love' (*Grecian Kindness*, lines 7–8); 'In vain you *vex* the Gods with your Petition' (*Verses put into a Lady's Prayer-book*, line 7).

There will be many readers who feel that that is where the 'real' Rochester is and that, in so far as his poems ever address true love, they do not have anything very interesting to say about it. Likewise, a case could be made out for the view that the Christian elements mentioned here are part and parcel of a project of merry blasphemy, as impish as it was impious. But as I have traced what seemed to me to be the impulses of emotion to their synapses, I have become more and more convinced of one thing: to Rochester, love, like religion, 'was either a mere Contrivance, or the most important thing that could be'.[32]

5 Letter from Henry Savile to Rochester, 25 June 1678

4

Rochester and Falstaff

HOWARD ERSKINE-HILL

'If sack and sugar be a sin, God help the wicked' was the saying of a merry fat
gentleman who lived in days of yore, loved a glass of wine, would be merry with
a friend and sometimes had an unlucky fancy for a wench. Now, dear Mr Savile,
forgive me if I confess that upon several occasions you have put me in mind of
this fat person ...

So Rochester wrote in June 1678 to the man who Frank Ellis has suggested
was the poet's closest friend.[1] Drinking and wenching hardly marked Henry
Savile out from Rochester himself, of course; neither did worldly intelligence,
and it is Savile's inclination to corpulence which completes the parallel.
As early, perhaps, as 1671 Rochester had written insultingly of Savile's 'fatt
Buttocks', and in 1677 he recalled an occasion when 'two large fat nudities
led the coranto round Rosamund's fair fountain [at Woodstock] while the
poor violated nymph wept to behold the strange decay of manly parts ...'
'P[rick] ... you showed but little of', added Rochester cruelly, but the 'two
folio volumes' certainly out weighed the lighter 'quartos' of his companions
in this debauch.[2]

That Rochester should have remembered Falstaff's paradoxical encomium
in his own defence from *1 Henry IV*, II.iv, or perhaps from a Restoration
performance of that play,[3] should not surprise us. 'If to be fat be to be hated,
then Pharaoh's lean kine are to be loved' (lines 458–60): the idiom may be
different from that of Rochester, but the ingenuity of the disputatious mind,
with all its paradoxical resources, is similar.

It was not only to Savile that Rochester alluded to Falstaff. He seems to
have expected that his wife would recall several salient points in Falstaff's
dramatic life, for, commenting on pictures of herself which she had sent him,

he wrote that despite a severe countenance, 'somwhat inclin'd to prayer & prophesy, yett there is an alacrity in the plump cheeke, that seemes to signify sack & sugar, & the sharp sighted nose has borrowed quickness from the sweete-smelling eye'.[4] As Jeremy Treglown notes in his commentary on this letter, not only does 'sack & sugar' recall Falstaff's defence of himself to the Prince in the tavern, but the word 'alacrity' recalls Falstaff's rueful remark from *The Merry Wives of Windsor* after he has been thrown into the Thames with the laundry, 'you may know by my size that I have a kind of alacrity in sinking' (III.v.12–13), while the 'sharp sighted nose' seems to recall Mistress Quickly's account of Falstaff's death in *Henry V*, 'his nose was as sharp as a pen' (II.iii.17). Neither are 'prayer & prophesy' out of keeping in this remembering of Falstaff, who had religious language ever ready on his lips: as he once said, 'I would I were a weaver; I could sing psalms or anything' (1 *Henry IV*, II.iv.125–7). When Theobald amended the detail immediately following the comment on Falstaff's sharp nose, in Mistress Quickly's speech, to 'a babbl'd of green fields' (line 19) this was partly convincing because it had Falstaff on his deathbed remembering the second verse of Psalm 23. As Treglown has remarked, Rochester 'depends on the reader to recognize a literary reference in order to catch his tone, to feel the full weight of his otherwise unobtrusive irony'.[5] The Earl and Countess of Rochester appear to have shared a quite close verbal knowledge of the career of Falstaff in Shakespeare, including a play, *Henry V*, which seems not to have been performed on the Restoration stage in Rochester's lifetime.[6]

It may be further remarked here that the joke about 'alacrity in sinking' was well appreciated in Rochester's circle, for it is made almost the climax of Dorset's brilliant satirical epistle *To Mr. Edward Howard, on his Incomparable, Incomprehensible Poem called 'The British Princes'*, where its context of similes makes it certain that the words constitute a link between *The Merry Wives of Windsor* and Pope's *The Art of Sinking in Poetry* and *The Dunciad*. Another member of Rochester's circle, George Etherege, was likewise impressed by the sayings of Falstaff, quoting, seven years after Rochester's death, 'They hate us youth' (1 *Henry IV*, II.ii. 82–3).[7]

Thus far it seems that Rochester knew three out of the four Falstaff plays of Shakespeare, at least so far as they presented Falstaff. Only 2 *Henry IV* appears unalluded to, somewhat surprising, we may think, when we recall the themes of age and impotence – Rochesterian themes also – to be found in the Falstaff scenes of this play. 'Is it not strange', asks Poins of Prince Hal as they spy on Falstaff and Doll Tearsheet, 'that desire should so many years outlive performance?' (2 *Henry IV*, II.iv.250–1). Mr Tom Jones, of Pembroke College, Cambridge, may have supplied, however, the missing piece of the jigsaw puzzle; he has noticed that in Rochester's *The Imperfect Enjoyment* the speaker's denunciation of his 'Worst part', his inadequate male member, 'when great Love the onsett does Command, / Base Recreant to thy Prince, thou durst not stand' (lines 60–1), there may be an echo of 2 *Henry IV*, where Pistol, arriving hot-foot in Justice Shallow's orchard in Gloucestershire with news of the accession of Henry V, repudiates a disparaging remark of Justice Silence, 'Puff! Puff in thy teeth, most recreant coward base!' (V.iii.91). 'Base Recreant', 'recreant . . . base', are, to be sure, pretty common terms of insult; nevertheless, the fact that Pistol's line turns on demands and opportunities arising from the accession to the throne of the Prince, his old tavern acquaintance Prince Hal (Silence being thus allegedly backward to support his new sovereign), and the fact that the speaker of *The Imperfect Enjoyment* sees his sexual failure as comparable to a failure of military loyalty to *his* sovereign (love), suggest that there is probably a significant echo here. If so, it should be appreciated that Rochester's speaker in this poem is in effect accusing his male member of being a Hector or a Pistol in minor sexual encounters, but a mere Puff in love.

From all this it may seem that Rochester is remembering phrases not only from theatrical performances of some of the Falstaff plays (which we would expect) but also from his reading of Shakespeare; the collocation of words suggests the reaction of a reader rather than the memory of an onlooker. What is, however, quite clear, is that Rochester's Falstaff was not just one dramatic character at one moment ('If sack and sugar be a sin', etc.) but a particular life stretching over several plays.

When Henry Savile replied to Rochester's letter comparing him to Falstaff, he responded not by writing about a literary creation as much as about a social type. Savile felt he had known Falstaffs:

> if the good Gentleman who loved Sack and Shugar soe well was so lucky as to bring mee into your mind I wishe there were more of them, though mee-thinks since the death of poor Sr Simon Fanshaw that sorte of excellent breed is almost extinguished, or at att least soe farr decayed that except an old Cavalier Corporall that I believe you have seen begging in St James's parke, there is noe more any such person than a Phoenix to bee found in these parts, a true fellow is like a Kingfisher, can onely breed in calme weather.[8]

Savile's associations with the Falstaffian ('poor Sr Simon Fanshaw' and the 'old Cavalier Corporall') remind us of what the late Professor A. J. Smith and Dame C. V. Wedgwood called 'the voice of fagged out Royalism', quoting Brome, 'I have been in love, and in debt, and in drink, / This many and many a year'.[9] But Savile's images of the phoenix and the kingfisher, in their teasingly self-promoting way, also suggest another quality: a capacity for perennial renewal which is also part of the Falstaffian in its wider alliance with Renaissance humanism, seen in Erasmus's *Praise of Folly*, Udall's *Ralph Roister Doister*, Rabelais, and other cases where the festive and cowardly seem the better part of valour and the very spirit of life.[10]

I now introduce a partial digression to ask how far there is a Falstaffian spirit in Savile's commentary on current affairs in this and subsequent letters. Savile had volunteered for active service in the navy in the Second and Third Dutch Wars, had been an outrageous sexual adventurer (for example, he was chased from Althrop to London by the Earl of Sunderland for violating the privacy of the Countess of Northumberland), suffering spectacular defeats and flights as well as some military and diplomatic success. He was a courtier and MP who fell out of royal favour through his independence of judgment but, in the end, he survived to fill diplomatic positions.[11] If Shakespeare's Falstaff ever summarises his innermost view of the world, it is perhaps in his comment in *1 Henry IV* on the beginnings of the rising against the King on the throne: 'Worcester is stol'n away tonight; thy father's beard is turned white with the news: you may buy land now as cheap as stinking mack'rel' (II.iv.348–50). Behind Falstaff's Gargantuan self-indulgence, behind the extraordinary reach of his comic eloquence, words like these are given to him by Shakespeare to show his recognition of the unedifying and corrupt world which so often underlies the realm of high politics and the reign of pleasure. Both Savile and Rochester adopt this tone of disenchanted realism in their commentaries on public affairs though, naturally, their letters of gossip are more diffuse in literary effect than any words of Shakespeare's Falstaff. The latter part of Savile's letter of 25 June 1678 on the 'excellent breed' of Falstaffs is a sceptical commentary on the current war fever and the desire of the House of Commons to discharge the army by the end of August, but just manages to rein in its underlying pessimism. In a later letter, in which Savile comes to admit the probability of another war, he mordantly notes some signs of the times:

> On Saturday last was a generall rendezvous of above 10000 men upon Hounslow heath where all the bloody doeings was that one souldier killed another for waking him when hee was asleep, who is to bee hanged for his paines but by ye assistance of the civill power . . . To shew military discipline, Sr Phillip Howard was suspended his employment for not obeying some orders the D. of Monmouth gave him in wch though his Grace bee found in the wrong it is thought fitt the other should suffer for examples sake to shew that orders must bee obeyed though never soe foolish.[12]

Rochester himself, writing to Savile with London news over a year later, as the first moves of the Popish Plot and the Succession Crisis were becoming apparent, shows his own blend of bluntness and terse irony. This is the letter which begins 'The lousiness of affairs in this place . . .' and goes on:

> The general heads under which this whole island may be considered are spies, beggars and rebels. The transpositions and mixtures of these make an agreeable variety: busy fools and cautious knaves are bred out of them . . . , hypocrisy being the only vice in decay amongst us. Few men here dissemble their being rascals and

no woman disowns being a whore. Mr O[ates] was tried two days ago for buggery and cleared. The next day he brought his action to the King's Bench against his accuser, being attended by the Earl of Shaftesbury and other peers to the number of seven, for the honour of the Protestant cause.[13]

Basil Greenslade, quoting the first part of this passage in his essay 'Affairs of State', is surely right to see in Rochester an idiom pointing towards that of Swift, and is also correct to see the politics of Court, Court patronage and Court gossip ('who, and who's togeather', as Rochester put it in *Artemiza to Chloe* (line 35)) as 'politics subjected to a highly personal focus'.[14] Greenslade is persuasive in seeing *this* realm of politics as closer to Clarendon's than Locke's, despite the large differences of belief and value between Clarendon and Rochester. By the same token, the political world of Rochester and Savile is closer to that of Elizabeth's last years than to the new notions of Whig and Tory which were to be dominant at the end of the seventeenth century.

Savile evidently regarded Falstaffianism as a product of times of peace. Perhaps Sir Simon Fanshaw and the old corporal had been truly Falstaffian only before the civil wars, but in any case Shakespeare for his part saw the matter differently, dramatising Falstaff as he so often did against a background, or amidst a foreground, of physical and military conflict. Rochester differs in another way from Shakespeare's conception when he writes to Savile of 'Love, Wine, or Wisdome (wch rule you by turnes)', and of 'that second bottle' which is 'the sincerest, wisest, & most impartiall downwright freind we have, [and] tells us truth of our selves, & forces us to speake truths of others, banishes flattery from our tongues and distrust from our Hearts, [and] setts us above the meane Pollicy of Court prudence'. Of what Rochester calls 'the three Buisnisses of this Age, Woemen, Polliticks & drinking', he tells Savile 'the last is the only exercise att wch you & I have nott prouv'd our selves Errant fumblers'.[15] Falstaff was no fumbling drinker, it is true, but so much taking in of the 'lusty juice' of the grape did not take him so far as all that from flattery, or so close as all that to sincerity and truth. Doubtless, however, Rochester exaggerates to make his point when he writes of the moral virtues of the second bottle.

To return to libertinism and hedonism: Rochester, like Savile in one way, may have idealised the Falstaffian life of 'Woemen, Polliticks & drinking' in which the last was at least one pleasure you could achieve really well. In July 1678 Rochester quotes to Savile (consciously or unconsciously changing the lines to apply to his own debilitated physical condition) 'a good old ballad' – something he may have felt that the 'merry fat gentleman who lived in days of yore' could have sung, 'But he who lives not wise and sober / Falls with the leaf still in October'.[16] Treglown identifies this as the drinking song from *Rollo, Duke of Normandy*, a play attributed to Fletcher, and performed, it turns out, on the Restoration stage;[17] he might have added that it is sung by the cook as part of an enormous banquet scene. It is an excellent song of an unmistakably Elizabethan or Jacobean character, staunch and vigorous, and totally lacking in the elegance and classic grace so often found in Rochester:

> Drinke to day and drowne all sorrow,
> You shall perhaps not doe it to morrow.
> Best while you have it use your breath,
> There is no drinking after death.
>
> Wine works the heart up, wakes the wit,
> There is no cure gainst age but it.
> It helps the head-ach, cough and tissick,
> And is for all diseases Physick.
>
> Then let us swill boyes for our health,
> Who drinkes well loves the common wealth.
> And he that will to bed goe sober,
> Falls with the leafe still in October.[18]

By comparison with Rochester's songs on 'Woemen . . . & drinking' the song from *Rollo, Duke of Normandy* is innocence itself. Several of Rochester's most brilliant lyrics might be instanced as entirely different: *Nestor* ('*Vulcan* contrive me such a Cupp'); *To a Lady, in a Letter*; *Love and Life* and *The Fall*. As for the first of these, I could not improve on Barbara Everett's description of it as 'a brilliant energy of human creation, teetering over a void'.[19] Something similar might be said of the elegantly yet outrageously symmetrical in *To a Lady, in a Letter*: the buoyant confidence that all must be well in the most libertine possible world, when each partner can have his or her own pleasure – the lady a potent male, the gentleman a potent wine – gains its aesthetic triumph at the end, at the same moment as it recognises that all this 'perfect bliss' amounts to nothing more than the emission and consumption of different fluids:

> Nor doe you thinke it worth your care
>   How empty and how dull
> The heads of your Admirers are
>   Soe that their Codds be full.
>
> All this you freely may Confesse
>   Yett wee nere disagree
> For did you love your pleasure lesse
>   You were noe Match for mee.
>
> Whilst I my pleasure to pursue
>   Whole nights am takeing in,
> The Lusty Juice of Grapes, take you
>   The Juice of Lusty Men.

(lines 21–32)

Nothing could be less Falstaffian than the libertinism of Rochester's *Love and Life*. Marianne Thormählen writes of the 'suave persuasiveness' of its male speaker (meaning that she for one is unpersuaded) and later alludes to 'the slick equivocator' who utters this poem.[20] It is certainly right to mention the conventional occasion and purpose upon which Rochester's words rest – a persuasion to sexual fulfilment, a disuasion from any expectation of constancy – but this is merely the groundwork of the poem. Such conventional professions need not raise epistemological issues, but here they do. Compare, for example, something nearer the milieu of Falstaff, Feste's song from *Twelfth Night*:

> What is love? 'Tis not hereafter;
> Present mirth hath present laughter;
>   What's to come is still unsure.
> In delay there lies no plenty,
> Then come and kiss me, sweet and twenty;
>   Youth's a stuff will not endure.
>
> (II.iii.46–51)

Each poem stresses the fragility of love and the uncertainty of the future, but there is a world of philosophical difference between saying 'What's to come is still unsure' and 'What ever is to come is not'. When the poem, albeit in pleading play, goes on to ask, 'How can it then be mine?' it questions the continuity of the self, thus relegating on new grounds the notion of fidelity in love. Rochester's poem has a conceptual sophistication lacking in its Cavalier predecessors, and is more analytic than the *carpe diem* tradition to which it partly belongs. Generally, the loneliness and fragility of love in this poem, with its metaphysical and religious terms all transposed upon the fleetingly sexual, make it seem far removed from Elizabethan representations of love, and the crowded physical world of Falstaff.

Like the above poems, *The Fall* has at least the confidence of grace and style, though it concludes by touching on a fear raised in more explicit form in the exchange between Poins and Prince Hal in *2 Henry IV* which we have already noticed: 'Is it not strange that desire should so many years outlive performance?'

> But we poore slaves to hope and fear
>   Are never of our Joyes secure:
> They lessen still as they draw nere
>   And none but dull delights endure.
>
> Then *Cloris* while I Duly pay
>   The nobler Tribute of a heart,
> Be not you soe severe to say
>   You Love me for a frayler part.
>
> (lines 9–16)

As A. J. Smith says of this, 'The irony is disturbing as well as frank. She is to keep up the pretence of a sentimental loyalty, though they both know that the reality is frailer, because their illusion of satisfaction and performance is all they may have to console them.'[21] *The Imperfect Enjoyment* is once again recalled: sexual failure is there much more plain, but there also the speaker's erected wit finally balances his defective will, rather as *To a Lady, in a Letter* balances rival bottle with rival fop. *The Fall* takes us closer, in one sense of love, to what A. J. Smith calls 'The failure of love', but in another sense of the word one might challenge the equation of 'sentimental loyalty' with 'the nobler Tribute of a heart'.

There is, however, one poem of Rochester which indulges a vision apparently able to quieten that sexual fear and make good that sexual failure with something better than wit: it is *Song. A Young Lady to her Antient Lover*. Here my discussion of Rochester and Falstaff proposes what is indeed no more than hypothesis, though I think it is an hypothesis worth considering. As Sarah Wintle has pointed out, readers have always been rather confused and disturbed by this poem, one of the more sexually explicit texts to be allowed into *Poems on Several Occasions* (1691), a publication apparently authorised by Rochester's family.[22] While a few precedents for poems recommending love or marriage between young women and old men have been found, for example David Farley-Hills's citation of Henry King's *Paradox. That it is best for a Young Maid to marry an Old Man*,[23] the more obvious tradition was one of warning against such a match and enjoyment of the discomfiture of the perennial January at the hands of May. Against that tradition, the very harmony of the young lady and her ancient lover looks paradoxical:

> Ancient Person for whome I
> All the Flutt'ring youth defie,
> Long be it e're thou grow old,
> Aking, shaking, Crazy, Cold;
> But still Continue as thou art
> Ancient person of my heart.
>
> On thy wither'd Lips and dry
> Which Like barren furrowes Lye
> Brooding kisses I will power
> Shall thy youthfull heate restore:
> Such kinde showers in Autumne fall
> And a Second spring recall;
> Nor from thee will ever part,
> Ancient Person of my heart.
>
> Thy nobler parts which but to name
> In owr Sex would be Counted shame,
> By ages frozen grasp possest

From their Ice shall be releast
And sooth'd by my reviveing hand
In former warmth and Vigour stand.

All a Lovers wish can reach
For thy Joy my Love shall teach
And for thy pleasure shall improve
All that Art can add to Love;
Yet still I'le Love thee without art
Antient person of my heart.[24]

(Song. A Young Lady to her Antient Lover)

A paradoxical wish-fulfilment, especially perhaps from the male viewpoint, the address of the 'Young Lady' has a further paradox enfolded within it: while she professes sincere love, 'without art', the whole poem displays her sexual experience and skill. This is clearly avowed at the end: 'All that Art can add to Love; / Yet still I'le Love thee without art'. Not only is there a reversal in which the female takes on the male part of impregnating the land, but one can see from the whole poem why Sarah Wintle invokes *Aretine's Postures* or *The School of Venus* in her discussion of it, though she claims no verbal link.[25] The speaker of the poem may seem more like a genuinely affectionate whore than the at first sight innocent 'Young Lady' of the title.

As Sarah Wintle does not propose *Aretine's Postures* as a demonstrable source for the poem, so I do not propose 2 *Henry IV*, II.iv. It does seem to me, however, that the scene between Falstaff and Doll to which I have already alluded probably prompted the ideas of Rochester's poem. If there is anything in my suggestion it would point to a response by the poet to the one Falstaffian text – 2 *Henry IV* – not alluded to in Rochester's letters, though possibly echoed in *The Imperfect Enjoyment*. Shakespeare's scene is, of course, full of paradoxes of its own, some marking the distance between Rochester and Falstaff that I have already recognised. Thus Falstaff's world is so crowded and intrusive here that hardly have Bardolph and Falstaff beaten off that noisy Hector, Pistol, and brought in the music, than the Prince and Poins, disguised as drawers, sneak on to the scene ready to make their unfeeling remarks. It seems probable that Mistress Quickly and perhaps Bardolph remain on stage, and in the midst of all this Falstaff and Doll exchange some tender words. The onlooker sees them as the Prince and Poins do: 'Saturn and Venus this year in conjunction!' (lines 252–3); doubtless Doll is no spring chicken, but Falstaff is much older as each of them acknowledges. This has emerged from the brief passage of intimate dialogue they were able to enjoy; Doll asks, after Pistol has been driven away, 'when wilt thou leave fighting a days and foining a nights, and begin to patch up thy old body for heaven?', to which Falstaff responds, 'do not bid me remember mine end' (lines 221–5). The intimate dialogue picks up again a little later:

Fal. Thou dost give me flattering busses.
Doll. By my troth, I kiss thee with a most constant heart.
Fal. I am old, I am old.
Doll. I love thee better than I love e'er a scurvy young boy of them all.
Fal. What stuff wilt have a kirtle of? I shall receive money a Thursday. Shalt have a
    cap to-morrow. A merry song, come. 'A grows late; we'll to bed. Thou't forget me
    when I am gone.
Doll. By my troth, thou't set me a-weeping, an thou say'st so.

(lines 258–69)

Like Rochester's 'Young Lady', Doll rejects youth to profess a constant love
for her ancient lover. What A. J. Smith writes about *The Fall* has a striking
applicability here: 'The irony is disturbing as well as frank. She is to keep up
the pretence of sentimental loyalty, though they both know that the reality is
frailer, because their illusion of satisfaction and performance is all they have
to console them.'[26]

The advantage of this formulation is that it allows for all the material
motive and changeable behaviour which Shakespeare's scene encompasses:
Falstaff wants kisses and warmth from Doll, probably more; Doll wants the
clothes and money Falstaff speaks of; Mistress Quickly may hope to recover
through Doll something of what Falstaff owes her. The scene may be regarded
as a play of self-interest (Falstaff, Doll, Mistress Quickly) or of voyeuristic
entertainment (Falstaff, the Prince and Poins). Further, both Falstaff and
Doll turn briefly against one another when the Prince and Poins unmask
(lines 286, 326–8), yet when the Prince and Poins are gone, and Falstaff
himself is sent for, both Doll and Mistress Quickly seem overwhelmed with
affection for him, though at this moment the possibility of some lucrative
whoring has apparently been snatched away. Then, at the very end of the scene,
Falstaff sends for Doll and, urged on by Mistress Quickly, she runs after him,
weeping as she goes. So this scene also seems a play of love. Shakespeare's scene
and Rochester's poem show comprehensive and balanced authorial minds:
Falstaff thinks of Doll as a whore but still appreciates the kisses and show of
love, if it is a show; the 'Young Lady', with art and yet without art, is still a
welcome presence to one oppressed by the prospect of old age. In neither
case can it be said that the woman feels no real affection for the old man.

Around 1980 David M. Vieth, the American editor of Rochester's *Complete
Poems* (1968), noticed what might have been noticed long before: that the three
stanzas of *Song. A Young Lady to her Antient Lover*, as it was then received,
were not equal in length, as we would expect of a song – and as is true of
Rochester's best-known songs – but that the second stanza was longer than
the first, and the third longer than the second. The first was of six lines, the
second eight, and the third twelve, all being bound together by the similar
refrain. Vieth saw the aptness of this for the poem's subject but, so far as

I know, it remained for Frank Ellis in his Penguin edition (1994) to write of the 'stanzas' tumescence'.[27] In Harold Love's edition the layout he adopts from the Hartwell manuscript counters but cannot refute this important point, since the fundamental divisions within the text are articulated by the three-fold refrain (see note 24). If one were *hearing* the poem, for example, one would only be aware of the increasing space and number of lines between one refrain and the next. It is thus significant that it is in the third and longest of the *Song*'s fundamental components that the 'nobler parts' of the 'Antient person' do 'sooth'd by my reviveing hand / In former warmth and Vigour stand' (lines 1, 15, 19–20).

I want to suggest, however, that there is something more here than a simple correspondence between an extending stanza and a reviving member. I think that this song by Rochester takes us back to the world of the 'merry fat gentleman who lived in days of yore' and of the 'good old ballad', 'Drinke to day and drowne all sorrow', while yet in the strangely ambiguous role of the 'Young Lady' taking account of all the material realities behind the tenderness of Doll to Falstaff. I therefore believe that in this poem Rochester avoids any temptation to think of the Falstaffian as a product of lost, halcyon days when one could believingly fish for kings, but rather as a condition from which one can arise from the apparently dead or senile, like Savile's phoenix, and do so with the assistance of a tender-hearted whore who is at least as loving as she is acquisitive. The stanzas do not merely lengthen, but expand in scope: they expand to explore the large Elizabethan dimensions of Falstaff ('Theirs was the Gyant Race, before the Flood' as Dryden would put it in *To My Dear Friend Mr Congreve*[28]), a huge and hugely envied capacity for physical enjoyment together with a widely circumspect understanding of the ways in which material interest and personal affection may cohabit without the one betraying the other. That, in the end, is what I think Rochester the explorer learned from contemplation of the whole career of Shakespeare's Falstaff.

When the Bitch growing bold, to my Pocket do's
    (creep.
Then slily she leaves me, and to revenge the Af-
    (front,
At once she bereaves me of Money and Cunt.
If by chance then I wake, hot-headed and drunk,
What a coil do I make for the loss of my Punk?
I storm, and I roar, and I fall in a rage,
And missing my Whore, I Bugger my Page.
Then Crop-sick all Morning, I rail at my Men,
And in Bed I lie yawning till Eleven agen.

Song.

Love a Woman! y'are an Ass,
    'Tis a most insipid Passion,
To Chuse out for Happiness
The idlest part of God's Creation.

Let the Porter and the Groom,
Things design'd for Dirty Slaves,
Drudg in Fair *Aurelia's* Womb,
To get Supplies for Age and Graves

Farewel Woman, I intend
Henceforth ev'ry Night to sit
With my Lewd Well-natur'd Friend,
Drinking, to engender Wit.

Then

Then give me Health, Wealth, Mirth, and Wine,
And it busie Love intrenches,
    There's a sweet soft Page of mine,
Do's the Trick worth Forty Wenches.

Song *to* Cloris.

Fair *Cloris* in a Pig-sty lay,
    Her tender Herd lay by her;
She slept, in murm'ring Gruntlings they
Complaining of the scorching Day,
    Her slumbers thus inspire.

She dreamt, while she with careful pains
    Her snowy Arms employ'd,
In Ivory Pails, to fill out Grains,
One of her Love-convicted Swains
    Thus hasting to her, cry'd;

Fly, *Nymph!* Oh fly! e're 'tis too late,
    A dear-lov'd Life to save;
Rescue your Bosom-Pig from Fate,
Who now expires, hung in the Gate
    That leads to yonder Cave.

My self had try'd to set him free,
    Rather than brought the News,
But I am so abhorr'd by thee,
That ev'n thy Darlings Life from me
    I know thou wou'dst refuse.

Struck

But whether Life, or Death, betide,

    In love 'tis equal Measure,

The Victor lives with empty Pride;

    The Vanquish'd die with Pleasure.

A SONG.

1.

Love a Woman! you're an Ass,

    'Tis a most insipid Passion;

To chuse out for your happiness,

    The silliest part of God's Creation.

2.

Let the Porter, and the Groom,

    Things design'd for dirty Slaves;

Drudge in fair *Aurelia's* Womb,

    To get Supplies for Age and Graves.

3. Farewel

3.

Farewell Woman, I intend,

    Henceforth, every night to sit

With my lewd well natur'd Friend,

    Drinking to engender Wit.

A

6 *Love to a Woman* in *Poems on Several Occasions* . . . 1680 (Tyrrell-Fisher copy)
and *Poems, etc. on Several Occasions: with Valentinian* . . . 1691 (cancel leaf)

5

Rochester's homoeroticism

PAUL HAMMOND

How is one to interpret those moments in Rochester's work when he turns aside from his concern with heterosexual desire and writes about erotic relations between men? What is the place of homoeroticism in his work? There is a problem of terminology here which requires to be addressed at the outset. Modern interpreters are inevitably caught within the conceptual structures which we have inherited or created, and in this case social and cultural historians investigating sexual relations between men in the early modern period have at their disposal a set of terms which may appear to be clear, but are actually of questionable integrity and usefulness.[1] We know that the word 'homosexual' is a nineteenth-century coinage which still carries with it traces of the medical, psychiatric and philosophical assumptions which attended its origins, and that it is therefore an anachronistic and virtually unusable term in a discussion of seventeenth-century society when applied as a noun; even as an adjective it is problematic. Yet we also know that the authentic seventeenth-century terms 'sodomy' and 'sodomite' are also problematic, since they are at once too specific – referring to a particular act, and one which is not limited to sex between men – and too general, evoking a complex category of moral, spiritual and political deviance, as Alan Bray showed in his pioneering study *Homosexuality in Renaissance England*.[2] That category of 'sodomy' is itself internally incoherent, as Foucault argued,[3] and when it is applied within particular texts and discourses it tends to forge relationships with other ways of conceptualising the political subject or individual selfhood which produce distortions and confusions in those other discourses.[4] As for the word 'homoeroticism', this denotes a desire for, or an erotic appreciation of, the male body which remains at the level of seeing, longing, and representing, rather than of acting: it applies to the glance rather than the touch. But this may be of only limited usefulness for Rochester's period. I have argued elsewhere[5] that (with the notable exception of Marvell)[6] the homoerotic appreciation of the male body virtually disappears from English literature in the later seventeenth century, to be replaced by texts which make either troubled or fascinated readings of bodies, clothes, and social spaces; these are representations fraught with epistemological anxiety rather than delighted appreciation.

We also have available the word 'homosocial', usefully promoted by Eve Kosofsky Sedgwick,[7] which refers to those intense male relationships which are part of – indeed, crucial to – the public social order, and whose complete lack of any erotic dimension is frequently insisted upon by those involved, sometimes in ways which are curiously over-emphatic. The boundary between homosocial and homosexual relations is generally policed and enforced with vigour, and yet in some areas of early modern culture, perhaps particularly in the Renaissance, an easy, unthreatening homoeroticism seems often to have coloured male friendship. Indeed, the problem of understanding how sexual relations between men were conceptualised in the early modern period could be formulated as the problem of how to read the shifting and contradictory conjunctions and disjunctions which our texts make between the homosocial and the homoerotic.

There is yet another boundary which we need to bear in mind: the one which marks out a distinction between sex between two adult males, and sex between a man and a boy. Were these perceived in the Restoration period as two separate phenomena, or as two aspects of the same desire, or were they perhaps not distinguished at all? When Rochester's poems evoke the sexual attractions of a 'boy' or a 'page', they never suggest his age, not even approximately. To some extent the words 'boy' and 'page' may be markers of social status and sexual role rather than of age.

In part, our difficulties in interpreting emotional and sexual relations between men in the early modern period are created by our own definitions and the historiography in which they are implicated, and I hope in this chapter to circumvent this problem by exploring how definitions of sexual relations between men were made and unmade in the Restoration period, firstly in the texts written by Rochester, and secondly in the processes through which those texts were received and altered as they were circulated both in manuscript and in print. An investigation of the reception of these poems may assist us in charting the range of possible contemporary meanings which were attributed to Rochester's allusions to sex between men.

We should avoid trying to make these references coalesce centripetally into a coherent mode of subjectivity or a recognisable form of an individual's sexual desire; in the case of Rochester – more than with most writers – there is a strong centrifugal impulse, a desire to lose selfhood in a series of roles and masks and voices; to lose, particularly, that mode of coherent selfhood which is predicated upon narrative continuity. His poetry often disturbs such continuity through the fragmentation of experience into discrete moments which may be severed from any possible narrative by abrupt changes of argument or of register. We need to learn to read discontinuities which are formed locally, within texts, by unexpected fissures and contiguities, if we are to begin to read the wider conceptual terrain which is formed around this subject.

So what kind of discursive field is shaped by those texts in which Rochester and his contemporaries refer to sexual relations between men? What continuities and discontinuities are brought into play? Some intriguing examples are provided by the correspondence between Rochester and his close friend Henry Savile. In a letter dated 16 October 1677, Savile asks Rochester about a rumour concerning his latest escapade:

> there has been such a story made concerning your last adventure as would perswade us grave men that you had stripd yourselfe of all your prudence as well as of your breeches which you will give a man leave to thinke impossible who knowes & admires your talents as much as I doe. After all if you have not caught cold and made yourselfe sick with your race, it is not one pinn matter for all the other circumstances of it though the same advantages have been taken of it heer that use to bee on any unseasonable pranke performed by your L^p.[8]

As Savile notes, Rochester's behaviour has frequently been open to misconstruction, and an example of this is provided by Thomas Hearne's interpretation of this same episode: 'This Lord . . . used sometimes with others of his companions to run naked, and particularly they did so once in Woodstocke park, upon a Sunday in the afternoon, expecting that several of the female sex would have been spectators, but not one appeared.'[9] Hearne interprets the episode as part of a habit ('used sometimes . . . to run naked'), as an act of sabbath-breaking, and as a form of exhibitionism which was designed to impress female spectators; but these women – who never appear in anyone's narrative – are merely part of Hearne's interpretation of Rochester's intentions. By supplying these absent women, Hearne makes this a story of homosocial play and heterosexually motivated display, which is certainly a comprehensible framework for the incident, but by no means the only possible reading.

Savile goes on to say:

> without you the towne is soe dull that the Dutch men thinke themselves in Holland and goe Yawning about as if they were att home, for Gods sake come & helpe to entertain them for I am quite spent and can not hope to have my Spirits ever revived but by your L^{ps} Kindnesse and company of which I esteem one & love the other above all the happiness I have ever enjoyed.[10]

Should we hear a series of sexual innuendoes in 'entertain . . . spent . . . Spirits . . . revived', and in Savile's earlier reference to Rochester's 'talents'? If so, how are they directed – homosocially (sharing a self-deprecating joke with a male friend) or homosexually (making an erotic invitation to Rochester)? The problem of interpretation extends to the word 'Kindnesse', which had a wide semantic field from 'affectionate friendship' to 'sexual compliance'. What assumptions about likely behaviour between men, and what assumptions about epistolary idiom (at this date, and in this social circle) would we need to invoke in order to argue this one way or the other?[11]

Rochester replied to Savile in a letter which is preserved only in a printed text published in the reign of William III,[12] when standards of public decency had changed – and when the questions which were being raised about the new king's sexual interests made any reference to sex between men a politically sensitive topic.[13] According to this text, Rochester explains the adventure in these terms:

> For the *hideous Deportment*, which you have heard of, concerning *running naked*, so much is true, that we went into the River *somewhat late in the Year*, and had a *frisk* for forty yards in the Meadow, *to dry ourselves*. I will appeal to the *King* and the *D.[uke]* if *they* had not done *as much*; nay, *my Lord-Chancellor*, and the *Archbishops both*, when they were *School-boys*.

This explanation constructs the incident as an impeccably homosocial occurrence, although the syntax mischievously allows us the image of the King, the Duke, the Lord Chancellor and the two Archbishops all running naked through a meadow, until the sentence establishes this as a hypothetical scene from childhood. Then Rochester reminds Savile of an occasion in the previous year,

> when *two large fat Nudities* led the Coranto round *Rosamond*'s fair Fountain, while the poor *violated Nymph wept* to behold the strange decay of *Manly Parts*, since the Days of her dear *Harry* the Second: *Pr-ck* (tis confess'd) you shew'd but little of, but for *A—* and *B—ks*, *(a filthier Ostentation! God wot!)* you expos'd more of *that nastiness* in *your two Folio Volumes*, than we *all together* in our *six Quarto's*.

This time, collective male nudity is presented both as grotesquely unappealing and as a performance staged for a female audience (as Hearne had imagined). These gestures of definition are perhaps answers to a homosexual interpretation of the incident which is implicit but never articulated in Savile's initial enquiry.

Rochester's letter then refers to Savile's request that he come to London to help entertain the Dutchmen who are in town with William of Orange, 'a thing I would avoid like killing *Punaises*, the filthy savour of *Dutch-Mirth* being *more terrible*'. But, he says, 'the Prince of *Orange* is exalted *above 'em*, and I cou'd wish myself in Town to serve him in some *refin'd Pleasures*; which, I fear, you are too much a *Dutchman* to think of'. What might these '*refined Pleasures*' be? Given William's reputation for homosexual liaisons (whether this was justified or not is immaterial in this context – it suffices that there were already rumours around which Rochester could have heard[14]), are these the '*refined Pleasures*' which Rochester jokes about providing him with? Was this the reason why this letter was omitted when the collection of *Familiar Letters* was reprinted in 1699?

One has to remember how the letter continues: 'The best Present I can make at this time is the *Bearer*, whom I beg you to take care of, that the King may hear his Tunes, when he is easie and private, because I am sure they will divert him extreamly'. An implicit connection with the previous sentence is apparently being made, but as the sentence unfolds Rochester turns out to be offering James Paisible not to William (or to Savile) but to Charles II, who is most unlikely to have been interested in this young Frenchman's services in anything other than a musical capacity. But Rochester's letter does manage to be suggestive about William of Orange within an impeccably polite phrasing which prevents the letter from being incriminatory should it fall into the wrong hands. This is a text which plays several different, teasing games with the reader, each of which is predicated upon the silent suggestion of sex between men.

Of a different tenor is the letter which Rochester wrote to Savile on 1 November 1679, when the latter was on an embassy in Paris:

> The News I have to send, and the sort alone which could be so to *you*, are things *Gyaris & carcere digna*,[15] which I dare not trust to *this pretty Fool the Bearer*, whom I heartily recommend to your *Favour* and *Protection*, and *whose Qualities* will recommend him more; and truly if it might suit with your *Character*, at your times of leisure, to [make] Mr. *Baptist*'s Acquaintance, the happy Consequence would be *singing*, and in which your *Excellence* might have a share not unworthy *the greatest Ambassadors*, nor to be despis'd even by a *Cardinal-legate*; the *greatest and gravest* of *this Court* of *both Sexes* have tasted his *Beauties*; and, I'll assure you, *Rome* gains upon us *here*, in *this point* mainly; and there is no part of the *Plot* carried with so much *Secresie* and *Vigour* as *this*. Proselytes, of consequence, are daily made, and my Lord S—'s *Imprisonment* is no *Check* to any.[16]

This time there can be no doubt as to the use which Savile is being invited to make of this second French servant.[17] But once again Rochester's text (at least, in so far as the *Familiar Letters* of 1697 preserves Rochester's original text) traces an intriguing connection between homosexual interests and political ones, linking two kinds of secrecy. This time the letter seems to suggest that the Roman Catholic community in London included a homosexual subculture – which is what John Kenyon proposed as an explanation for the surprising ease with which Titus Oates was accepted into Roman Catholic circles.[18] Another form of ambiguity resides in the phrase, 'Proselytes, of consequence, are daily made': are these 'people made proselytes as a consequence of tasting Baptist's beauties', or 'proselytes of great consequence in society'? And to what

are these proselytes being converted? But the problem with this reading of the letter – taking it as a comment on current sexual practices in London society – is that it so obviously depends for its effect on giving a witty twist to the old commonplace associating Rome with sodomy. It is also a self-conscious rhetorical performance, and the quotation from Juvenal is in this respect perfectly apt. Once again, we are presented with a teasing, posing text, whose syntactical twists incite but ward off interpretation.

I would like to turn now to the question of how homosexual relations are represented in Rochester's poems, and how the wording of those poems was altered during their textual transmission.[19]

The most curious case is the poem *Love to a Woman*. In the version which editors have agreed is closest to Rochester's original, it clearly fashions a stance which rejects erotic involvement with women in favour of the homosocial pleasures of the all-male drinking session, and, if necessary, the sexual pleasures provided by a page. The poem makes a clear distinction within this all-male milieu, for it is the friend who provides companionship and wit, and the page who supplies the sex:

Song.

Love a *Woman*! y'are an *Ass*,
'Tis a most insipid Passion,
To choose out for your happiness!
The idlest part of *Gods Creation*.

Let the *Porter*, and the *Groome*,
Things design'd for dirty *Slaves*,
Drudge in fair *Aurelias Womb*,
To get supplies for Age, and Graves.

Farewel *Woman*, I intend,
Henceforth, ev'ry *Night* to sit,
With my lewd well natur'd *Friend*,
Drinking, to engender *Wit*.

Then give me *Health*, *Wealth*, *Mirth*, and *Wine*,
And if busie *Love*, intrenches,
There's a sweet soft *Page*, of mine,
Does the trick worth *Forty Wenches*.

This is the text as it appears in the first printed collection of Rochester's poetry, the *Poems on Several Occasions by the Right Honourable, the E. of R—* ('Antwerp', 1680),[20] a thoroughly disreputable edition which appeared shortly after Rochester's death. Though it is difficult, and often impossible, to date the circulation of Rochester's poems in manuscript, it seems unlikely on present evidence that this poem had achieved much currency before the publication of the 1680 edition. It survives in only six known manuscripts,[21] none of which can be dated earlier than 1680. In these manuscripts its relationship to Rochester's other songs is odd, for although it is consistently associated with a group of thirteen songs and erotic poems which are probably by Rochester, it is detached from this sequence and placed by various manuscripts in different positions along with the song beginning 'Amintor lov'd, and liv'd in pain' (whose authorship is unknown), the obscene verses 'In the Fields of Lincolns Inn' (probably by Sir Charles Sedley), and the song 'As trembling prisoners stand at bar' (by Alexander Radcliffe).[22] So *Love to a Woman* is found in a liminal position at the point where a coherent collection of poems securely attributable to Rochester dissolves into poems articulating a generally libertine ethos.[23] The uncertainty which attends the position of this poem might be construed as evidence of uncertainty as to its authorship were it not that these poems are generally presented without attributions, and *Love to a Woman* is included in the 1691 edition, which is not known to make any false attributions. So I would suggest that it may be the homosexual flourish in the final stanza which has caused it to be detached from the other pieces. The 1680 edition places it after the verses 'I Rise at Eleven', the quintessential description of a Restoration rake's day, and a poem which also includes a reference to sex with a page. Evidently someone thought that this was an appropriate juxtaposition.

In 1685 a revised version of the 1680 collection was published by A. Thorncome,[24] in which much of the explicit sexual language is bowdlerised. Thorncome's intervention extends to the complete eradication of the homosexual reference in this poem:

> Then give me Health, Wealth, Mirth and Wine,
> And if Busie Love intrenches,
> There's a sweet soft Love of mine,
> Does the trick worth forty Wenches.[25]

If this stanza still has some sort of point, the antithesis between 'Love' and 'Wenches' presumably now suggests a distinction between the poet's own girlfriend and the prostitutes who are no better at 'the trick' than she is.

In the careful edition which Jacob Tonson published in 1691[26] the poem was at first set up in much the same form that it had taken in *1680*, but as David Vieth pointed out, while the volume was being printed a cancel leaf was substituted which removed the final stanza.[27] This is more than an act of bowdlerisation, for it creates a significantly different poem from the four-stanza version which readers had been used to up to that point, and which we now take for granted. It places the poem securely within the boundaries of homosocial companionship, putting any homosexual interests beyond the pale and drawing an invisible but firm line between homosocial and homosexual pleasures. The final turn of the poem now occurs on the idea that the engendering of wit is the only form of procreation for a sensible man, rather than the suggestion that sex with a page is the only form of sexual pleasure for a sensible man. The poem in this form is a pleasing and witty performance which would not have been out of place (at least in tone, if not in sentiment) in a volume by Lovelace or Waller.[28]

But it was not only printed editions which had problems with this final stanza. The manuscript transmission of Rochester's poetry was just as much subject to censorship, this time by individual scribes. In the manuscript owned by Pierre Danchin, the entire poem is heavily obliterated, so what one reader carefully copied out, a subsequent owner rejected as unacceptable. Moreover, those witnesses which do preserve the poem show an interesting uncertainty at crucial points. The actual sexual act at which the page is so adept is variously called 'the trick',[29] 'the feat',[30] or 'the thing',[31] a set of variants which cannot be explained palaeographically. As for the boy himself, he is either a 'sweet soft Page' (as the 1680 edition calls him) or a 'Soft Young Page' (in the 1691 edition before cancellation). The copyist of one manuscript[32] was evidently somewhat distracted by seeing the use of 'soft' to describe the page, and wrote the word in the previous line as well ('soft love' rather than 'busy love'). So the textual tradition reveals various forms of uncertainty and unease around the very point at which one has to conceptualise the male speaker's male lover, and the sexual act in which they engage.

Another poem which displays significant textual instability around a homosexual reference is *The Disabled Debauchee*, one stanza of which runs thus:

> Nor shall our *Love-fits Cloris* be forgot,
> When each the well-look'd *Link-Boy*, strove t'enjoy
> And the best Kiss, was the deciding *Lot*,
> Whether the *Boy* us'd you, or I the *Boy*.[33]

This is the text of the poem in the 1680 and 1685 editions; once again the 1691 edition was altered as it went through the press, and corrected copies omit this stanza as do four of the manuscripts.[34] As in the case of the alterations to *Love to a Woman* this has the effect of changing the poem's semantic field and consolidating the homosocial environment which it imagines. Actually, the second-person address to 'Cloris' here awkwardly disrupts the prevailing sense that this poem is spoken by the rake to his younger companions (who are addressed as 'you' in lines 18 and 47). Some of the witnesses which do include this stanza alter the wording in ways which betray anxiety about what is being said. Two manuscripts have 'best Lov'd' for 'well-look'd', and although 'loved' is palaeographically a possible misreading of 'looked' it serves to remove the reference to the boy's beauty. Four manuscripts omit the word 'Boy' in the first line, a variant which might possibly be generated by a sensitivity to the niceties of metre, but which is more plausibly interpreted as a preference for imprecision. Three other manuscripts read 'sought' instead of 'strove', making the sexually motivated combat less vigorous. The two witnesses which read 'our deciding lot' instead of 'the deciding lot' make the game one which took place between the speaker and Cloris, thus blurring the obvious inter-pretation that each in turn kisses the boy, who then decides which of the two kisses was the best, and gives the winner a suitable reward.[35]

Most strikingly, whereas the 1680 and 1685 editions print the last line of this stanza as 'Whether the *Boy* us'd you, or I the *Boy*', all but two of the manuscripts which record this line have not 'us'd' but 'fucked'.[36] The 1680 edition is not noted for its coyness, and happily prints 'fuck', 'fucking' and 'fuckt' elsewhere in heterosexual encounters.[37] The manuscript tradition sug-gests that Rochester wrote 'fucked', and that whoever was responsible for *1680* (or for the copy-text which it was using) changed the word in this particular instance because it was too explicit a reference to homosexual intercourse. Nevertheless, the very imprecision of 'us'd' ironically creates a new field of meaning, a wider range of sexual possibilities than 'fuck'd'. Bodleian MS Don. b. 8 makes a confused attempt to deal with this point in a different way by removing the homosexual reference entirely and recording the last line as 'Whether yᵉ Boy you fucke, or you yᵉ Boy'.[38] Even the most careful student of Aretino's postures would have difficulty making sense of those arrangements.

A similar act of censorship in *1680* is found in *The Imperfect Enjoyment*. In the *1680* text we read:

> Stiffly resolv'd, twou'd carelessly invade,
> *Woman* or *Boy*, nor ought its fury staid,
> Where e're it pierc'd, a *Cunt* it found or made.[39]

Whereas *1680* reads '*Woman* or *Boy*', all but two of the extant manuscripts apparently read 'Woman or man'.[40] The consensus of manuscript witnesses points to Rochester having written 'Man', and so once again the text has been rewritten in order to change the way in which sex between men is imagined, in this case transforming it from the encounter of two adults to what was apparently the less unacceptable paradigm of adult and boy.[41] The 1685 edi-tion rewrites the lines even more drastically:

> Stiffly resolv'd, twou'd carelessly invade,
> Where it essay'd, nor ought its fury staid,
> Where e're it pierc'd, entrance it found or made.[42]

But one also has to ask whether this poem is, in any case, really interested in sexual relations between men. The reference is perfunctory, and the casual phrasing suggests that the gender of the partner is immaterial, though at the same time the line 'Where e're it pierc'd, a *Cunt* it found or made' makes it clear that the male body is no more than a convenient substitute for the female. There is in fact no trace here of homoeroticism, no real responsive-ness to the sexual attractions of the male body.

I wish to turn now to a very different case, the song *Nestor* ('*Vulcan* contrive me such a Cup'). This is an adaptation of a poem attributed to Anacreon (number 17 in Renaissance editions of Anacreon; now number 4 in the *Anacreontea*), with some touches added from a second (once 18, now 5).[43] Vulcan is asked to decorate the drinking bowl:

> But carve thereon a spreading *Vine*,
>   Then add Two lovely *Boys*;
> Their Limbs in Amorous folds intwine,
>   The *Type* of future joys.
>
> *Cupid*, and *Bacchus*, my *Saints* are,
>   May drink, and Love, still reign,
> With *Wine*, I wash away my cares,
>   And then to *Cunt* again.[44]

In the first stanza Rochester sounds a note which has no exact precedent in the Greek text of *Anacreontea* 4:

> ποίησον ἀμπέλους μοι
> καὶ βότρυας κατ' αὐτῶν
> καὶ μαινάδας τρυγώσας,
> ποίει δὲ ληνὸν οἴνου,
> ληνοβάτας πατοῦντας,
> τοὺς σατύρους γελῶντας
> καὶ χρυσοῦς τοὺς Ἔρωτας
> καὶ Κυθέρην γελῶσαν
> ὁμοῦ καλῷ Λυαίῳ,
> Ἔρωτα κἀφροδίτην.[45]

Instead, the image of the two boys seems to have come from *Anacreontea* 5:

> ὑπ' ἄμπελον εὐπέταλον
> εὐβότρυον κομῶσαν
> σύναπτε κούρους εὐπρεπεῖς,
> ἂν μὴ Φοῖβος ἀθύρῃ.[46]

Here the *kourous euprepeis* ('good-looking youths') have become the 'lovely *Boys*' of Rochester's poem, but in neither of the Anacreontic poems is there any precedent for the last two lines of the stanza, 'Their Limbs in Amorous folds intwine, / The *Type* of future joys'.

Two of Rochester's contemporary admirers, Oldham and Lee, reacted to this poem in ways which suggest their disapproval of (or at least their lack of interest in) the homoerotic penultimate stanza. In *An Ode of Anacreon Paraphras'd: The Cup* (1683), Oldham writes:

Draw me first a spreading Vine,
Make its Arms the Bowl entwine,
With kind embraces, such as I
Twist about my loving she.
Let its Boughs o're-spread above
Scenes of Drinking, Scenes of Love:
Draw next the Patron of that Tree,
Draw *Bacchus* and soft *Cupid* by;
Draw them both in toping Shapes,
Their Temples crown'd with cluster'd Grapes:
Make them lean against the Cup,
As 'twere to keep their Figures up:
And when their reeling Forms I view,
I'll think them drunk, and be so too:
   The Gods shall my examples be,
   The Gods, thus drunk in Effigy.[47]

Oldham has taken over Rochester's rhyme of 'vine' and 'entwine', but he makes it clear that to his imagination it is the vine which is entwined around the bowl, like the poet embracing his girl. Bacchus and Cupid are drawn in 'toping Shapes', leaning against the cup rather than mutually entwined, and serve as an encouragement to the poet to drink rather than make love.

A second response to Rochester's poem may be traced in Nathaniel Lee's play *The Princess of Cleve* (staged 1682), in which Nemours says:

the Fury of Wine and Fury of Women possess me waking and sleeping; let me Dream of nothing but dimpl'd Cheeks, and laughing Lips, and flowing Bowls, Venus be my Star, and Whoring my House, and Death I defie thee. Thus sung Rosidore in the Urn.[48]

Whether or not this is a direct allusion to this particular poem, Rochester's poetry generally, and his reputation, have been purged of any homoeroticism through the thoroughly conventional insistence on wine and women. And this care to dissociate Rochester from homoerotic pleasure is particularly remarkable since elsewhere in the play Lee makes Nemours express homosexual interests in conversation with his eunuch Bellamore.[49]

But homoeroticism is already displaced within Rochester's poem itself. In the final stanza Cupid and Bacchus, the gods of love and of wine, promise the satisfactions of drink and (as Rochester puts it with shocking crudity) '*Cunt*'. This movement between the two stanzas presents a problem for the reader. One possible interpretation is that the two lovely boys turn out to be Cupid and Bacchus, and so the 'future joys' promised by these boys (which we thought were going to be the pleasures of homosexual sex) are defined instead as '*Wine*' and '*Cunt*'. An alternative reading is that the speaker's ideal world encompasses all these pleasures. So is Cupid an exclusive or inclusive symbol, the god of sexual pleasure in its various forms, or only of hetero-sexual pleasure? Does the gap between the stanzas mark a connection or a disjunction? There is also a shocking disjunction tonally as we move from the graceful sensuousness of the penultimate stanza to the graceless obscenity of the final line. This is a shock which several witnesses attempt to modify: *1691* and two manuscripts[50] read 'Love', which curiously has the inadvertent effect of keeping the homoerotic possibilities in play at the end of the poem. Some manuscripts try to make the ending return to drink ('And then to fill again') or to a named lover ('And then to *Phill*: again', Phill being a curiously androgynous name). All these changes, in their different ways, are responses to a perceived incoherence of tone and desire. So, if we think that the *1680* text is what Rochester wrote, how do we read the contrast between the homoerotic lyricism and the heterosexual crudity? The teasingly uncertain syntax and register through which this libertine milieu is constructed man-age to offer the prospect of homoerotic pleasure without quite establishing it as part of the speaker's own fantasy.

Moreover, as Marianne Thormählen astutely observes, the references to homosexual sex are conditional or unrealised:[51] the boys here are the type of *future* joys; the page is available *if* busy love entrenches, but we do not know that it will; the linkboy's decision is unknown, so we do not know whether the disabled debauchee ever did get to fuck him. She makes this point in the context of showing that such a conditional mood and temporal displacement also generally characterise Rochester's descriptions of sex with women; but I think that in the case of sex with men or boys there is a further grammat-ical distancing which one can observe. In *Nestor* the words 'I', 'me' and 'my' occur seven times, but not once in the stanza describing the boys: the speaker never explicitly owns this prospect. In *Love to a Woman* the syntax changes at the end of the poem: after 'I intend . . . to sit . . . Drinking' and 'give me *Health, Wealth, Mirth,* and *Wine*', the first person singular retreats: 'There's a sweet soft *Page*, of mine, / Does the Trick'. In *The Imperfect Enjoyment* it is the speaker's penis which is the grammatical subject, and the whole point of that poem, of course, is the way it functions independently of the speaker's desire.

These grammatical displacements of the speaker from the representation of sex between men contribute to forming the libertine pose. There is in some instances an epigrammatic shape to the lines – 'Whether the boy fucked you, or I the boy' – which marks them as tendentious gestures. The persona which governs such utterances is presented in a convenient summary in the verses beginning 'I Rise at Eleven', which are part of the Rochester apocrypha, and actually precede *Love to a Woman* in *1680*. The rake has been robbed by a prostitute, who has left him asleep:

> If by chance then I wake, hot-headed, and drunk,
> What a coyle do I make for the loss of my *Punk?*
> I storm, and I roar, and I fall in a rage,
> And missing my *Whore*, I bugger my *Page.*[52]

Again there is an epigrammatic punch to the line. This act seems to be produced more by anger and frustration than by desire, an assertion of power rather than an act of love. Indeed, *1685* rewrites the lines in just this spirit:

> I storm, and I roar, and I fall in a rage,
> And missing my *Lass*, I fall on my *Page*:[53]

Here 'fall on' could simply mean 'beat', with no sexual implications.

It is interesting, in the light of the grammatical caution of Rochester's own poems, that while the anonymous rake is made to dramatise himself quite freely here, the lines which I have quoted are not included when the verses are presented as part of an anecdote about Dorset and Rochester in a letter from Godfrey Thacker to the Earl of Huntington:

> My Lord Buckhurst and Lord Rochester being in company, a suddaine Malancholly possest him Rochester inquiring the reason hee answered hee was troubled at Rochesters lude way of living, and in these verses over the leafe exprest it
>
> > You rise at Eleaven
> > And dine at two
> > you get drunk at seaven
> > And have nothing to doe
> > you goe to a wentch but for feare of a clapp
> > you spend in your hand or spue in her lapp.[54]

We cannot know whether Thacker omitted the lines about the page, or whether they were added when the verses were worked up for publication; but in any case it seems clear that they can prove acceptable as part of the mythology of the anonymous rake, but not as part of a narrative about named individuals.

Here again we meet a boundary. In other instances we noticed that a line of demarcation ran between sex with a boy and sex with a man: this was one of the boundaries which *1680* maintained. In the preparation of the 1691 edition there were evidently second thoughts about including the last stanza of *Love to a Woman*, and in its final form *1691* omits the homosexual references both in that poem and in *The Disabled Debauchee*. Yet it prints *Nestor* in full, perhaps because there the reference forms an ecphrasis rather than part of a narrative. The manuscript tradition may have served as a convenient mode for the circulation of material which was too hot for printers to handle, but within that medium too there are many examples of censorship, revealing a range of sensitivities on this subject. It does not appear, however, that the manuscript tradition includes any evidence that Rochester's poems were altered to make them *more* explicit, as happened in the case of some Restoration satires.[55]

One of the crucial differences between Rochester's references to heterosexual and to homosexual sex is that while both are caught up in his endless posing (and in the reflexive commentaries which in turn expose those poses as egoistic fictions) homosexual sex is never included within a grammar of love, or a syntax of subjectivity; it belongs to epigram rather than narrative, and the isolated moments which present it do not take on that extra dimension of existential contemplation which we find associated with reflection on erotic experience in Rochester's finest poems. There are, I would suggest, two kinds of narrative silence in Rochester, two kinds of disjunction: one, which frames the homosexual references, marks them as part of a libertine mythology, and wards off autobiographical inferences; the other, found in heterosexual contexts, separates the present from the past and the future, and evokes absence as part of an acute act of self-awareness which calls into question the modes through which selfhood may be thought. Homosexual possibilities never function like that for Rochester. They form no part of the grounds for subjectivity.

That homosexual sex is supplementary, always a sign of something else, may be seen in the two plays with which Rochester is associated, *Sodom* and *Valentinian*. About the first I have nothing to add to what I have already said elsewhere,[56] that its frisson depends upon the reader sharing its essentially conservative assumption that sodomy is the ultimate form of transgression against society, nature and God. The play reduces the male body to members and orifices, and, whatever else one might call it, it is hardly homoerotic, in that it shows little imaginative delight in the sexual attraction of the male body.

However, Rochester's adaptation of Fletcher's *Valentinian* is more interesting in this respect, while still perhaps operating within the same conceptual framework as *Sodom*.[57] In one of the passages which Rochester added, Valentinian reacts to the failure of his procurers to obtain for him Lucina, the wife of Maximus. He claims that her chastity is, in fact, one of the things which he most admires about her, and that he would have been disappointed if she had indeed yielded to his servants' persuasions. He then tells his servant Chylax:

> I'le play to night.
> You, sawcy Fool! send privately away
> For *Lycias* hither by the Garden Gate,
> That sweet-fac'd Eunuch that sung
> In *Maximus*'s Grove the other day,
> And in my Closet keep him till I come.

(It is curious that the fourth line here, which describes Lycias, is three syllables short: is something missing? Why should the text stumble over the description of the boy's attractions?) And when Valentinian has left, Chylax comments:

> 'Tis a soft Rogue, this *Lycias*
> And rightly understood,
> Hee's worth a thousand Womens Nicenesses!
> The Love of Women moves even with their Lust,
> Who therefore still are fond, but seldom just:
> Their Love is Usury, while they pretend,
> To gain the Pleasure double which they lend.
> But a dear Boy's disinterested Flame
> Gives Pleasure, and for meer love gathers pain;
>   "In him alone Fondness sincere does prove,
>   And the kind tender Naked Boy is Love.[58]

From this perspective, a boy will be a more satisfying lover because he receives no pleasure himself, acting out of pure affection for his partner, whereas women are always seeking (and faking) their own sexual gratification. This of course figures the boy once again as a replacement for a woman; and the comparison is made on an ostensibly logical, pragmatic basis, rather than being driven by any distinctive personalised desire.

After the death of Lucina, Valentinian and Lycias appear together in the final scene of the play, which opens with 'Valentinian *and the* Eunuch *discover'd on a Couch*'.[59] The Emperor says:

> Oh let me press these balmy Lips all day,
> And bathe my Love-scorch'd Soul in thy moist Kisses.
> Now by my Joys thou art all sweet and soft,
> And thou shalt be the Altar of my Love,
> Upon thy Beauties hourly will I offer,
> And pour out Pleasure and blest Sacrifice,
> To the dear memory of my *Lucina*,
> No God, nor Goddess ever was ador'd
> With such Religion, as my Love shall be.
> For in these charming Raptures of my Soul,
> Claspt in thy Arms, I'le waste my self away,
> And rob the ruin'd World of their great Lord,
> While to the Honour of *Lucina*'s Name,
> I leave Mankind to mourn the loss for ever.[60]

Although the speech opens with Valentinian showing some appreciation of Lycias's sensual attractions, it soon becomes clear that, as in the previous quotation, the boy's function is to replace the woman; more specifically in this case he provides a human altar on which Valentinian may make sacrifice to the memory of Lucina. Any embrace is but part of a ritual of regret for the absent woman, any worship offered is worship of her, and when Valentinian expires in the boy's arms it will not be in a climax of homosexual pleasure but in a self-destructive act of mourning.

Both these speeches are placed at a moment when the Emperor has been thwarted in his attempt to possess Lucina, and both use Lycias to chart a stage in the degradation of Valentinian. In the first example, he has just announced that he finds Lucina's chastity sexually exciting, and is going to alter his seduction strategy to incorporate this new realisation. In the second, he is appropriating the memory of Lucina – over which he has no rights – and exploiting Lycias in a perverted ritual mourning. When the avengers break in to murder Valentinian they pay virtually no attention to Lycias: no one remarks on Valentinian's homosexual dalliance, and with good reason, because it is offered to us principally as the signifier of corruption. It is not made visible in and for itself, but functions metonymically as the sign of a larger category of deviance. Moreover, this is coupled with blasphemy, as Valentinian imagines all this as a religious ritual. In Rochester's imagination, then, the simulacrum of homosexual pleasure with a youth can appropriately function as a sign of a perverse and blasphemous heterosexual obsession. It is a way of conceptualising sex between men which would surely have satisfied the most censorious Restoration divine.

6

Love in the ayre: Rochester's songs and their music

NICHOLAS FISHER

Writing almost a century after Rochester's death, Samuel Johnson observed in his essay on the poet:

> As he cannot be supposed to have found leisure for any course of continued study, his pieces are commonly short, such as one fit of resolution would produce . . .
>
> His songs have no particular character: they tell, like other songs, in smooth and easy language, of scorn and kindness, dismission and desertion, absence and inconstancy, with the common places of artificial courtship. They are commonly smooth and easy; but have little nature, and little sentiment.[1]

Johnson was acquainted with the main body of Rochester's verse, although it appears that he did not personally select the poems that appear in *The Works of the English Poets*; Boswell reports that Johnson gave an edition of Rochester's poetry to his friend George Steevens 'to castrate for the edition of the poets, to which he was to write Prefaces'.[2] It may be deduced that the edition Boswell is referring to is one of the two entitled *The Works of John Earl of Rochester* that Tonson published in 1714 and again in 1732, because *The Works of the English Poets* includes thirty-six poems that almost exactly replicate Tonson's contents in terms of selection, order and readings (the 'postscript' to *A Satyre against Reason and Mankind* that is included did not appear in the earlier Tonson editions of 1691, 1696 and 1705). Of the seven poems not reprinted, five are songs that could be deemed unacceptable on religious grounds (*The Fall*, with its depiction of the Garden of Eden as allowing the most pleasurable sexual relations), on moral grounds (*Love to a Woman*, with its advocacy of homosexual relations) or on grounds of taste (*Song. A Young Lady to her Antient Lover*, 'Faire Cloris in a Pigsty lay' and *To a Lady, in a Letter* describe various aspects of sexual pleasure).[3] This choice

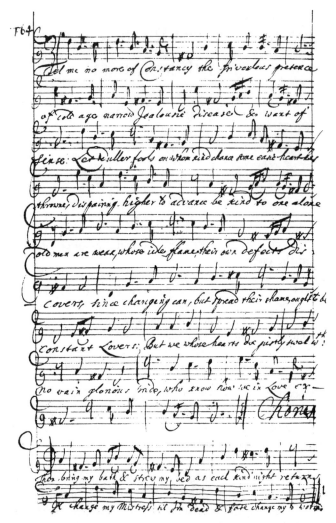

7 Setting (before 1675) of 'Tel me no more of Constancy' by
John Jackson. The text for bars 47–50 has been accidentally omitted

seems arbitrary, for on similar grounds of taste 'As Chloris full of harmless thought' (describing a fortuitous sexual encounter) and 'Phillis, be gentler I advise' (a less witty and subtle invitation than Donne's *The Flea* and Marvell's *To his Coy Mistress*) could as readily have been excluded. Simply on the evidence of these two songs, let alone the omitted songs which Johnson would have read in his Tonson edition, there is sufficient individuality to give the lie to the assertion that Rochester's songs 'have no particular character' and, *pace* Jeremy Treglown, this 'dismission' of Rochester's poetry itself merits prompt dismissal.[4] For once, the judgment of 'that great Cham of literature, Samuel Johnson' is questionable, for he seems to have followed too unhesitatingly Pope's superficial assessment that Rochester, along with the Earl of Dorset, 'should be considered as holiday writers – as gentlemen that diverted themselves now and then with poetry, rather than as poets'.[5] These words, arguably, are more illustrative of Pope than Rochester, and reflect Pope's mixed reactions to Rochester rather than a dispassionate critical analysis of his writing: though criticising Rochester's 'very bad versification sometimes', he marked approvingly in his copy of Tonson's 1696 edition of Rochester's work twelve of the poems (including four songs), and when he edited Mulgrave's works in 1723 he chose to neutralise the latter's censure of Rochester's poetry in the *Essay on Satire*.[6]

A clear indication that Rochester took greater pains over his work than Pope's 'holiday writer' tag suggests is provided by Burnet in his biography, where he reports that 'He would often go into the Country, and be for some months wholly imployed in Study, or the Sallies of his Wit: Which he came to direct chiefly to *Satyre*'.[7] This statement contradicts Johnson's assertion that Rochester would not have found 'leisure for any course of continued study', a statement supported by the admission in one of the poet's letters to Henry Savile that he has been reading the Roman historian Livy while in the country. Burnet's use of the word 'chiefly' indicates that he recognised that Rochester's 'Sallies of his Wit' were employed both in the satires and in the shorter pieces, and implies that the latter were not the result of just 'one fit of resolution'. This latter interpretation of the poet's work is strengthened later in the biography by Rochester's assertion that a similar amount of effort was demanded of 'earnest Prayer', solving 'a *Problem* in *Euclid*' or writing 'a Copy of Verses'.[8]

Firm evidence to support the presence of a greater artfulness than was appreciated by Pope or Johnson exists in the holograph text of the poem *To a Lady, in a Letter*. Vieth has described the work as 'one of Rochester's cleverest lyrics and one of the finest songs of the late seventeenth century', and the three significantly variant texts available provide, as Walker stresses in his edition, a 'rare opportunity to see a poem by Rochester in the process of revision'.[9] The subtle changes in words and focus are graphically seen in the opening stanza:

How happy Cloris (were they free)
   Might our Enjoyments prove,
But you wth formall Jealousie
   Are still tormenting Love.   (Version A)

How happy* Cloris, & how free
   Would these enjoyments prouve,
But you wth formall jealousy
   Are still tormenting Love.   (Version B)
                     *altered to 'perfect' in manuscript

Such perfect Blisse faire Chloris, wee
   In our Enjoyment prove
'Tis pitty restless Jealiousy
   Should Mingle with our Love.   (Version C)

The tone in the first two versions differs greatly from that in the final version: versions A and B reflect on the part of the speaker a frustration, perhaps even anger, concerning Cloris's 'formall Jealousie', but in version C (which also contains an additional two verses) the accusatory approach has been replaced by a style that is both relaxed and urbane. What these changes demonstrate to a marked and highly sophisticated degree is Rochester's sensitivity to tone and nuance, and they evidence his distinctive ability to achieve a substantially different effect by means of minimal adjustment to a word or line.[10]

Treglown is probably correct to observe that many of Rochester's pieces were 'apparently rapidly composed'. The impromptus and epigrams obviously fall into this category, and, whether or not they *were* improvised, contemporary accounts associate Rochester with this skill; what he seems to exemplify are two distinct poetic facilities – inspiration and craftsmanship. Treglown's implicitly pejorative comment is effectively answered, too, by the critique of David Vieth:

> as a poet, he is noteworthy for his discriminating ear and his sure touch. Though many of his revised readings will seem, to the average ear, neither better nor worse than the words he canceled, they must have appealed to his superior sensitivity to language. Also, the list reveals very few instances in which Rochester altered a reading, then returned later to his original thought. Evidently he possessed rare facility in finding exactly the words he wanted to body forth his conceptions.[11]

In similar vein, Marianne Thormählen, author in 1993 of the most extensive examination hitherto of Rochester's poetry, specifically adjudged five of his songs to have been 'unsurpassed in their time' (three of which Johnson included: *The Mistress, Love and Life* and 'Absent from thee'). A comment on Rochester later in Johnson's essay, 'The glare of his general character diffused itself upon his writings', indicates that even an outstanding critic was unable to separate his reaction to the reputation from his response to the writing, and, with regard to the latter, Johnson's response to Rochester's lyrics can be seen to have been at variance with general taste during the seventeenth and eighteenth centuries.[12]

In his lifetime, Rochester was recognised as the writer of two distinct strands of verse: love lyrics and 'sharp Satyrs'. The anonymous *Advice to Apollo*, written in about 1678, makes this clear:

> Rochester's easie Muse does still improve
> Each hour thy little wealthy *World* of Love,
> (That *World* in which each Muse is thought a Queen)
> That he must be forgiv'n in Charity then;
> Tho his sharp Satyrs have offended thee.[13]

What the poet is indicating here is that Rochester was seen as a master of both the smooth versification needed for songs and the rougher verse associated with satire. At his death, there was a powerful and convincing outpouring of grief by his fellow poets: Aphra Behn, Thomas Flatman, Samuel Holland, John Oldham, Anne Wharton, Samuel Woodford and two anonymous writers contributed verses, with those by Behn eliciting a verse response from Wharton (to which the former replied in kind) and those by Wharton attracting poetical responses from John Grubham Howe, Edmund Waller and Robert Wolseley. Although most of the poets, like Holland, identified Rochester's 'pointed Wit [which] . . . / So Justly lasht our Foppish Times' as worthy of special mention, Aphra Behn combined in her lament the observation 'Satyr has lost its Art, its Sting is gone' (line 27) with the comment 'He was but lent this duller World t'improve / In all the charms of Poetry and Love' (lines 7–8); Rochester's niece Anne Wharton, too, referred to the 'artful music [that] hung / Upon his useful kind instructing tongue'.[14]

The most explicit link of Rochester with Apollo's 'little wealthy *World* of Love', however, was made by John Oldham, 'the most talented of Rochester's literary disciples'.[15] In an extended elegy of more than 250 lines entitled *Bion: A Pastoral, in Imitation of the Greek of Moschus, bewailing the Death of the Earl of Rochester*, he chose to focus upon Rochester as a writer of songs: 'the lov'd Swain is gone, / And with him all the Art of graceful Song' (lines 21–22).[16] The cumulative effect of the series of extravagant claims and compliments, set against a background of musical imagery and reference, is to leave the reader in absolutely no doubt as to Rochester's contribution to the form, for example:

> In every Wood, on every Tree, and Bush
> The Lark, the Linnet, Nightingale, and Thrush,
> And all the feather'd Choir, that us'd to throng
> In list'ning flocks to learn his well-tun'd Song;
> Now each in the sad Con[s]ort bear a part,
> And with kind Notes repay their Teachers Art:
> Ye Turtles too (I charge you) here assist,

Let not your murmurs in the crowd be mist:
To the dear Swain do not ungrateful prove,
That taught you how to sing and how to love.

(lines 89–98)

Pan only e're can equal thee in Song,

(line 109)

With thee, sweet *Bion*, all the grace of Song,
And all the *Muses* boasted Art is gone:

(lines 131–2)

If I am reckon'd not unblest in Song,
'Tis what I ow to thy all-teaching tongue:

(lines 191–2)

Maevius still lives; still let him live for me,
He, and his Pipe shall ne'r my envy be:
None e're that heard thy sweet, thy Artful Tongue,
Will grate their ears with his rough untun'd Song.

(lines 218–21)

It is clear that 'song' here is not simply a synecdoche for 'poetry', and that, apart from feeling that the older poet had influenced his own verse, Oldham believed that Rochester's writing was artful, graceful, tuneful and sweet: the phrases 'well-tun'd Song ... taught you how to sing and how to love ... rough untun'd Song' show that Oldham particularly wished to establish in *Bion* the importance of this aspect of Rochester's work.[17] After all, Dorimant, the character in Etherege's *The Man of Mode, or, Sᵣ Fopling Flutter* (1676) held to be based on the personality of Rochester, shows a fondness for such writing by frequently having on his lips verse by Waller (who, in Dryden's words, was famed for 'the sweetness of [his] lyric poesy'[18]), and Act I ends with Dorimant singing as he leaves the stage.

Confirmation of such association of Rochester with song is supported by the contents, and the arrangement, of the first three published editions of Rochester's poems. A not inconsiderable proportion of the sixty-one poems in *Poems on Several Occasions by the Right Honourable the E. of R—* published in 1680 (hereafter referred to as *1680*) consist of songs, sandwiched as a group between works that are obviously not love poems: 'Upon Nothing' (pp. 51–4) and *Actus Primus Scena Prima* (pp. 76–7). Nineteen of the twenty-three poems in this group contain the word 'song' in the title, and their placement together initiated a procedure that was followed by Thorncome five years later in *Poems on Several Occasions. By the R. H. the E. of R.* (hereafter referred to as *1685*) which included fifteen 'songs' amongst a group of twenty-one love poems, and, more influentially, in the series of editions published by the Tonsons between 1691 and 1732, in which almost half (seventeen) of the thirty-nine poems in the volume had 'song' in their title. The practice of clustering the songs together is paralleled by some of the early manuscript miscellanies: Yale University Library MS Osborn b.105, whose link with *1680* has been detailed by David Vieth, evidences an identical clustering in the parts of the original manuscript that survive, and further significant examples are provided by four other manuscripts derived from various scriptoria.[19] The Badminton MS contains a cluster of fourteen songs, eleven of which are by Rochester, and ten of which appear as a group in *1680* and Tonson's 1691 edition; the Gyldenstolpe MS groups the same fourteen songs, but in a different order; the Harbin MS has a cluster of four songs separated by some of Rochester's letters from another cluster of eight songs, seven of which follow the order of *1680*; and MS Osborn fb 334 (previously known as the Hartwell MS) contains fourteen of Rochester's poems titled 'Song', of which two different groupings of eight follow the order (but not the readings) of the songs in *1680* and the Harbin MS.[20] Accumulatively this evidence demonstrates an even greater contemporary perception of Rochester as a song writer than has usually been acknowledged.

In the introduction to his 1948 edition of Rochester's verse, the poet Ronald Duncan observed, 'Rochester's positive achievement is his contribution to the tradition of song', but he also cautioned, 'Not every poem printed in the anthologies under the loose title of "Song" is capable of being sung'.[21] To date, the extent to which Rochester's verses were combined with music has been virtually ignored, and it would be understandable, therefore, for the modern reader to assume that Rochester's songs were not sung. Keith Walker listed twelve settings in an appendix to his 1984 edition (see p. 70 below), and Frank Ellis ten years later in his Penguin edition drew upon Claude Simpson's classic work on the British broadside ballad to indicate other tunes to which it would have been possible to sing Rochester's verse.[22] While these editors have alerted readers to the possibility that a number of Rochester's lyrics were sung, the impression given has been that such poems were the exception rather than the rule. Harold Love, however, in a stimulating paper based on a careful examination of the ordering of five manuscripts and *1680*, has recently concluded the reverse: 'a lyric by Rochester . . . was probably written for sung performance at some Court occasion rather than as an abstract love poem'. Love identified three basic groupings, and 'polite' and indecent collections, of the songs; this led him to hypothesise that 'the balance of probability must lie with the scribal sequences having derived from one or more collections assembled by Rochester himself for presentation or . . . for the use of musicians' in the form of a small manuscript *liber carminum* at Court on perhaps more than one occasion (the contents depending on the particular recipient).[23] The part of the hypothesis concerning sung performance is convincing, but less so is the suggestion that Rochester himself assembled collections of his work (which contrasts interestingly with Pope's idea that Rochester was diffident about the circulation of his poetry). As Love freely admits, there is no actual evidence that Rochester ever produced or envisaged a collection of his 'works', which weakens the argument, and it is as possible that a centrally placed courtier such as Henry Bulkely, the Master of the Household, or Will Chiffinch, Keeper of the Closet, or someone close to them, might have acted as the repository for the songs presented by Rochester at Court. The significant contribution of Love's hypothesis, though, is to strengthen the likelihood that Rochester was particularly recognised during his lifetime (and after his death) as a writer of songs.

The probability of Rochester's songs having been 'written for sung performance' is further enhanced when the musical settings, and the contents of word books, dating from the poet's lifetime and the century or so after his death are more closely examined. In his edition, Walker lists twelve musical settings of all or part of eight poems by Rochester that date from the last quarter of the seventeenth century, only three of which, marked below by an asterisk, were published before Rochester's death; they begin:

*'All my past life is mine no more' (Henry Bowman) in *Songs for i, 2 & 3 Voyces*, 1678
'All my past Life is mine no more' in *Songs set by Signior Pietro Reggio* [1680]
'All my past Life is mine no more' (John Blow) in *The Theater of Music . . .* 1685 and *Wit and Mirth: or, Pills to Purge Melancholy*, 1700
*'Give me leave to raile at you' (Henry Bowman) in *Songs for i 2 & 3 Voyces*, 1678
'Injurious charmer of my vanquisht heart' (Lewis Grabue) in *Pastoralle* [1684]
'Insulting Beauty you mis-spend' (Anon.) in *Thesaurus Musicus . . . the Fourth Book*, 1695
'Kindness hath resistless charmes' [v. 2 of 'Injurious Charmer'] (Lewis Grabue) in *Pastoralle* [1684]
'Phillis, be gentler, I advise' (Thomas Tudway) in *The Theater of Music . . .* 1685
'Too late, alas, I must confess' (Samuel Ackeroyde) in *Mercurius Musicus*, 1700
'What cruel pains Corinna takes' (Moses Snow) in *The Theater of Music . . . 1685.*
*'While Cloe full of harmless thoughts' (James Hart) in *New Ayres and Dialogues*, 1678.

To this list may be added the anonymous engraved setting of 'As Cloris full of Harmless thoughts' (British Library Huntington MS 1601 (*c.* 1700)); the anonymous manuscript setting of 'Phillis be Gentler I advise' (Bodleian Library MS Mus.Sch.F.572 (before 1700)); a setting by John Jackson of 'Tel me no more of Constancy' (British Library Add.MS 29396 (before 1675: figure 7)); and an association of *Seigneur Dildoe* with the ballad tune 'Peggy's gone over sea with the soldier' (Bodleian MS Don.b.8). There were also further printings of Blow's setting of 'All my past Life is mine no more' in *The Gentleman's Journal*, 1693; and Hart's setting of 'While Cloe full of harmless thoughts' in *New Ayres, Dialogues and Trialogues*, 1678 and *Choice Ayres & Songs*, 1679. When the eighteenth-century settings are taken into account also, there survives a total of twenty-six settings of fifteen of Rochester's songs.[24]

The absence of printed musical settings for some of Rochester's 'songs' should not be taken as a definitive indication that particular verses were not set to music; the existence of single manuscript settings of 'Phillis, be gentler, I advise' and 'Tell mee noe more of Constancy' emphasises the chance survival of what was an ephemeral and occasional art form. The presence of Rochester's songs in collections clearly intended as wordbooks for singers is indicative both of the possibility that many settings have failed to survive, and also that the publisher expected the singer or singers to select from the sources available tunes that would fit the metre of particular songs. Sir Carr Scroope's song 'As Amoret with Phillis sat' from Etherege's *The Man of Mode*, for example, was set by the Master of the King's Musick, Nicholas Staggins, but, sharing the same ballad metre as Rochester's 'As Chloris full of harmless thought', it became associated with Rochester's song to the extent that when Staggins's tune was printed in *Youth's Delight on the Flagelet*, 9th edition (c. 1690), it was headed 'When Clori[s] full of harmless thoughts'.[25] Six of Rochester's poems appeared during his lifetime in *A New Collection of the Choicest Songs*, 1676, and *The Last and Best Edition of New Songs*, 1677, and a further nine songs appeared in 1688 in *The Triumph of Wit* (although their titles might suggest otherwise, there are no musical settings in *A New Collection . . .* 1676, and *The Last and Best Edition . . .* 1677); they begin:

'All my past life is mine noe more': *The Triumph of Wit*
'As Chloris full of harmless thought': *The Last and Best Edition*
'Att Last you'l force mee to confess': *A New Collection*
'Give me leave to raile at you': *The Triumph of Wit*
'How blest was the Created State': *The Triumph of Wit*
'How happy Cloris (were they free)': *A New Collection*; *The Last and Best Edition*
'I swive as well as others do': *The Triumph of Wit*
'Phillis, be gentler I advice': *The Triumph of Wit*
'Such perfect Blisse faire Chloris': *A New Collection*; *The Last and Best Edition*
'Tell me no more of constancy': *A New Collection*
'To this moment a Rebell, I throw down my Arms': *The Triumph of Wit*
'Vulcan contrive me such a Cup': *The Triumph of Wit*
'What Cruel pains Corinna takes': *The Triumph of Wit*
'While on those lovely looks I gaze': *A New Collection*; *The Last and Best Edition*; *The Triumph of Wit*.

The likelihood of these verses having been sung is increased on two counts: firstly, the existence of seventeenth-century settings for half of these songs (reckoning the songs beginning 'As Chloris full . . .' and 'While Chloe full . . .', and 'Too late, alas . . .' and 'At last you'l force . . .' to be variations of the same song); and, secondly, the evidence in *A New Collection*, for example, that the printer was already aware of eight-line musical settings for 'Tell me no more of constancy' and 'Such perfect Blisse faire Chloris', for the five quatrains of 'Tell me no more of constancy' are set out as two eight-line verses, and the final verse printed with an indication that it should be repeated in order to fit an eight-line tune:

> Then bring my Bath, and strew my bed,
>   as each kind night returns,
> Ile change a Mistress till i'me dead,
> and fate change me for worms,
> Then bring my Bath, &c.

> (sig. A7r)

Similarly, although 'Such perfect Blisse, faire Chloris' is printed in seven quatrains, an eight-line tune is strongly suggested by the repeat indicated for the last verse (the song 'Was it a Queen, or else a Cowlady', for example, printed in four quatrains on the previous page, lacks such a marking):

> All this you freely may confess,
>   yet we'd ne'r disagree;
> For, did you love your pleasure less,
>   you were no mate for me, &c.

> (sig. A4v)

In the eighteenth century, Rochester's songs continued to appear both in word books (indicated below by an asterisk) and in new settings, largely utilising the *corpus* already in circulation but in two cases, marked below by italics, selecting verses not previously printed with music; they begin:

'All my past life is mine no more' (Anon.)
*'As Chloris full of harmless thought'
'Give me leave to raile on you' (John Blundevile)
*'How happy Cloris (were they free)'
*'I cannot change as others do'
*'Injurious Charmer of my vanquisht Heart'
*'Kindness has resistless charms'
Love bid me hope (Abiel Whichello)
My dear Mistress has a heart (Tommaso Giordani, Thomas Arne)
*'To this moment a Rebell, I throw down'
'Vulcan contrive me such a Cup' (Fisher Tench, Anon.)
*'What Cruel pains Corinna takes'
'While on those lovely looks I gaze' (John Sheeles).

This choice of verses set to music or included in wordbooks evidences a consistent association of Rochester with love poetry (or at least with the battle between the sexes in various guises); despite the inclusion of 'Vulcan contrive me such a Cup' amongst 'drinking songs' in Ritson's *A Select Collection of English Songs with their original airs*, 1783, it can be argued that with the declaration '*Bacchus*, and *Venus*, my saints are' in the anonymous setting in *An Antidote against Melancholy*, 1749, a concern with love is not entirely absent. With the proviso that several of the excluded poems that contain sexually explicit material *could* have been sung at some private gathering – examples such as *Love to a Woman* and 'Faire Cloris in a Pigsty lay' come readily to mind – the songs detailed in the listings above share to a greater or lesser extent an urbanity and wit, or, at least, do so once sanitised of potentially offensive words or sentiment; the last line of 'Vulcan contrive me such a Cup', for example, as printed in *1680* was 'And then to *Cunt* again', but for the anonymous 1749 setting became softened to 'And then to love again'. It is relevant to add that only one of the impolite songs, *Seigneur Dildoe*, was identified with specific music (although the tune 'Peggy's gone over sea with the soldier' could also be used, for example, with the obscene verses 'Quoth the *Dutchess of Cleveland*'), so the overwhelming impression given by the settings of Rochester's songs was of a poet whose writing complied with good taste.

What becomes apparent is that Rochester's songs had an existence (and therefore an audience) apart from the various collected editions of his poetry. The poem 'My dear Mistris', for example, was given the heading 'Song' by its first printer (*Miscellany Poems*, 1685), but was entitled *The Fickle Fair* in the settings by Thomas Arne and Tommaso Giordani in 1760 and 1784 respectively. The point is made more forcefully by what can be discerned to have been Rochester's most popular lyric, 'As Chloris full of harmless thought', which unusually exists in six printed sources before 1680: in the form of the broadside *Corydon & Cloris or, The Wanton Sheepherdess* [?1676], the miscellany entitled *The Wits Academy or, The Muses Delight*, 1677, the wordbook *The Last and Best Edition of New Songs*, 1677, and in three printings of a setting by James Hart (*New Ayres and Dialogues*, 1678, *New Ayres, Dialogues and Trialogues*, 1678, and *Choice Ayres & Songs*, 1679). These different printed sources, and the evident tailoring of Rochester's lines to accommodate a variety of taste, are strongly indicative of the song's appeal to different social groups, and it further appeared in wordbooks and musical miscellanies on at least a dozen occasions during the eighteenth century.

The adjustments made to Rochester's verses seem strongly indicative of oral musical transmission. Haphazardly in four of the eighteenth-century versions, for example, the tree under which Chloris was lying is described as a 'Myrtle' rather than a 'Willow'; both trees are traditionally associated with grief for unrequited love or the loss of a mate, but whereas the willow is redolent of the English pastoral tradition (as exemplified by Desdemona's 'song of "willow"' in *Othello*, IV.iii), the myrtle has a classical association through Phaedra, the wife of Theseus, repairing to such a tree to observe longingly her stepson Hippolytus training naked at Troezen.[26] In addition, although the variant opening words 'While Cloe full of harmless thoughts' appeared only in *New Ayres and Dialogues* and *New Ayres, Dialogues and Trialogues* in 1678, and were not repeated in later editions, the description of the shepherd as 'youthful' rather than 'comely', and the phrase 'Pomp and Train' rather than 'pompous train', were adopted from *Choyce Ayres & Songs*, 1679 onwards; the description of Chloris's eyes as 'Virgins Eyes' was softened to 'lovely Eyes' in *1680*, *1685*, *1691*, the engraved BL Huntington MS 1601, and then only in *An Antidote against Melancholy*, 1749 and *The Convivial Songster*, [1782]; and in *New Ayres and Dialogues*, 1678, *The Choice*, 1729 and *An Antidote against Melancholy*, 1749, the shepherdess is described as lying trembling for fear *she* rather than *he* 'should comply'. For the setting printed in *An Antidote against Melancholy*, 1749, the text is dislocated to the extent that the original third verse is placed after the fifth verse, allowing the description of Chloris's amorous feelings to refer to her awakened, rather than awakening, passion.

The music associated with the settings of Rochester's songs reflects their time. In the 'airy' seventeenth-century settings, the influence of the Court and theatres is paramount, as titles of three of the collections reflect: *Choice Ayres & Songs To Sing to the Theorbo-Lute or Bass-Viol, Being Most of the Newest* Ayres *and* Songs, *Sung at* Court, *And at the Publick* Theatres. Composed by several Gentlemen of His Majesties Musick, and others, 1679; *The Newest Collection of the Choicest Songs, As they are Sung at Court, Theatre, Musick-schools, Balls, etc. with Musical Notes*, 1683; and *The Theater of Music: or, A Choice Collection of the newest and best* Songs *Sung at the Court, and Public Theaters, The* Words *composed by the most ingenious* Wits *of the Age, and set to Music by the greatest Masters in that* Science, 1685. I have to disagree with Harold Love when, having commented that 'the quality of the lyrics was as important as that of the music', he observes that in the 1685 collection, the '*Words* composed by the most ingenious *Wits* of the Age' have priority over the settings: in reality, the situation is reminiscent of that which Rochester describes in *A Satyre against Reason and Mankind*: 'For *Witts* are treated just like common *Whores*, / First they're enjoy'd, and then kickt out of *Doores*' (lines 37–8). The normal practice is for only the composer to be regularly identified, the 'most ingenious *Wits*' tending to remain firmly anonymous (in the first volume of the collection, Rochester has the distinction of being the only author named), and it is striking to find Dryden admitting in the preface to *Albion and Albanius: an Opera* (1685) the extent to which in writing the libretto he had subjugated his poetic instincts to what he perceived to be the demands of the music:

there is no maintaining the purity of English in short measures, where the rhyme returns so quick, and is so often female, or double rhyme, which is not natural to our tongue, because it consists too much of monosyllables, and those too most commonly clogged with consonants; for which reason I am often forced to coin new words, revive some that are antiquated, and botch others; as if I had not served out my time in poetry, but was bound apprentice to some doggerel rhymer, who makes songs to tunes, and sings them for a livelihood.[27]

If the leading professional poet of the day was willing to defer so publicly to a composer, it is perhaps not surprising that, in the three song collections referred to above, the poets were only rarely credited with having provided the lyrics, Rochester specifically in the settings of 'All my past life is mine noe more' by Pietro Reggio (1680) and John Blow (1685), and 'As Chloris full of harmless thought' (Anon., c. 1700). The basic point regarding the value placed on the lyrics is valid, none the less, for the collections include verse by most of the important poets of the period, including Aphra Behn, Cowley, Dorset, Dryden, Etherege, Oldham and Sedley.[28]

The range of composers who set Rochester's verses in the seventeenth century reveals the centrality of Court and theatre in relation to the artistic life of the time. Given that 'Every play had to have its songs',[29] it is hardly surprising that settings should have been made of the songs in his play *Valentinian*: 'Give me leave to raile at you' by Henry Bowman (fl. 1670–85) and (the second verse only, beginning 'Injurious charmer of my vanquisht heart') by the Catalan composer and onetime Master of the King's Musick Lewis Grabue (fl. 1665–94), who also set 'Kindness hath resistless charms'. Samuel Ackeroyde (fl. 1684–1706) regularly wrote music for the theatre, and it is feasible that his setting of 'Too late, alas, I must confess' (figure 8) enjoyed a theatrical context. Several composers had connections with the royal music-making: James Hart (1647–1718), whose setting of 'While Cloe full of harmless thoughts' appeared in print first, was a Gentleman of the Chapel Royal as well as composer of some sixty songs; John Blow (1649–1708), the organist of Westminster Abbey and erstwhile teacher of Henry Purcell, was a brilliant and prolific composer, writing songs (including Rochester's 'All my past life is mine noe more'), church music, music for the harpsichord and the masque *Venus and Adonis*; John Blundevile (c. 1650–1721) left the Chapel Royal at the same time as Blow and after a period as a lay clerk at Ely Cathedral became Master of the Choristers at York Minster; Thomas Tudway (c. 1650–1726), a member of the Chapel Royal who subsequently became Professor of Music at Cambridge, wrote church music in the tradition of Blow, and set some songs (including a setting of 'Phillis, be gentler I advice'); Moses Snow (c. 1650–1702) was an organist and member of both the Chapel Royal and the King's Vocal Musick, and left his setting of Rochester's 'What cruel pains Corinna takes' among a considerable body of songs; and John Jackson (d. 1688), the composer of apparently the earliest setting to survive

8 Setting of 'Too late, alas, I must confess' by Samuel Ackeroyde

('Tel me no more of Constancy': British Library Add.MS 29396), was Master of the Choristers at Wells Cathedral between 1680 and 1681, but may have had a Court connection some years prior to that. In the wider society, the Italian Signior Pietro Reggio (1632–85) was a singer and player who enjoyed a social cachet, performing, for example, in the homes of the diarists Samuel Pepys and John Evelyn.[30]

Although few, if any, of these settings are familiar today even to musical scholars, Keith Walker's comment in relation to twelve seventeenth-century settings, 'few of these settings are of musical interest', seems to merit some qualification.[31] He has a point, certainly, in respect of the two trios composed by Henry Bowman ('All my past life is mine no more', 'Give me leave to raile at you'), but though they are basic and uninspired, they would have undoubtedly given pleasure to the domestic performers for whom they were intended. They are the exception, though, for most of the other settings are professionally competent, albeit simple, unpretentious and easy on the ear; in general they seem to have been designed for the purpose of setting a mood in the theatre, or allowing a change of scenery, a function that they would have performed more than adequately. This is true even when the setting of the words is clumsy, as in two examples by, perhaps unsurprisingly, the foreign composers Lewis Grabue (whose manner of setting words made Pepys 'sick'[32]) and Pietro Reggio:

with vaine pre – tence fals – hood there – in might lye

A Excerpt from 'Injurious charmer of my vanquisht heart' (Grabue)

and

Then talke not of In – con – stan – -cy,

B Excerpt from 'All my past Life is mine no more' (Pietro Reggio)

The contrast with the workmanlike setting of the same line by Blow is instructive:

Then talk not of In – con – stan – cy,

C Excerpt from 'All my past Life is mine no more' (Blow)

One of the settings listed by Walker is Samuel Ackeroyde's 'Too late, alas, I must confess', a composition that displays real musicianship and would challenge a professional singer (figure 8). It begins in 4/4 time, changes in the second part to 3/8 time, and with its variation of notes for the repeated 'must confess' and 'kinder', its word painting on 'art', 'move' and 'madness', and its anticipation of a Handelian fluidity, it is positively virtuosic. In terms of sophistication, it is matched only by the setting 'My dear Mistress has a Heart' which Thomas Arne (1710–78) was to write some sixty years later: this setting, too, with its changes of rhythm, leaps, ornamentation, variety and clever accompaniment, would have also stretched the resources of a professional singer (figure 9).

9 Setting of 'My dear Mistress' by Thomas Arne

While the settings by Ackeroyde and Arne represent high peaks in terms of musical achievement, the variety of the settings and the number of competent musicians who provided them during the seventeenth and eighteenth centuries allow the settings of Rochester's verse to reflect changes to musical taste and practice over a period of one hundred years.[33] Following the death of Queen Mary in 1694, William III's lack of interest in music resulted in the Court giving a reduced lead in musical taste, and this, coupled with the increased wealth of London and national stability, facilitated the development of a more cosmopolitan influence. Charles II had earlier, for reasons of personal taste as well as policy, been a great proponent of French musical influences, modelling his 'Four and Twenty Fiddlers', for example, on the '24 violons du roi' at Versailles. Even before his death, though, the influence of Italian musicians was being felt in London; as Dryden observed:

All who are conversant in the Italian cannot but observe that it is the softest, the sweetest, the most harmonious, not only of any modern tongue, but even beyond any of the learned. It seems indeed to have been invented for the sake of poetry and music.[34]

With the accession of William and Mary in 1689, political mistrust of the French found expression in a developing taste for Italian musical styles, a taste that was to lead during the early decades of the eighteenth century to the flourishing in this country of Italian opera and the musical achievements of Handel. Throughout the century, the theatre maintained its position as a major cultural focus, as the setting of 'My dear Mistress has a heart' by the Naples-born Tommaso Giordani (c. 1733–1800) illustrates; he spent the years between 1768 and 1783 in London, during the course of which he prolifically composed sequences of odes, songs and operas and developed a close association with the King's Theatre in the Haymarket. Although it has been suggested that, because there was still a career available for the professional musician in the Court, church or theatre, the structure of London's music-making did not alter to any great extent during the first half of the eighteenth century, what in reality differed was the number of concerts and musical entertainments offered in response to the increasing wealth of a growingly confident middle class. Contrasting with the all-pervasive influence of the Court under the Restoration Stuart monarchs was now the form of entertainment promoted at the pleasure gardens, a point neatly made by the setting of 'My dear Mistress has a Heart' by Arne, the outstanding English composer of the century: the sheet is headed 'The Fickle Fair. A new French Horn-Song. Sung by Mr. Lowe, and Miss Falkner, at Marybone Gardens' (figure 9).

The settings of Rochester's songs that survive demonstrate an association between the poet's words and music that existed during his lifetime, and continued to exist for the century or so after his death. Not only do these settings amply support, therefore, the proposition by Ronald Duncan and Harold Love that the poet's lyrics were intended to be sung, but they clearly show that his verse had an influence upon social taste (albeit most often anonymously) through the eighteenth century that was not accorded his other writing.[35] In an entirely fitting parallel with the sequence of poetical tributes that appeared at Rochester's death, there exist three settings of Flatman's elegy 'As on his deathbed Strephon gasping lay' by Blundevile, Blow and William Turner (1651–1740), Oldham's moving poem perhaps having disqualified itself by its length. The setting by Blundevile exists only in a manuscript of his songs dated c. 1720[36] (though it is reasonable to expect the composition to have been written within a few months of Rochester's death), but the outstanding, emotionally powerful setting by Blow was included in John Playford's influential collection Choice Ayres and Songs ... the Third Book, 1681, and Turner's modest but elegant version in The Newest Collection of the Choicest Songs in 1683. Written by three individuals close to the centre of contemporary

musical life who had had considerable experience of providing the accompaniment for the verses of the 'most ingenious *Wits* of the Age', these settings
provide an impressive and symbolic testimony to Rochester's stature as perceived by musicians, and indicate that for composers as well as poets, Rochester
possessed a special lyrical talent that was widely recognised and genuinely
mourned:

> Listen, ye Virgins to his charming Song,
> Eternal Musick dwelt upon his Tongue.
> The Gods of Love and Wit inspir'd his Pen,
> And Love and Beauty was his glorious Theam.
> (Aphra Behn, Prologue to *Valentinian*, 1685, lines 39–42)

Plate 1

Portrait of the Earl of Rochester attributed to Sir Peter Lely

Plate 2

Portrait of the Earl of Rochester by an unknown artist

7

Lord Rochester's monkey (again)

KEITH WALKER

As would be expected, Rochester did not share the attitude to animals almost universally held in the seventeenth century. This generally held attitude can be illustrated by some choice quotations from right-thinking men of the time, although they appear quaint to us. 'All things were at first created, and are continually order'd for the Best and that principally for the Benefit and Pleasure of Man', wrote Richard Bentley in 1692, or, as Boileau's Doctor (as 'imitated' by John Oldham) expressed the idea:

> Man is ... Lord of the Universe;
> For him was this fair frame of Nature made,
> And all the Creatures for his use and aid:
> To him alone of all the living kind,
> Has bounteous Heav'n the reas'ning gift assign'd.[1]

Rochester's view was different: animals exist for many purposes but also to point up the folly and presumption of Men, whom they so closely resemble, and who consider they are so superior; whereas it is the animals who trust their instincts and do not rely on reason who are the wiser. Like many noblemen of his time, Rochester kept a pet monkey, and it is perhaps no coincidence that monkeys appear twice in significant passages in Rochester's verse: in *A Satyre against Reason and Mankind* and in *A Letter from Artemiza in the Towne to Chloe in the Countrey*.

In *Against Reason and Mankind*, Rochester's speaker laments being 'One of those strange prodigious Creatures Man' and says that he would rather be 'a Dog, a Monky, or a Bear' (lines 2, 5); at this point in Boileau's eighth satire, Rochester's 'source' for his poem, there is no monkey (in Oldham's 'imitation' of Boileau there's a *'freakish Ape'* introduced by an *adversarius*). As

1608 August 26 Munday

KING IAMES MADE ME TO RVN; FOR LIFE FROM DEADMANS RIDING
I RAN TO GOREIL GATE, WHERE DEATH FOR ME WAS BIDING

10 The saloon at Ditchley Park, Oxfordshire, and one of the brass inscriptions (1608–10) beneath the six stags' heads formerly in Ditchley House, Rochester's childhood home. The early inspiration, perhaps, for Rochester's *persona* poems. The inscriptions are transcribed in Thomas Hearne, *Reliquiae Hearniae . . .* (Oxford, 1857), p. 397

Thomas Rymer, one of Rochester's earliest critics, commented of Rochester's satire, 'You wou'd take his *Monkey* for a Man of *Metaphysicks*'.[2] Whatever Rymer meant by this rather cryptic sentence, it seems clear that he saw, not in the famous 'monkey portrait' (see below), which he cannot have viewed, but in Rochester's general treatment of monkeys, something unusual and significant.

Secondly, in *Artemiza to Chloe*, there is the monkey who actually appears, so to speak, as a character. Artemiza is describing a visit from a 'fine Lady':

> Shee to the Window runns, where she had spy'de
> Her much esteem'd deare Freind the Monkey ti'de.
> With fourty smiles, as many Antick bows,
> As if 't had beene the Lady of the House,
> The dirty chatt'ring Monster she embrac't,
> And made it this fine tender speech att last.
> Kisse mee, thou curious Miniature of Man;
> How odde thou art? How pritty? How Japan?
> Oh I could live, and dye with thee – then on
> For halfe an houre in Complement shee runne.

(lines 137–46)

There is much that could be said about this vividly realised scene, but it is enough to note how close to humans, and human behaviour, monkeys are.

Monkeys also appear elsewhere in Rochester's writing. The ape in *Tunbridge Wells*, in contrast to the two previous, fulfils a more diagrammatic function:

> So the beargarden Ape on his Steed mounted
> No longer is a Jackanaps accounted
> But is by vertue of his Trumpery then
> Call'd by the name of the young Gentleman.
> Bless me thought I what thing is man that thus
> In all his shapes he is rediculous:
> Our selves with noise of reason wee do please
> In vaine; Humanity's our worst disease.
> Thrice happy beasts are, who because they be
> Of reason void, are so of Foppery.
> Faith I was so asham'd that with remorse
> I us'd the insolence to mount my horse
> For he doing only things fitt for his nature
> Did seem to me, by much, the wiser Creature.

(lines 174–87)

And in a chilling revelation of Rochester's knowledge of what was in all likelihood common seventeenth-century practice, Aecius reminds Proculus in the fifth Act of *Valentinian*, 'When Monkey's grow mischievous, they are whipt, / Chain'd up and whipt' (V.i.41–2).[3] Finally, in a letter to Savile Rochester writes:

For my own part, I'm taking pains not to die without knowing how to live on when I have brought it about. But most human affairs are carried on at the same nonsensical rate, which makes me (who am now grown superstitious [= religious]) think it a fault to laugh at the monkey we have here when I compare his condition with mankind.[4]

The most famous monkey connected with Rochester, however, is the monkey in Huysmans's portrait of Rochester. So powerful a hold has this icon taken over Rochester scholars that Graham Greene entitled his biography *Lord Rochester's Monkey*, without ever discussing the meaning of the monkey in the picture; a discussion of the meaning of the monkey has subsequently been performed with quite awesome Teutonic thoroughness in an essay by Hans-Joachim Zimmermann published in a *Festschrift* for Erwin Wolff in 1984.[5]

Jacob Huysmans (1633–96) was born and trained in Antwerp (the painter's name, by the way, was at the Restoration, and should be now, pronounced 'Housmans'). A Catholic, he came to England during the Restoration, and was taken up by his co-religionist Catherine of Braganza, whom he painted in a variety of poses; Pepys, who visited his studio in 1664, wrote that he was 'said to exceed Lilly [Lely]'. There are two versions of his 'monkey portrait' of Rochester: one, the property of Lord Brooke, was formerly in Warwick Castle, but the owner took it with him when he left the country to live abroad; the other is a copy, which is now on display in the National Portrait Gallery, London (see plate 2). Both are widely reproduced. The simplest way to tell the original portrait and the copy apart is that in the copy Rochester has long red shoulder tabs divided at the ends; by making the costume appear more military these tabs have the effect of attempting to 'normalise' the portrait.[6]

Huysmans is reputed to have been influenced by earlier satirical painters, but nothing of satire can be seen in his portraits of women of the court. One unusual (indeed, in my experience, unique) feature of his 'monkey' portrait is the monkey itself. Huysmans had painted animals in portraits before: the portrait of Queen Catherine of Braganza now at Windsor Castle shows her seated,

> her right arm resting on drapery, her left hand on the head of a lamb, her long dark hair over her shoulder; she wears a white satin gown with pearl ornaments, a large hat lined with mauve satin and a mauve satin scarf across her lap. A cupid with flowers behind the lamb; another lamb in the right foreground, a duck and duckling in a pool in left foreground. Background in dark trees, and sky with cupids flying.[7]

In other words, the picture is completely conventional, if at the same time absurd. I should add that the queen is frowning, possibly at the Baroque carry-on around her, and the cupid looks apprehensive about something unexplained. The animals in this painting may be sentimental and prettified, but they are not offensive to decorum like a monkey.

The most truly absurd painting by Huysmans is one entitled 'The Duke of Monmouth, as Saint John the Baptist'. (At the Restoration, glaring incongruities such as this were common in paintings but even by contemporary standards this is a ludicrous depiction.) Pepys describes Monmouth as 'the most skittish, leaping gallant that ever I saw, alway in action, vaulting or leaping or clambering' – hardly a description one would expect to apply to John the Baptist.[8] The painting, which *is* confident in execution, shows a nearly naked Monmouth, seated, holding a staff; a sheep rests on his left arm. He is dressed in what can only be described as 'an off-the shoulder number' (forgive the choice of words – it is the only one that adequately does justice to the sheer vulgarity of the painting). His pink robes billow up to reveal a shapely leg.[9]

People tend to see in Huysmans's portrait of Rochester what they want to see. The neatest and the most egregious example (but all too typical) is that by Charles Norman:

> The portrait . . . depicts a man who has found nothing to satisfy him. Over the lace and the ribboned gown, framed by twin cascades of hair [it is really a wig], his face peers cynically and sadly at the painter and the world, his left hand holding a sheaf of manuscripts, his right outstretched in the act of crowning a monkey – his own – with the poet's bays. His face has the pallor, his eyes the fixed gaze, of a man with a mortal illness.[10]

The presence of the monkey, though, as I have argued, is a calculated offence to our expectations. We expect an aristocrat to have himself painted primarily as an act of memorial; he might surround himself with dogs, or horses, or possibly a library or an ample estate, or even with a wife and children, but never with an animal so lascivious, or dirty, or so unpredictable, as a monkey. It is so ungrand.

In two other portraits of Rochester, there is no monkey. In a further portrait in the National Portrait Gallery, by an unknown artist, he is dressed in armour, wearing a sword and holding a staff, and in a similarly conventional depiction by Lely in the Victoria and Albert Museum, London, Rochester is standing, in rich Court clothes very much as in the Huysmans picture, apparently wearing an armorial breast-plate.[11] These paintings date, of course, from the 1660s when Rochester still was, and would have thought of himself as, an active soldier.

Rochester must have discussed the composition of the Huysmans painting with the artist. We know from a letter to his wife that Rochester had a lively appreciation of portraits:

> Deare Wife I receiv'd y^r three pictures & am in a greate fright least they should bee like you, by the biggnes of y^e heade I should apprehend you farr gone in y^e Ricketts, by the severity of the Count'nance, somwhat inclin'd to prayer & prophesy, yet there is an alacrity [=liveliness] in the plump cheeke, that seemes to signify sack & sugar, & the sharp sighted nose has borrow'd quickness from the sweete smelling

eye, I never saw a chin smile before, a mouth frowne, & a forhead mump [grimace], truly y⁰ Artist has done his part, (god keep him humble) & a fine man hee is if his excellencyes doe not puff him up like his pictures.[12]

It is even possible that this passage refers to a time when Huysmans was engaged in painting Rochester; certainly the remarks at the end suggest personal knowledge of what portrait painters may have been like.

Does the monkey, then, satirise some enemy of Rochester? Dryden has been suggested, a suggestion enthusiastically endorsed by Zimmermann. I shall entertain it here. The relationship between Dryden and Rochester was uneasy at best and underwent several vicissitudes. There are certain fixed points to be borne in mind: first, that Rochester and Dryden were separated by a huge social void; second, that the literary point at issue in their quarrels was that Dryden, as Harold Love has observed, felt (or arrogated to himself) the right to arbitrate on literary matters:

> Dryden's real crime was not hastiness, nor least of all carelessness, nor even that he wrote for money, but that he claimed an authority to distinguish good writing from bad, which Rochester regarded as among the hereditary privileges of the aristocracy.[13]

I will simply list the main points in the relationship between Rochester and Dryden, which must have begun early, perhaps as early as the 1660s:

1 Rochester may have had a hand in Dryden's appointment as poet laureate in April 1668.
2 Rochester's friend Buckingham in *The Rehearsal* (1672) mocks Dryden as 'Mr. Bayes'.
3 Dryden's choice of Mulgrave, Rochester's enemy, as patron, signalled in the dedication of *Aureng-Zebe* (1676).
4 Rochester's criticism of Dryden in *An Allusion to Horace* (late 1675), copiously naming him.
5 Dryden's attack on Shadwell (whom Rochester had praised in *An Allusion to Horace*) in *Mac Flecknoe*, written 1676, could be seen as an attack on Rochester as Shadwell's patron.
6 Dryden's ferocious and sustained assault on Rochester and the Court poets in the preface to *All for Love* (1678). Dryden does not name Rochester here, but (among much oblique abuse) implicitly compares him to an ass hiding in a lion's skin, alluding to Aesop's fable of the ass who tries on a lion's skin to frighten other animals, but is exposed as an ass by his braying.[14]

In a letter to his chum Henry Savile in the spring of 1676, Rochester comments,

> You write me word that I'm out of favour with a certain poet [generally agreed to be Dryden] whom I have ever admired for the disproportion of him and his attributes. He is a rarity which I cannot but be fond of, as one would be of a hog that could fiddle, or a singing owl.[15]

The tone is quizzically wondering, rather than outraged or angry, and I suggest that it is near to the feeling of the Huysmans portrait too.

Dryden, it seems, was hurt by Huysmans's portrayal of him. I find this quite reasonable. He would be additionally hurt by Rochester's attack in *An Allusion to Horace* (in so far as it *is* an attack), and would feel bitter. Ten years later, in *The Hind and the Panther*, he slightingly refers to 'the *Buffoon Ape*, as Atheists use' (line 39), a clear and at the same time an obscure reference to Rochester's monkey in the picture. We have already seen some of the ways Rochester 'uses' the monkey in the portrait, and the 'atheist' is, of course, Rochester.

All commentators on Huysmans's picture, including Zimmermann, assume that the monkey is in the process of being crowned, but Rochester's outstretched right arm can be read differently. In order for someone to be crowned, even with a laurel wreath, the crown is held with both hands, and not between forefinger and thumb with the other fingers spread (although Huysmans may have copied this characteristic hand-position from Van Dyck, a painter who was his master in other respects), and the person holding the crown looks at the person or animal that is about to be crowned. Far from being, therefore, a coronation of the monkey with the laureate's bays, it may be a *de*-laureation ceremony, reminding the monkey (Dryden) of a hypothetical threat made in *An Allusion to Horace*: 'Nor dare I from his sacred Temples tear / That Lawrell which he best deservs to wear' (lines 79–80). So then, Rochester, as Apollo, not glancing with bemused (aristocratic?) indulgence at the monkey, is looking at us, and the monkey is looking up expectantly towards Rochester, proffering him a page torn out of the book the monkey is holding.

Huysmans, as I hope I have shown, was not a skilful enough painter to embody the more subtle interpretations of the painting that have been proposed and are canvassed by Zimmermann; certainty on these points is therefore unattainable. The attitude towards Dryden seems to me a bemused and tolerant exasperation, and, while it may also be condescending, it is very far from the terrible brutality of Rochester's rejection, in which he also 'uses' a monkey, of Sir Carr Scroope:

> To Rack and torture thy unmeaning brain
> In *Satyrs* Praise, to a low untuned strain
> In Thee was most Impertinent and vain
> When in thy person we more clerely see
> That *Satyr's* of Divine Authority
> For God made one on Man when he made Thee
> To show there are some Men as there are Apes
> Fram'd for meer sport who differ but in shapes:
> In Thee are all those Contradictions Joyn'd,
> That make an Ass prodigious and refin'd.[16]

Upon Nothing.
A POEM.

By a Person of Honour.

Nothing, thou Elder-Brother, *Eve* to shade,
Thou had'st a Being e're the World was made,
Well fixt alone, of ending not afraid.

E're Time and Place were, Time and Place were not,
When primitive Nothing, Something strait begot;
Then all proceeded from the great united What!

Something, the General Attribute of all,
Sever'd from Thee its sole Original,
Into thy boundless Self, must undistinguisht fall.

Yet Something, did thy Nothing Power command,
And from thy Fruitful Emptinesses Hand,
Snatch Men, Beasts, Birds, Fire, Water, Air and Land.

Matter, the wicked'st Offspring of thy Race,
By Form assisted, flew from thy Embrace,
And Rebel Light obscur'd thy Rev'rend dusky Face.

With Form and Matter, Time and Place did joyn;
Body, thy Foe, with these did Leagues combine,
To spoyl thy Peaceful Reign, and ruin all thy Line.

But Turn-Coat Time, assists the Foe in vain;
And bribed by Thee, destroys their short-lived Reign,
And to thy hungry Womb, drives back the Slaves again.

Thy Mysteries are hid from *Laick* Eyes,
And the Divine alone by warrant pries
Into thy Bosom, where thy Truth in private lies.

Yet this of thee, the Wife may truly say,
Thou from the Virtuous, nothing takes away,
And to be part of thee, the Wicked wisely Pray.

Great Negative! how vainly would the Wife
Enquire, Design, Distinguish, Teach, Devise,
Did'st not thou stand to point their Blind Philoso-
(phies;

Is, or is not, the Two great Ends of Fate,
Of True or False, the Subject of debate,
That perfects or destroys designs of State.

When they have wrackt the Politicians Breast,
Within thy Bosom most securely Rest,
Reduc'd to Thee are least, tho safe and best.

But Nothing, why doth Something still permit,
That Sacred Monarchs should at Council sit
With Persons thought, at best, for Nothing fit?

Whilst weighty Something, modestly abstains
Fro Princes Courts, & fro the States-mans brains,
And Nothing there like stately Nothing Reigns.

Nothing, that dwells with Fools, in grave disguise,
For whom they Rev'rend Forms & Shapes devise,
Lawn Sleeves, and Furrs, and Gowns, when they
(look VVife.

French Truth, *Dutch* Prowess, *British* Policy,
Hybernian Learning, *Scotch* Civility,
Spaniards Dispatch, *Danes* Wit are seen in Thee.

The Great Mans gratitude to his best Friend,
Court promises, *whores* vows, tow'rds thee, I bend,
Flow Swift, Fly into Thee, and severs in the End.

FINIS.

11 One of the two broadside versions of *Upon Nothing. A Poem* [1679]

8

The missing foot of *Upon Nothing,* and other mysteries of creation

David Quentin

In John Lennard's *Poetry Handbook*, subtitled 'A Guide to Reading Poetry for Pleasure and Practical Criticism', there is a section intended to bring comfort to worried A-level students and undergraduates, and it advises them when confronted with a poem in an exam to 'make a short technical description', after which it assures them they will suffer 'an embarrassment of things to remark', top of the list being 'metrical conformity and deviation'.[1] Armed with this advice, a practical criticism examinee would be overjoyed to reach the line 42 of Rochester's *Upon Nothing*, 'And Nothing there, like stately Nothing Reigns'.[2] Unlike the hexameter one has come to expect at the end of each stanza, this line has but ten syllables. It is missing a foot on the end, a foot that is all too easy to imagine reigning at the end of the line like stately Nothing itself. Surely if any example of metrical deviation has semantic value contingent upon its context, this does. But did Rochester put it there with that purpose in mind? Is there a contemporary theory of contingent metrical semantics to justify our reading of a putative empty sixth foot? In 1690, Sir William Temple wrote that the Greek name for poets, and this would have been no news to anyone, signified 'makers or Creators, such as raise admirable Frames and Fabricks out of nothing'.[3] The purpose of this chapter is to decide whether there is anything in the qualities of Nothing generally, and Rochester's Nothing particularly, to help answer this question of the relationship between frame and fabric in his poem.

It is by no means a critical contrivance to expect of *Upon Nothing* an elucidation of an aspect of poetics. To write of Nothing that it had 'a Being e're the World was made', which Rochester does in the second line of this poem, is to alert the reader to the linguistic ontology of Nothing. The word is anomalous; the 'no' denotes absence of 'thing', but it operates like an adjective. 'Nothing ... / Thou had'st a Being e're the World was made' is grammatically similar to 'wild thing, you make my heart sing', or any other sentence in which a qualified thing is the subject of an active verb. The word makes non-existence an accident, rather than an absence, of body. In the Rochester, the verb is the very verb 'to have being', which emphasises the spurious existence afforded Nothing by its having a name. 'This word *nothing* is a name', as Hobbes puts it in *De Corpore*, 'which yet cannot be the name of any thing'.[4] This is what led Parmenides to warn us in such strenuous terms of the dangers of the path of 'is not', for 'you could not know what is not ... nor indicate it'.[5] To indicate Nothing is to give to Nothing a local habitation and a name, which is of course the preserve of the lunatic, the lover and the poet. A poem which indicates Nothing, then, is a sort of poem squared. Puttenham wrote that poets are makers 'such as we may say of God who ... made all the world of nought'.[6] A poem about Nothing would therefore be a parody of the very process of poetic creation.

What then of the relationship in seventeenth-century poetics between form and content, frame and fabric? Sir William Temple's observation about poetry originating in Nothing is nicely balanced between the two, and that poetry is 'making' in these two distinct fields, what Harington described as 'the two parts of poetry',[7] is widely acknowledged by the theorists of the seventeenth century and their Elizabethan forebears. There is, however, a consensus that the frame is less important than the fabric. Hobbes writes that 'they that take for poesy whatsoever is writ in verse ... they err', or as Sidney put it, 'it is not rhyming and versing that maketh a poet', and for Sidney, poetry seems for the most part to be roughly synonymous with fiction.[8] According to William Drummond, Jonson was occasionally prepared to maintain that 'verses stood by sense without either colours or accent',[9] and so much of the debate in the field of poetics over the course of this period appears to be about what should go on within the arbitrary prescribed limits of poetic form, rather than concerning itself with the nature of that arbitrary prescription. Bacon writes that 'poesie is a part of learning in measure of words for the most part restrained, but in all other points extreamely licensed',[10] and goes on to discuss at length the licence of fiction while barely mentioning again the restraint of measure. Ironically, this theoretical predilection for the idea of fiction was held responsible for the kind of restrictive evils we moderns associate with prescribed verse. Sir William Alexander writes that 'many would bound the boundless Liberty of a Poet, binding him only to the Birth of his own Brains', against which position Davenant replies 'how much pleasure they loose ... who take away the liberty of a Poet, and fetter his feet in the shackles of an Historian'.[11]

The poet is nevertheless, as Jonson puts it 'tyed ... to numbers', and there is no doubt that poets were to get them right according to what Dryden was happy to refer to by the end of the century as the 'mechanical rules' of English prosody.[12] Jonson, it will be recalled, thought that Donne deserved hanging for not keeping of accent.[13] 'The counting of the Syllables is the least part of the Poet's Work', wrote Robert Wolseley in the preface to *Valentinian*, exemplifying the overall ethos that metre is a pre-existing requirement; the actual poetry goes into the words that fulfil that requirement.[14] 'Though the Laws of Verse . . . put great constraint upon the natural course of Language', writes Hobbes, 'yet the Poet, having liberty to depart from what is obstinate, and to chuse somewhat else that is more obedient to such Laws, and no less fit for his purpose, shall not be, neither by the measure nor the necessity of Rime, excused'.[15]

Hobbes dismisses Herbert's experiments in the most primitive of formally mimetic modes; 'in a . . . Sonnet, a man may vary his measures, and seek glory from a needlesse difficulty, as he that contrived verses into the form of . . . a paire of Wings'.[16] In this he is in accord with the prevalent sense that the relationship between form and content is arbitrary. According to Samuel Daniel, form is *of necessity* an arbitrary restriction unrelated to content, 'especially seeing our passions are often without measure', as he points out.[17] When Chapman claims a semantic quality to verse in the following lines 'Our Monosyllables so kindly fall, / And meete, opposde in rhyme, as they did kisse',[18] he clearly does not mean this kissing to relate to the content of the rhymed lines; he is, after all, writing about a martial epic. Davenant alerts us to the pitfalls of trying to extract sense from the formal and metrical properties of verse when he writes to Hobbes, 'I shall say a little why I have chosen my interwoven *Stanza* of four, though I am not oblig'd to excuse the choice; for numbers in Verse must, like distinct kinds of Musick, be expos'd to the uncertain and different taste of several Eares'.[19]

As it happens, this indeterminacy is exemplified in criticism of *Upon Nothing*, the stanza form of which has been variously interpreted as assertive of the triumph of measure,[20] evocative of the chaotic,[21] and even indicative of an elegiac and ultimately finite largeness whose precision makes the heterodoxy of the poem more subversive.[22] Incidentally, the stanza occurs in Dryden's translation of the *Aeneid*. This is from the dedicatory letter to the Earl of Mulgrave: 'Spenser has also given me the boldness to make use sometimes of his alexandrine line . . . it adds a certain majesty to the verse, when 'tis used with judgment, and stops the sense from overflowing into another line'. Shortly afterwards, he writes 'I frequently make use of triplet rhymes, and for the same reason, because they bound the sense. And therefore, I generally join these two licences together, and make the last verse of the triplet a Pindaric [i.e. an Alexandrine]: for, besides the majesty which it gives, it confines the sense within the barriers of three lines, which would languish if it were lengthened into four'.[23] The business about majesty is a fiction. 'When 'tis used with judgement' means when the line is so written as not to fall apart into two trimeters, or when the content of the line is itself majestical. There is nothing majestical, for example, in the Alexandrine from *Upon Nothing* 'And to be part of thee, the wicked wisely Pray' (line 27), with its obvious caesura in the middle, and its alliteration on the paradoxical and distinctly unmajestical topic of the wicked wisely praying for oblivion. Dryden's fictitious hexametrical majesty is intended to excuse the manifest licence he is taking in order to keep his sense within his verses, a motivation he is happy to admit. But there is another excuse in the mention of Spenser, the evocation of a prosodic convention, an arbitrary limit defined by precedent.

Puttenham insists that 'the Poet makes and contriues out of his owne braine both the verse and the matter of his poeme', not 'by any paterne or mould, as the Platonicks . . . do phantastically suppose'.[24] But anyone reading his manual, however taxonomic it might be in intention, could take one of the verse forms therein and use it as a pattern or mould for his own poem. In any case, formal prescription comes into play, at the very latest, as soon as the first stanza of a stanzaic poem is written; and certainly, if one sits down to write a sonnet, the standard sonnet forms exist already, as formal conventions, waiting to be given tangible existence by the words one writes on the page. As regards metre, does Puttenham expect us to believe what Jonson calls the observing of accent to have been re-invented anew for every poem written? If verse is made of naught then, whether Puttenham likes it or not, there is alongside that naught an empty pattern or mould such as the Platonicks do phantastically suppose. Verse form, to paraphrase Rochester, has a being ere the poem is made.

That form pre-exists substance is acknowledged by Sidney as an occasional phenomenon in bad rhymed verse: 'It will be found', he writes, 'that one verse did but beget another'.[25] It is famously celebrated, however, by Daniel: 'Ryme', he tells us, 'is no impediment to [the poet's] conceit, but rather giues him wings to mount, and carries him, not out of his course, but as it were beyond his power.'[26] Jonson's claim that he wrote all his poems first in prose and then versified them would appear to contradict this theory, but even he I think could not deny Sidney's assertion that if rhyme is to be done well it requires 'ordering at the first what should be at the last', a clear statement of the pre-existing and prescriptive nature of poetic form, rather more convincing than his earlier suggestion that verse is merely ornament to matter.[27] This aspect of poetics is modelled in terms of the creation of the cosmos. Pre-existing prescriptive form is justified as analogous to the Pythagorean, and indeed Platonic, idea that the Universe is ordered by number. Campion writes that 'the world is made by Simmetry and proportion, and is in that respect compared to Musick, and Musick to Poetry'.[28] Even Sidney, despite his insistence that 'it is not rhyming and versifying that maketh a poet', acknowledges poetry's 'planet-like music'.[29]

Nevertheless, it is to be assumed that matter as well as formal prescription pre-exists the poem; it is rare that poets fill formal requirements with unpremeditated words and see what emerges. This pre-existing matter is also understood cosmogonically, in this case as primordial chaos: 'The body of our imagination', asks Daniel, 'being as an Vnformed *Chaos* without fashion, without day, if by the diuine power of the spirit it be wrought into an Orbe of order and forme, is it not more pleasing to Nature?'[30] In the same vein, Dryden describes primordial poetic matter as 'a confused mass of thoughts, tumbling over one another in the dark'.[31] So where is Nothing in all this, the Nothing from which Puttenham, Theseus, Sir William Temple and the rest think poetry is made? There hardly seems space for it if symmetry and chaos have coexisted all along.

Clearly, the ubiquitous metaphor of God and the poet as analogous creators *ex nihilo* brings with it a complex cosmogonical problem, as indeed do most cosmogonies irrespective of their application in poetics. Genesis conflates chaos and non-existence by stating that the earth was both formless and void. It represents a point midway between the ancient Mesopotamian cosmogonies in which it originated, according to which Chaos precedes the ordering intelligence of the creator, and medieval Christian doctrine, according to which God is the sole originator of all things and creates out of nothing.[32] Substance cannot be made out of nothing, because if body came into being, there would have been a time when it was not, and this is to take the Parmenidean path of 'is not', which way error lies. But body must have come into being during the creation, because otherwise God would not be the sole originator of all things, being therefore coeval with chaos.

Though this latter position is clearly heretical, it survived the Thomist onslaught[33] and lived on into the Renaissance for two reasons. Firstly, the doctrine of creation *ex nihilo* does not fit with the Old Testament, which admits only creation from the seas of chaos, except in two verses, Genesis 1.2 and 2 Maccabees 7.28, in which creation *ex nihilo* is hardly positively endorsed. Secondly, the classical tradition in favour of the chaos narrative is strong, particularly in Plato's *Timaeus*, the only Platonic dialogue to have had a significant doctrinal influence over the medieval period,[34] and also in Ovid's *Metamorphoses*, the creation narrative of which is thoroughly rooted in the Hesiodic cosmogony of chaos.

Nevertheless, Renaissance poets by no means forgot that the world was made of nothing too, and the coexistence of nothing and chaos is imagined sequentially. When Romeo comes across what he calls a 'Misshapen chaos of well-seeming forms', he exclaims 'O brawling love, O loving hate, / O anything of nothing first create'.[35] When Donne in the 'Nocturnall upon S. Lucies day' is transformed from one of 'two Chaosses', into a quintessence of nothingness, he becomes the elixir 'of the first nothing'.[36] Romeo is presumably not a doctrinal expert, and in Donne the primacy of Nothing is both a concession to orthodoxy and an integral part of his metaphor. Spenser's solution to the problem of the coexistence of Nothing and chaos, in the Garden of Adonis passage of the *Faerie Queene*, however, engages much more directly with the actual ontological problem of creation. He writes that

> in the wide wombe of the world there lyes,
> In hatefull darknesse and in deep horrore,
> An huge eternall Chaos, which supplyes
> The substances of natures fruitfull progenyes.
>
> All things from thence doe their first being fetch,
> And borrow matter.[37]

Chaos here partakes of the origins of things; it is in the womb of the world, not the world itself. The matter from which temporal tangible things are made exists prior to the existence of those things, and, as Spenser goes on to indicate, it exists after those things to which it has given substance cease to exist:

> That substance is eterne, and bideth so,
> Ne when the life decayes, and forme does fade,
> Doth it consume, and into nothing go.
>
> (*Faerie Queene*, III.vi.37)

Tangible reality is clearly then not substance, but the temporary combination of substance and form; substance itself does not partake of the order of reality in which things are or are not. An absence, a 'nothing', in tangible reality before or after the existence of a thing means that its matter is in the realm of pure substance, the womb of the world.

This ontology is Platonic: it comes from the *Timaeus*, in which there are three orders of being: the realm of pure form, the realm of pure substance which is a homogeneous chaos, and the space in which the combination of form and substance is manifest. Plato helps us here with an analogy that reverses the qualities of substance and tangible reality. Eternal substance is like a sheet of gold, into which shapes are pressed. The tangible world has the ontological status of those shapes while visible as impressions in the gold. In this cosmology, 'nothing', has the status of space, the absence of impressions in the gold being equivalent to nothing in tangible reality. When Donne partakes of the first nothing he is re-begot 'of absence, darkness, death, things which are not'; things, in fact, which, like 'nothing', are merely names denoting absences.

Here, then, is a cosmogony of poetry. Poetry, like Plato's cosmos, has three orders of being: the pre-existing conventions of metre and poetic form, imagined as we have seen as the eternal numbers according to which the world was made; the pre-existing substance of the poet's thoughts, imagined as we have seen as a chaos; and the nothing that is the absence of a poem before it has been written. It is this nothing that is the backbone of my contention that the relationship between form and content in poetry written according to the theories of the Elizabethans and their successors is arbitrary, not collaborative. Nothing is what form and content have in common before they are combined in the tangible world of the poem. Their only accident in common is absence. 'Because I count it without reason', writes Sir John Harington of a Latin epigram, 'I will English it without rhyme',[38] giving rhyme and reason a mutual contingency that is ontological and nothing more.

In fact, just as the tangible world is imperfect, so the actual poem is imperfect; it will be recalled that Hobbes described how the sense is not aided but compromised by metre, and that Dryden described the licences he took with metre to contain the sense. Is there any space left for a collaborative understanding of form and content? It could be argued, and I would agree, that the imaginative links between cosmology and poetics faded over the course of the seventeenth century, and a collaborative understanding of form and content crept in. In 1674, apparently the year of composition of Rochester's poem, Thomas Rymer wrote of a verse of Virgil's: 'the *numbers* are so ratling that nothing can be more repugnant to the general repose and silence which the Poet describes'.[39] He is anticipating Pope's dictum 'The *Sound* must seem an *Eccho* to the Sense',[40] which, though it implies no semantic of metrical *deviation*, certainly implies a secondary acoustic semantic, to which metre and verse form might contribute. So what of Rochester himself? Was he heir to the Elizabethan cosmogony of poetics or was he a pioneer of formal mimeticism? Does the missing foot mean Nothing, or does it not mean anything at all?

Rochester's cosmogony in *Upon Nothing* is principally concerned with a question that does not arise in the cosmology of poetics, the old question of why nothing should become something in the first place. 'What need', asked Parmenides, 'would have driven [that which is] later rather than earlier, beginning from the nothing, to grow?'[41] If nothing had a being ere the world was made, in that before the world was made, nothing existed, then what made the world? Of course in line 6 Rochester tells us that 'What' did indeed make the world, where 'What' is the creator God shaved to infinitesimal thickness by Occam's razor. 'What' is that which existed along with primitive Nothing and caused it to become something. The problem is explored through a paradoxical chronology; the creation happened at the moment when time began, and at that moment Nothing something *straight* begot, and then, presumably a 'then' of chronological succession rather than simultaneity, 'all proceeded from the great united What!'. In this stanza, 'Something' is synonymous with the 'What'; it was begot at the very moment when time began and all, that is everything, proceeded from it. If everything proceeded from it after it itself came into being then it must be no thing, which is why Nothing begot it straight: that first something is in fact coeval with Nothing and partakes of it. This explains how the primal Nothing can be predicated by a past participle in line 3: Nothing is 'Well fixt' because it was fixed by that generative principle that is and is not nothing, that does not partake of existence, but must exist to cause existence. Nothing and the 'great united What!' begot each other at that eternity of infinitesimal duration at the beginning of time. The third and fourth stanzas restate the paradox. Line 7 points out that something is 'the General Attribute of all', and line 10 reminds us that the existence of all is contingent upon the prior existence of something. Nevertheless, this paradox having been exploited long enough, we suddenly find ourselves on familiar territory in stanzas 5 and 6.

Nothing has a kind of extended family; we saw it in Donne's 'absence, darkness, death, things which are not', and we see it here. 'Matter' is the offspring of Nothing's 'Race', and assisted by form it combines to ruin Nothing's 'Line', by producing body, Nothing's 'Foe'. Clearly body is opposed to Nothing, but it is preceded by rebellious agents that partake of Nothing. Matter has been held in Nothing's embrace since the moment of creation. This is just the kind of ontology we found in Spenser, and in line 21 Spenser's very womb image is recalled. A Lucretian version of the same ontology is explored in Rochester's eschatological Nothing poem, the translation from Seneca beginning 'After Death nothing is, and nothing Death'.[42] 'Dead', he writes, 'we become the Lumber of the World: / And to that Mass of Matter shall be swept, / Where things destroy'd, with things unborn are kept' (lines 8–10). Here is that same identity of non-entity that makes unformed matter a kind of nothing, coeval with the Nothing into which form and matter become body. When Hobbes discusses what he calls *Materia Prima* in *De Corpore*, he says of it that it is body in general, it is just a name, and it is nothing.[43] He explains this with the following analogy. If one were to invent a name for the substance that can be either water or ice, it would refer to water and ice in general, it would be just a name, and it would be nothing. Body in general, then, is primordial matter, which is no thing, and corresponds exactly to that kind of nothing that is chaos in Plato or Spenser. It goes without saying that form too is not in itself tangible body, and is therefore also no thing. Just as we found in ontology and poetics elsewhere, form and matter, prior to creation, are only linked by common familial ties with primordial absence.

This is roughly in accord with Cowley's *Davideis*, apparently one of the sources of *Upon Nothing*. Cowley's creation narrative has an unusually comprehensive cosmogony of poetics. Having just previously narrated that '*All* . . . / From out the womb of *fertile Nothing* ris',[44] he sets up the following analogy:

As first a various unform'd *Hint* we find
Rise in some god-like *Poets* fertile *Mind*,
Till all the parts and words their places take,
And with just marches *verse* and *musick* make;
Such was *Gods Poem*, this *Worlds* new *Essay*;
So wild and rude in its first draught it lay;
Th'ungovern'd parts no *Correspondence* knew,
An artless *war* from thwarting *Motions* grew;
Till they to *Number* and fixt rules were brought
By the *eternal Minds Poetique Thought*.

(p. 253)

Cowley has already explained that God's '*spirit* contains / The well-knit *Mass*, from him each Creature gains/ *Being*' (p. 251); in other words, the primordial stuff has no more tangible being than the 'fixt rules' with which it will be combined, and according to which it will be knit by the spirit of God. The 'first draught' was a '*Hint*' of being.

I do not, however, consider my anti-mimetic argument about Rochester's metre to be proved by his acknowledgment of this orthodox post-Renaissance cosmogony of poetics. It is clearly the very act of bringing something out of nothing that interests Rochester, not the mechanical details of that act, or the different kinds of nothing that in combination produce something. If stanzas five and six are merely toeing the orthodox ontological line of his time for want of a more interesting cosmogony to explore, we cannot necessarily expect of Rochester an engagement with their implications for poetics generally, and for the ontology of the sixth foot of the 42nd line of his poem specifically. Furthermore, were I to consider my point proved, it would automatically undermine itself. My inferences pertaining to 'Well fixt' in line 3, for example, are invalid if 'Well fixt' is there to make up the Alexandrine. If form and content in poetry are indeed an unsatisfactory compromise between arbitrary numbers and matter without measure, then 'Well fixt' could so easily be an addition to an original pentameter 'And art alone of ending not afraid'. The line is much smoother as a pentameter without 'Well fixt' than it is as a hexameter with a caesura after the first syllable and a trochee for a second foot. 'Well fixt' is not even necessary for the sense. Is it just there to ratify the numbers? The same could be asked of the word 'strait' in line 5, so central to my contention that the generative principle is coeval with Nothing. Is the word in fact not there for its sense of chronological immediacy, but because it makes up the pentameter in the way that having 'did beget' instead of 'begot' would do, but without necessitating a change of rhyme? In denying the semantic properties of metrical feet, does the poetic cosmogony of the time by implication deny the semantic properties of the words required to fill them?

Such a denial would certainly explain Rochester's interest in the paradoxical nature of the creative act itself rather than the process by which that act occurs. If the correlation between cosmogony and poetics does inhere in this poem, the question, 'What quality in nothing causes it to become something?' is analogous to the question, 'What quality in the absence of a poem causes the poet to sacrifice his measureless pre-poetic chaos on the altar of arbitrary form?' It will be recalled that to write a poem upon nothing is to satirise the very process of poetical composition. If this poem argues for a pervasive semantic ambiguity in poetry as a result of poetry's compromisive nature, then it thereby shows why the very process of poetical composition is so deserving of such satire. In the field of poetics it is a great united why? Twice in the first seven stanzas Rochester reminds us that all this creation will fall back into the boundless self of Nothing, driven back into its womb, and I am reminded of the end of Daniel's *Defence of Ryme*, where having defended the arbitrary limit of form as creating an orb of order out of chaos, he tells us, the very *mise en page* tailing off into nothing, that 'we must heerein be content to submit ourselves to the law of time, which in few yeeres wil make al that for which we now contend Nothing'.[45]

Appealing to Rochester's other pronouncements on poetry is not entirely helpful. He does advocate respect for a vague kind of formal prescription in *An Allusion to Horace*: 'within due proportions circumscribe / What e're you write' (lines 20–1) but this is no mechanical formalism, for he mocks Dryden for finding Fletcher and Beaumont 'uncorrect' (line 82) and appears to espouse a doctrine of liberty from extremes of prescription, without positive advocacy of a semantics of metrical deviation. He makes it clear, in the Sidneyan vein of denying the definitive status of form and metre in poetry, that 'Five hundred Verses every morning writt / Proves you no more a Poet than a Witt' (lines 93–4), and in *An Epistolary Essay* asks 'Why shoud my prostituted sence be drawn / To ev'ry Rule their mustie Customes spawn?' (lines 85–6), though of course it is not clear on whose behalf. Nevertheless he appears to show tendencies towards collaborative poetics in the imitation of Boileau, when he mocks Halfwit's exclamation 'There's fine Poetry! you'd sweare 'twere Prose, / Soe little on the Sense, the Rhymes impose' (*Satyr.* [*Timon*], lines 119–20), an exclamation based on the theoretical assumption that form and content are arbitrarily linked, and the less the two impose on each other, the better both are.

The most positive theory, however, to emerge from Rochester's explicit engagements with poetics seems to advocate sheer hard work. In *An Allusion to Horace* he advises that the poet 'Compare each Phrase, Examine every Line, / Weigh every word, and every thought refine' (lines 100–1). But this is by no means an advocacy of formal and semantic collaboration, it argues rather for the Hobbesian considered approach to minimum compromise mocked in the figure of Halfwit. In any case, I do not believe a word of it. I am much happier believing as Rochester's own thoughts on the matter the sentiment expressed in the epistolary essay; 'But 'tis your choice whether you'l read or no. / If likewise of your smelling it were so: / I'd fart just as I write, for my own ease' (lines 34–6). It seems unlikely that Rochester, so adept at disseminating the image of himself as the readiest way to hell, would want us to extrapolate from his advice to other poets an image of him hunched over a paper cross-hatched with deletions, trying to impress us with his compared phrases, examined lines, weighted words and refined thoughts. On the contrary, it is much more likely that he would wish to be thought of as concerning himself with idle nothing, than with poetry.

I say 'idle' nothing with good reason.[46] Idleness is a primordial quality as Wycliffe shows in his 1388 *Genesis*, in which he, not inaccurately, translates the Vulgate's 'inanis' as 'idle'; 'the erthe was idel and voide'. Creation in Rochester spoils Nothing's 'Peaceful Reign' (line 18), a reign in which matter and Nothing would have lain in eternal embrace if it were not for the activities of 'the great united What!' (line 6). Nothing is, as we have seen, a womb, and according to Rochester in *Love to a Woman*, the womb is the 'dullest part of Gods Creation' (line 4). This poem shares certain concerns with *Upon Nothing*: it denounces the normal processes of procreation in the way that *Upon Nothing* satirises creation itself, on the grounds that created things are fated eventually to become nothing. To 'Drudg in fair *Aurelias* womb' like a slave, is only to 'gett supplies for Age and Graves' (lines 7–8), the same process as turncoat Time's driving of Nothing's slaves back to her 'hungry Womb' (line 21) in *Upon Nothing*. In both cases the effort required to snatch things from the idleness of Nothing's womb serves only to return those things to it. That 'slaves' are required to sate Nothing's hunger only adds to the picture of Nothing's decadent idleness.

The idleness of Nothing, however, reflects on its encomiast. In the song *Love to a Woman* he gives the alternative to reproductive drudgery in idle parts, which is (as well as busy love with a personage of parts less idle) engendering wit. But this is clearly an idle pursuit; not choosing out for one's happiness the idlest part of God's creation gives one the leisure, that 'the Porter and the Groom' (line 5) do not have, to be idle oneself. *Upon Nothing* is certainly the result of an engendering of wit; in permitting himself to satirise creation rather than engaging in procreation, might Rochester be putting into practice the idleness that he has thereby earned himself?

In *Paradoxica Epidemica*, Rosalie Colie identifies two main kinds of writing about nothing, the one being the simple and superficial use of the linguistic and ontological paradox of nothing to produce amusing trivialities, in which category she places Rochester's poem, and the other being the use of nothing to articulate large-scale tragic themes, as in Shakespeare's tragedies. The former category is poetry with a mock subject, the latter is poetry in which the true subject is the human race. But if the former is poetry with a mock subject, then it too must have a true subject, and I think that subject is the author. This is well exemplified by another work in the category of 'entirely trivial', Fielding's essay *On Nothing*, in which he writes towards the end 'surely it becomes a wise man to regard Nothing with the utmost awe and adoration; to pursue it with all his parts and pains; and to sacrifice to it his ease . . . and his present happiness'.[47] Fielding implies that the truly wise man pursues only ease and happiness, a pursuit manifestly engaged in by the encomiast of Nothing, for whom the subject itself is nothing, and the facility and paradoxical pleasure of its praise is everything. Of course the passage explicitly states that the wise man *is* the encomiast of Nothing, a man not just characterised by his interest in the topic of Nothing, and his pursuit of ease, but also characterised as not regarding anything with awe; he is a leisured satirist, who does nothing with any great sincerity of endeavour. This is the Rochester with whom we are familiar, a man who blasphemes his God and libels kings for his own and our amusement, a man who writes great poetry about nothing at all. Is the careful weighing of syllables appropriate to such a man?

Fortunately, it does not matter to us if this self-image of the encomiast of Nothing is a fiction or not. If, bearing in mind the Davenant Metrical Indeterminacy Principle,[48] we adopt a new interpretation of the missing foot of line 42, the question of whether there is a semantically active empty foot there is solved. Let us interpret it, not as signifying stately Nothing reigning at the end of the line, but as indicative of Rochester's leisured carelessness, in which case it makes no difference if it is a genuine metrical error, or a carefully considered strategy to portray himself as too much at his ease to care about or even notice a metrical error. The effect is the same. It is in any case no great interpretative leap thus to unite the two sides of an argument which has only ever been about whether the missing foot means Nothing, or does not mean anything at all. It was perhaps overly optimistic to expect an unequivocal answer to the question, 'Is there or is there not an empty sixth foot at the end of line 42?', or an unequivocal answer to the question, 'Is there or is there not a semantics of metre?', from the poem itself, a poem which as much as anything can, or indeed as only Nothing can, blurs the distinction between those two great ends of Fate, 'Is', and 'is not'.

Artemiza to Chloe: Rochester's 'female' epistle

GILLIAN MANNING

In a virulent, anti-feminist satire of 1691, Robert Gould invokes Rochester, and appropriates lines 26–7 from *A Letter from Artemiza in the Towne to Chloe in the Countrey*:

> Hast thou not heard what Rochester declares?
> That Man of Men . . .
> He tells thee, *Whore's the like reproachful Name,*
> *As Poetress* – the luckless Twins of Shame.[1]

Pace Gould, I should like to consider some of what (on balance) I take to be the predominantly female-friendly perspectives of Rochester's *Artemiza to Chloe*. These I suggest result largely from the controlling viewpoint of Artemiza, the poem's chief speaker and fictive composer, and the techniques and strategies employed to construct and define this view point: in particular a complex intertextual web of significance. Before discussing this, however, a few contextual details may be noted relating, firstly, to Rochester himself, and, secondly, to the poem's reception.

Despite Rochester's reputation among both contemporary and later readers as a misogynistic rake, and the perpetrator of some obscene, anti-female verse, there is evidence that he was regarded with affectionate respect, both as friend and literary mentor, by at least two women writers: his niece, Anne Wharton, and Aphra Behn. Wharton's elegy on her uncle describes generally how

> He civiliz'd the rude and taught the young,
> Made Fools grow wise; such artful magick hung
> Upon his useful kind instructing Tongue,

(lines 20–2)

12 Anne Lee, Marchioness of Wharton. *Engraving after Sir Peter Lely*

and more personally recalls her assisted *gradus ad Parnassum*:

> He led thee up the steep and high Ascent
> To Poetry, the Sacred Way he went.
> He taught thy Infant Muse the Art betime
> Tho' then the way was difficult to climb.[2]

Behn's own elegy for Rochester caused Wharton to reply in complimentary vein with *To Mrs. A. Behn, On what she writ of the Earl of Rochester*, a poem which in turn elicited a politely supportive response from the established writer: *To Mrs. W. On her Excellent Verses (Writ in Praise of some I had made on the Earl of Rochester) Written in a Fit of Sickness*. Here Behn describes an inspiring vision: a visitation by the 'Lovely *Phantom*' of her late fellow-poet, 'the Great, the God-like *Rochester*', whom she depicts as continuing to offer her the same gracious, if characteristically stringent, artistic advice as he had in his lifetime:

> It did advance, and with a Generous Look,
> To me Addrest, to worthless me it spoke:
> With the same wonted Grace my Muse it prais'd,
> With the same Goodness did my Faults Correct:
> And Careful of the Fame himself first rais'd
> Obligingly it School'd my loose Neglect.[3]

Interestingly, the penultimate line suggests also that Rochester had been in some way instrumental in helping to establish Behn's literary reputation.

If Rochester himself encouraged both Behn and Wharton in their writing, so *Artemiza to Chloe* may have prompted several other women writers to engage with some of its materials and techniques. I am discounting here the many eighteenth-century writers, male and female, who merely cite the poem, or who, like Gould, appropriate the occasional line or phrase for their own ends, and note only those who appear effectively to enter into creative dialogue with Rochester's poem: taking up and developing issues central to the latter work, especially women's views on love, attitudes to men and the predicament of the woman poet in a predominantly hostile or dismissive society. Given such titles as *Chloe to Sabina, An Epistle to Artemisia. On Fame*, and perhaps also *Cloe to Artimesa*, it seems arguable that these works are deliberately flagged as bearing some relation to Rochester's tour de force of ventriloquism, *Artemiza to Chloe*.[4] If so, then it might suggest that several Restoration and eighteenth-century women poets read *Artemiza to Chloe* not as a satire relating primarily to the misogynistic tradition which includes Juvenal's sixth satire, Boileau's tenth satire and Pope's *Epistle to a Lady*, but as a less biased, though still complex and rigorous, assessment of the contemporary female condition. Endorsing such an approach, I shall first canvass some possible implications of Artemiza's name, and then discuss two key related, though neglected, aspects of the poem: its allusions to specific texts, and the significance of its epistolary nature.

Artemiza hardly seems to have been a popular name, and it is unlikely that Rochester's decision to bestow it on his protagonist was simply casual, especially since he gives proper names only to Artemiza and Timon, of the main speakers in his major satires.[5] The possible implications of Artemiza's name proposed by recent readers have been diverse and numerous. As in Timon's case, however, all seem broadly compatible and relevant to Rochester's portrayal of his speaker, and some would also seem to offer significant hints as to the precise nature of Artemiza's role, character and situation.

Weinbrot is the first critic to consider the matter of Artemiza's name in any detail, though, in consequence of his somewhat sensational reading of the poem, he is moved to fancy that, as part of the process of her gradual corruption, Artemiza may have been persuaded to 'forget the background of chastity and female heroism and fidelity associated with her name'. However, he usefully outlines the stories concerning the two most famous bearers of the name, the classical queens and heroines Artemisia of Caria, and Artemisia of Halicarnassus, and he also implies a possible additional link between Rochester's Artemiza and Artemis, the 'perpetually celibate goddess of the chase'. Of the two celebrated queens, Artemisia of Caria was perhaps the better known in the seventeenth century, but writers often confounded the two figures. Jonson, for instance, in his *Masque of Queens*, rightly describes Artemisia of Caria as 'renowm'd for her chastety and love to her Husband, *Mausolus*, whose bones, (after he was dead) she preseru'd in ashes, and drunke in wine, making her selfe his tombe', but mistakenly attributes to the same lady the 'excellence of spirit' and more than manly prowess displayed by her namesake, Artemisia of Halicarnassus, who fought to such effect with Xerxes against the Greeks at Salamis. Since Rochester could hardly have been unaware, either of the famous stories concerning the two queens or of the commonly accepted derivation of the name Artemisia from that of the goddess Artemis (whose festivals were, in addition, called Artemisia), it seems probable that his intention in using the name was to suggest a range of possible implications and associations to enhance the subtlety and signific-ance of his protagonist's persona. There may also be a slighter, more playful and contemporary reference to the high-minded Princess Artemise of La Calprenède's popular romance *La Cléopâtre*.[6]

Clearly, a good many of the characteristics noted above appear applic-able in varying degrees to Rochester's Artemiza, if rather more ironically, or obliquely, than some readers have suggested. For instance, it seems inappro-priate in view of the poem's elusive nature, and the lack of positive evidence, that Artemiza should be seen as 'virginal', or at least that her 'apparent non-engagement in sexual relationships [should attributed to] the affinity with her namesake, Artemis'.[7] Equally unsubstantiated is Weinbrot's theory that

Artemiza may have been led, in the course of the poem, to reject such an affinity. If, as seems probable, Rochester is alluding more lightly, tenuously and creatively to Artemiza's possible affinities both with Artemis and with the two heroic, classical queens, there is no more reason necessarily to suppose Artemiza herself a virgin, like Artemis, or (after Weinbrot) a hitherto principled lady who has had a recent change of lifestyle, than to suppose her, for example, a faithful and devoted widow, like Artemisia of Caria. Since Artemiza's letter appears designed to offer (albeit indirectly) both information and advice (to stimulate, not merely interest in, but thoughtful assessment of, various attitudes and patterns of conduct open to women, especially in the sphere of love and sexual relationships), it seems reasonable to hold that her name carries associations variously suggestive of Artemis's role as the patron of young girls and approver of chastity, as well, perhaps, as of her liking for a simple life in rural surroundings (Chloe's name, incidentally, bears the literal meaning, 'young plant' or 'green shoot').[8] Clearly, such allusions, like those relating to the two queens, relate only in subtle or ironic ways to Artemiza's own views, situation, and activities; Chloe may be in the country, but Artemiza herself is writing from 'this Lewd Towne' (line 33). Also, Chloe may be young and innocent, but while she is not, perhaps, 'lust[ing] for the game of gossip' in quite the manner that one critic suggests,[9] it is evident that, in Artemiza's view, Chloe is at least looking to be brought up to date with the latest gossip and news of love affairs about town, and in fact Artemiza makes this the pretext for diverting the course of her letter into rather more demanding channels. Moreover, though obviously disapproving of the 'fine Lady' (line 74) and her libertine notions, Artemiza makes no explicit attempt to define the kind of views and practice that she herself might endorse with regard to love. Even her lament for 'that lost thing (Love)' (lines 36–53) can hardly be taken as a direct, unequivocal encouragement to the practice either of a species of idealised, sublimated passion that might be acceptable to an Artemis, or of the kind of chaste, devoted love exemplified by Artemisia of Caria.[10]

In contrast to the two latter figures, Artemisia of Halicarnassus would seem to constitute a more ambiguous exemplar. Though indisputably courageous and great-hearted, according to Herodotus she escaped personal disaster at Salamis only by an action as ruthless and cunning as it was resourceful and daring.[11] In Rochester's poem, Artemiza's wary, self-mocking, but determined venture 'for the Bayes' (line 7) might seem to carry a witty allusion to her heroic namesake's exploits in the famous sea-battle; even the imagery used in these lines (7–13) is appropriately, if fortuitously, naval. Nor is the implied parallel quite of the sort to be found in *Timon*, where, by comparison with a classical heroic figure, a modern counterpart is diminished. Though Artemiza's poem is intimate and conversational, rather than heroic in kind, this seems appropriate, in view both of the debased and unheroic nature of the age she depicts, and of the disasters already encountered by more impetuous and hubristic male writers. Moreover, her preoccupations and, finally, her achievement are not trivial, while it is arguable that her courage and craft serve worthier ends than did those of Artemisia of Halicarnassus.

Perhaps the most important of the possible implications brought together by Rochester in naming his speaker 'Artemiza' was first touched on by Rothstein, who notes succinctly (though inaccurately) that '"Artemisia", in Latin, is wormwood', and suggests that 'the letter showers the bitter medicine of urban vice on sheltered innocence', the latter being, as we have seen, in his view somewhat less innocent than may at first sight appear. Everett makes much the same point, remarking that the 'word "Artemisia" means the species of bitter herb that contains the plant wormwood, and the poet may have thought this "flower of Artemis"a good name for his sharp-tongued virginal heroine'.[12]

In fact, the nature and significance of Rochester's herbal allusion seem likely to be more extensive and complex than either of these readers suggests. *Artemisia* is the Latin name not for wormwood (the Latin for which is *absinthium*) but for mugwort, a plant which, according to Pliny, resembles wormwood in appearance, but which, up to the eighteenth century at least, does not appear to have been considered of the same species. Thus the properties which a seventeenth-century reader would have associated with *Artemisia* are those connected with the mugwort, rather than with the wormwood, plant. English herbalists of the sixteenth and seventeenth centuries leaned heavily upon Pliny, and their esteem for the many useful properties of mugwort would have rendered it a familiar plant to both professional and amateur physicians. It seems to have been quite well known, too, by its Latin name; Elisha Coles, for instance, in his popular *English Dictionary* (1676) has as his (somewhat selective) entry for 'Artemisia': 'Queen of Halicarnassus, also Mug-wort'. The general character of the species is described by Gerard as 'hot, and dry in the second degree, and somewhat astringent', and the little group of plants then considered to belong to the species is credited with diverse properties, often either of a protective or a bracing nature. Gerard notes, for example, that mugwort prevents weariness, and serves as a protection against 'poysonsome medicines', and the effects of the sun and 'wilde beast[s]', besides being 'drunke against *Opium*'. It was best known, however, for its supposed efficacy in treating women's diseases, and Pliny suggests that it may derive its Latin name from 'Artemis Ilithyia, because the plant is specific for the troubles of women', though he also notes that it may have been named after 'Artemisia, the wife of Mausolus'.[13]

In view of Rochester's well-attested interest both in 'Books of Physick' and in the more practical aspects of the subject, it seems likely that he would have been familiar with the works of such standard herbalists as John Gerard and John Parkinson, and perhaps, too, with the relevant portions of Pliny's *Natural History*.[14] Moreover, his decision to call his main speaker Artemiza, perhaps with allusion to the herb of the same name, may have been partly influenced by the example of his favourite English poet, Cowley. Cowley not only shared Rochester's interest in physick, but had also studied medicine professionally, and his friend Sprat records how, in the course of these studies, Cowley 'proceeded to the Consideration of Simples; and having furnish'd himself with Books of that Nature, he retir'd into a fruitful part of *Kent*, where every Field and Wood might show him the real Figures of those Plants of which he read'. As a result of this sojourn, he composed a Latin poem concerning plants, which was published in six books in 1668, though Books I and II had appeared already in 1662.[15] Both these books may well have engaged Rochester's interest, and the second may have given him a hint for *Artemiza to Chloe*, since it concerns only those herbs which are used specifically in the treatment of women's conditions, and which Cowley characterises as female themselves, giving a prominent role to *Artemisia*. Nahum Tate, in his introduction to the complete English translation of the *Six Books of Plants*, gives the scene of the second book as 'the Physick-Garden at *Oxford*', and the occasion, a council of those herbs which 'come under the Female Province, and are serviceable in Generation or Birth'.[16] The assembly of plants begins at twelve on an April night, and is finally abruptly adjourned by its president, *Artemisia*, when just before dawn, the gardener is seen approaching in urgent search of herbs to ease his wife's labour pains, whereupon the plants hastily retreat to their beds. Throughout the poem, *Artemisia* plays a dominant and controlling role: as president of the council, her title is '*Mat[er] herbarum*', she delivers the opening speech of the meeting, prescribes the topic for discussion and bids each herb speak in turn and give an account of its properties and duties in combating female disease.[17] Later, when the discussion has turned into impassioned altercation, she contributes an important speech in a successful move to conciliate a number of herbs who react furiously to being attacked as abortifacients by their fellows. Before steering the debate into other channels, *Artemisia* admits that she herself shares the maligned properties of the former group, and points out judiciously their usefulness in times of disease, remarking that herbs intended to prove helpful remedies can hardly be blamed if they are misused.

It seems probable that Rochester knew Cowley's *Sex Libri Plantarum*, especially since his father, Henry Wilmot, receives a respectful mention in Book VI, which, though ostensibly devoted to trees, is largely concerned with relating 'the History of the late Rebellion, the King's Affliction and Return, and the beginning of the *Dutch* Wars'. It seems equally likely that Cowley's characterisation of *Artemisia* in Book II, and his general handling there of the herbs 'under the Female Province', may have proved a contributory factor in Rochester's naming his main speaker Artemiza.[18] The implications of a possible herbal allusion in Rochester's choice of name for his female protagonist are not far to seek, and are compatible with the range of other such allusions already mooted. Several of *Artemisia*'s more diverse medicinal properties, as an astringent, as an antidote to opium and as a protection against poisons and weariness, seem metaphorically applicable to the character and function of Rochester's Artemiza. Her sharp wit and perceptive insights regarding herself and others often appear astringent, and her narrative is far from anodyne. In view of the herb's reputed capacity to prevent weariness, her final reference to her own and Chloe's tiredness may be something of a joke on Rochester's part, as well as a conventionally witty way to conclude a letter.[19] More seriously, Artemiza's obliquely presented, but powerfully pejorative, disclosures concerning the corrupt state of love in 'this lewd Towne' (line 33), may parallel mugwort's discutient properties, and its supposed efficacy against poisons. There may also be a more general allusion, of a kind similar to that in *Tunbridge Wells*, to the traditional concept of satire as a form of physick.

Mugwort's specific reputation for being helpful in the treatment of women's diseases, relates self-evidently to Rochester's Artemiza, in that she endorses at least a positive moral stance regarding the corrupt views and practices her letter describes, if not a prescriptive code of wholesome ethics by which they should be countered. Moreover, Rochester, like Cowley, gives his speaker, Artemiza, the leading, authoritative role, in a poem where the characters, view points and preoccupations are almost exclusively female. Again, while Cowley's *Artemisia* sees her true function as cleansing and health-bringing, she laments that, as one of the '*Ecbolicks*',[20] she may be wickedly misapplied to produce abortions. Equally, Artemiza fears that her poem, whatever its intrinsic merits, may be maliciously received and abused by 'th'ill-humour'd' (line 22).

In all, then, Rochester brings together a range of possible allusions – medical, literary, historical and mythological – most of them familiar, and some already often interlinked, or even confounded. All combine to enrich the poem's significance and to add depth and definition to Artemiza's complex role and character. Of the various possible allusions suggested by Artemiza's name, however, it is those relating to her herbal namesake which are central to the poem's themes and subject. Such allusions supply a unifying metaphor to the whole poem. This links together a chain of associations which extends throughout the work, and adds resonance to such details as the 'Diseas'd' state of Corinna at her nadir (line 203), her final poisoning of her duped protector and, by contrast, 'That Cordiall dropp' (line 44) which Artemiza, at the outset, suggests might once have more truly figured the nature and function of love.

Artemiza's 'Cordiall dropp' not only contributes to the medicinal and disease-linked imagery and detail which inform the poem as a whole, but is also one of many intertextual allusions to be found throughout the work. The significance of these allusions, however, and in some cases even their presence, has been largely overlooked; in consequence, some important hints as to the poem's general tone and character have been missed, and its degree of literariness underestimated. Readers have in the main been content to note the undoubted general similarities which exist between *Artemiza to Chloe* and some of the stage comedies of the period, though Vieth has pointed out more specifically that the poem shares a group of related ideas with Etherege's *The Man of Mode*.[21] In addition, however, *Artemiza to Chloe* contains a range of precise and often pointed allusions to poetic and philosophical works. While some of these references are of limited and local significance, others play a major role in focusing the prime concerns of the poem. All combine to provide a context which is not only appropriate to the refined character and literary sensibility of the writer and true-wit, Artemiza, but which also define the pretensions of her counter-type, the 'fine Lady'.

The allusions of relatively local significance include the lines in which Artemiza describes love as 'That Cordiall dropp Heav'n in our Cup has throwne, / To make the nauseous draught of Life goe downe' (lines 44–5). This well-known couplet seems to refer to a famous passage in *De Rerum Natura*, which first appears in Book I, lines 936–47, and is later repeated verbatim in Book IV, lines 11–22.[22] Here Lucretius likens his practice of conveying in pleasing poetic form a doctrine which in itself may appear as rather harsh or unacceptable to that of physicians who persuade children to drink bitter medicines by coating the rim of their patients' cups with honey. Rochester appropriates Lucretius's thought and expression in a characteristically inventive manner. As suggested above, Lucretius's medical simile (similar in concept to Cowley's reference to his books of herbs as '*small Pills . . . gilt with a certain brightness of Style*'), is neatly absorbed into the medicinal metaphor associated with Artemiza's name, and may even touch on her epistolary strategy of promising Chloe gossip, and in fact presenting her with entertaining, but morally (if obliquely) pointed, portraits.[23] As regards its specific context, moreover, it underlines the ironic ambivalence of Artemiza's lament for 'that lost thing (Love)' (line 38). In Lucretius, the patients are described as deceived but not betrayed by the doctors' ruse, since by this means they are restored to health, and the writer expresses similar confidence in the efficacy of his bitter but intrinsically wholesome philosophic 'draught'. Artemiza, however, presents both the gift of love and heaven's action in bestowing it on humanity, in a rather more dubious light. Unlike the careful pagan physicians in Lucretius, who coat the rims of sick children's cups with honey, an ostensibly Christian 'Heav'n' is described by Artemiza as having 'throwne' a mere 'dropp' of sweetened and heartening (or perhaps only heart-affecting) liquid into 'our Cup',[24] in an effort to bribe hapless humanity into swallowing the 'draught of Life' which is not merely bitter but 'nauseous', and for which no compensatory properties are claimed.

Elsewhere in Rochester's poem, apparent allusions to works by Boileau, Sidney and Hobbes are put to similarly ironic purposes. These appropriations may be grouped together, since they all serve primarily to define various aspects of the pretensions of the 'fine Lady' (line 74). The Boileau reference occurs in this character's first speech to the assembled company when, preparatory to holding forth on why women should prefer fools as lovers, she remarks: 'When I was marry'd, Fooles were a la mode, / The Men of Witt were then held incommode' (lines 103–4). The lines to which Rochester alludes here occur in Boileau's first satire (itself loosely based on Juvenal's third satire). The speaker, a penurious poet, about to leave Paris where his talents have been despised and neglected, comments bitterly that: 'Un Poëte à la Cour fut jadis à la mode: / Mais des Fous aujourd'hui c'est le plus incommode' (lines 109–10).[25] In adapting these lines for use by his affected francophile, Rochester has followed Boileau's rhyme, but wittily varied the sense. In Boileau's satire, the honest speaker laments the time, now long since past, when true poets, rather than fools, were favoured at Court. By contrast, in Rochester's poem, the overbearing female fop recalls the time of her youth when fashionable women favoured fools as lovers above 'Men of Witt', and makes it plain that she, at least, has not changed her tastes in this respect. Having pronounced this opinion, she then proceeds to give her reasons for holding it, and her following speech contains several allusions which either ironically conflict with her viewpoint, or confirm that lack of 'discretion' later remarked on by Artemiza (lines 166–8); in the course of the strictures of the 'fine Lady' upon 'Men of Witt', she argues that such men should be avoided as less easy to deceive than fools, and advises that:

> Woman, who is an Arrant Bird of night,
> Bold in the Duske, before a Fooles dull sight,
> Should flye, when Reason brings the glaring light.
>
> (lines 121–3)

These last lines may owe something to Sidney's seventy-first sonnet in *Astrophil and Stella*, which describes:

> all vices' overthrow,
> Not by rude force, but sweetest soveraigntie
> Of reason, from whose light those night-birds flie.
>
> (lines 5–7)[26]

Rochester adjusts this sentiment to accord with the views of a speaker who fails to share even the qualified idealism regarding love expressed by Sidney's Astrophil, let alone the Platonism of the famous Petrarchan original (*Rime*, 248) to which Sidney alludes. Where, in Sidney's lines, the 'night-birds' represent man's vices, gently but inexorably put to flight by the light of Stella's virtuous reason, in the Rochester passage, by contrast, it is 'Woman' who is labelled 'an Arrant Bird of night', and advised to fly from the harsh and oppressive glare of man's excoriating reason. By inverting the terms of

Sidney's sonnet, Rochester stresses the degree to which the 'fine Lady', in cheerfully degrading the status accorded woman (and reason) in an earlier less 'ill-bred' age, conforms to the lamentable pattern of behaviour previously decried by Artemiza (lines 54–8).

The coolly rationalistic and amoral argument of the 'fine Lady' is grounded on self-interest and a desire to maintain at least a limited form of dominance over men. As such, it might appear to owe something directly to Hobbes, but any reference here to *Leviathan*, however, serves merely to pinpoint the 'fine Lady''s deficiencies. The libertine lady may have fashionable Hobbist pretensions, and she is certainly not without intelligence, but she lacks judgment, the one attribute essential not merely to a philosopher but to any person of good sense:

> All the good qualityes, that ever blest
> A Woman, soe distinguisht from the rest,
> Except discretion onely; she possest.

> (lines 166–8)

The term 'discretion', that is, judgment, may relate to a chapter in *Leviathan*, where Hobbes praises the importance of the 'Vertue . . . called DISCRETION', arguing that without it, even people of intelligence and imagination may run to folly:

> And in any Discourse whatsoever, if the defect of Discretion be apparent, how extravagant soever the Fancy be, the whole discourse will be taken for a signe of want of wit; and so will it never when the Discretion is manifest, though the Fancy be never so ordinary.[27]

In Hobbes's view, want of 'discretion' signifies 'want of wit' (and vice versa), wit being the very faculty upon which the 'fine Lady' prides herself, as her mock-modest disclaimer plainly reveals (lines 171–2). The lack of self-knowledge which she displays in this respect, and which Artemiza shrewdly points out (lines 164–5), merely confirms the former's essential lack of 'discretion'. Moreover, in general terms, the 'fine Lady' may be seen as exemplifying in her speech and behaviour what Hobbes in the same chapter calls 'GIDDINESSE, and *Distraction*', and which he claims results from 'hav[ing] Passions indifferently for everything'.[28] The 'fine Lady' feels no strong desire for anything, or anyone, in particular – being akin in this regard to those female libertines of whom Artemiza earlier remarks: 'To an exact perfection they have wrought / The Action *Love*, the Passion is forgott' (lines 63–6). The prime concern of the 'fine Lady' is not with her own desires, but with conforming to fashionable tastes; hence her behaviour towards her hostess's pet monkey, behaviour which, far from being 'warm, friendly, and sexual', therefore rendering her 'more bestial than the beast she courts', is essentially affected and dispassionate.[29] To the 'fine Lady', the animal (like a lover) is merely a fashionable property, to be picked up and dropped at will. Such 'indifference' convicts her, again, of lack of judgment, since, according to Hobbes, a person who is 'indifferent . . . cannot possibly have either a great Fancy, or much Judgement. For the Thoughts, are to the Desires, as Scouts, and Spies, to range abroad, and find the way to the things Desired: All Stedinesse of the minds motion, and all quicknesse of the same, proceeding from thence.'[30] The terms used by the lady in condemning the 'Men of Witt' for their wary and critical approach to women recall those employed by Hobbes in defining why 'indifferent' people (of whom she herself is one) lack judgment.

These local allusions to the works of such diverse writers as Hobbes, Sidney and Boileau indirectly confirm and substantiate Artemiza's assessment of the 'fine Lady' as 'a Foole of Parts' (line 161), one whose lack of the fundamental qualities of judgment and good sense perverts her undoubted gifts of intelligence and percipience. Thus, in a sense, the 'fine Lady' represents a more dangerous and disturbing exemplum than Corinna, whose tale she relates with a patronising scorn, and complacently insistent wit. Weinbrot complains that at the close of this narrative, 'Rochester has [Artemiza] ignore an opportunity to reject the lady's values and, instead, diminishes her earlier criticisms', adding that 'we are more impressed with . . . Artemisia's amusement, delight, and exasperation than with any desire to expose or punish'.[31] In the face of such a tale and such a teller, however, there seems little that even the most rabid moralist might add by way of further exposure. In fact, it is hard to know which is the more disturbing: the inexorable process of corruption which leads Corinna from her state of heedless and deceived innocence, to eventual triumph as cheat, whore and murderess; or the distorted lens which the loquacious narrator brings to bear upon this history. Moral condemnation features here only as a passing reference to Corinna's 'Man of Witt' (line 198), and serves merely to bear out the narrator's defined 'Rule' (line 177). In essence, the 'fine Lady' invites her audience to ignore all the obvious moral enormities exemplified in her tale, and to deprecate instead the meanness and folly of its chief characters. Thus Corinna's dupe and his family are viewed as receiving their just deserts as fools, while Corinna herself is regarded as a whore of attainments too mediocre, and too painfully acquired, to occasion any great wonder or admiration. In her own eyes, the teller is relating a common story of common and foolish people, the main purpose of which is to illustrate and confirm her own previously proclaimed views, and to enable her to display what she takes to be her own vastly superior wit, judgment and accomplishments. Lengthy or more strident criticism from Artemiza at this stage of her letter would be superfluous: she has already plainly indicated her disapproval of the 'fine Lady', comprehensively indicting, by a variety of means, the latter's character, manners and opinions. The story of Corinna, and the figure cut by its narrator are left to

Rochester's coat of arms in Wadham College cloister, sculpted by A. John Poole

Portrait of Henry Savile (1642–87) by Sir Godfrey Kneller (detail)

Whitehall from St James's Park, *c.* 1675, by Hendrick Danckerts

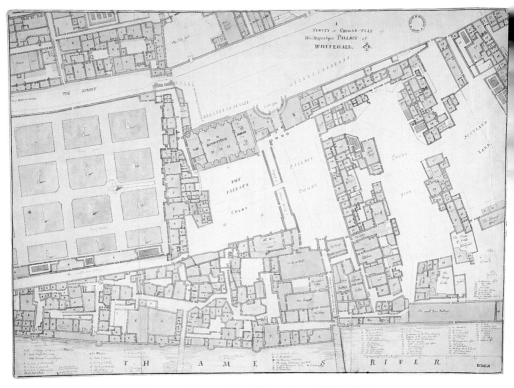

Ralph Greatorex's part plan of the palace of Whitehall *c.* 1670

speak for themselves, and Artemiza pauses only to add a tersely dismissive comment, and to promise Chloe accounts of more such 'infamous' characters and events, before briskly concluding her letter.

While it is clear that Artemiza unreservedly condemns the 'fine Lady', Corinna and all their works, it is less immediately obvious what kind of positive attitudes (if any) she may endorse regarding the areas of concern uppermost in her letter. At no point does she presume to offer Chloe direct advice, let alone to dogmatise in the opinionated manner favoured by the 'fine Lady', nor does she make any explicit attempt to define the kind of views or practice she herself might approve or seek to promote with regard to love, life or literature. None the less, her letter, though often brilliantly entertaining, treats serious issues in a complex and thoughtful way that clearly distinguishes it from the familiar verse epistle that is merely trying to be witty, and is concerned with presenting gossip or trivia. As noted earlier, Artemiza (albeit with characteristic tact) fails to comply with what she assumes is Chloe's desire to hear the latest details of the love affairs about town, and, though some of her letter's basic materials are sufficiently scandalous to satisfy the most avid gossip, their handling and careful positioning within the letter's sophisticated structure ensure their subjection to oblique but powerful condemnation. The reader is left in no doubt that they are present on the grounds not of sheer sensationalism but of their relevance to the letter's essentially moral themes and focus. Though Artemiza seems wary of offering anything very direct or explicit by way of positive advice or definition, her whole approach being characterised by an ironic, tentative, oblique and even somewhat devious quality, this seems appropriate given the nature of her enterprise. Not only is it fitting to the refined and complex character of her moral and literary preoccupations, which are themselves subtly intertwined with her roles as woman, friend, correspondent and poet, but it suits also with the decorum of the literary mode which is used to encompass all these: the familiar moral epistle. It seems likely, moreover, that in *Artemiza to Chloe*, Rochester is both alluding to and seeking to emulate the practice of the greatest master of this kind, Horace.

Reference in *Artemiza to Chloe* to the famous first line of Horace's *Epistles*, I.vi, seems to be of a different kind from some of the literary allusions discussed above. Firstly, it could hardly be missed, and seems intended to be recognised, in contrast to some of the other allusions, such as that to the Sidney sonnet, or to Boileau's first satire, where recognition of the source may constitute more in the way of an additional bonus than an absolute requirement for readers.[32] Secondly, it seems to serve more than a purely local function – in fact one might argue that to an extent it informs the whole poem. Thirdly, it occurs not on one occasion but on several, each time in a slightly varied form, echoing through the poem like a musical motif. The allusion first occurs quite early in the poem, in the course of Artemiza's deprecating account of the injurious views and practices of fashionable women, who, not content with debasing both their own status, and that of love, by their libertinism, do not even take account of their personal preferences in choosing lovers but seek instead to conform to whatever is the current taste in men among their modish acquaintance. Artemiza records with some astonishment their attempts to justify this practice: ''Tis below Witt, they tell you, to admire, / And e'ne without approving they desire' (lines 64–5). Rochester is referring here to 'nil admirari', the opening words of *Epistles*, I.vi, in which Horace advises his friend Numicius that the only sure way of leading a happy and virtuous life is to cultivate a philosophic attitude of calm, moderation and independent rational judgment: to avoid violent extremes of emotion, whether of fear or desire, and to crave nothing in excess. The misuse of this axiom by the fashionable female libertines whom Artemiza decries is only one of several instances in the poem of the misapplication of this or other aphorisms. In the case related by Artemiza, the irony is clear: that the advice 'nil admirari' should be used to justify the kind of fashionable and pointless libertinism of the women in question could hardly be further removed from its intended moral and philosophic purpose. The failure of understanding revealed by this misapplication only underlines the women's grievous lack of the 'witt' to which they lay such claim.

A further allusion to 'nil admirari' occurs in the first address of the 'fine Lady' to the company (line 107), and is apparently conflated both with the glance at *Leviathan* noted above and perhaps more importantly with a reference to the second of Seneca's *Epistulae Morales*. Rochester would seem to make several references to the Seneca epistle, and the first of these occurs at the beginning of the poem, where Artemiza is warily reflecting on the risks involved in writing poetry. Hammond notes in lines 7–10 of Rochester's poem 'a variant of the traditional image of the poet as explorer', and he implies a possible connection with a phrase from Seneca, *Epistles*, II.5–6: 'non tamquam transfuga, sed tamquam explorator'.[33] In this epistle, Seneca offers his friend, Lucilius, advice on reading habits, and recommends using his own custom of selecting each day from an approved author a single thought or saying for careful consideration. He then remarks that he took his thought for today from Epicurus, adding that he is accustomed to make such forays into the rival philosophic camp, 'non tamquam transfuga, sed tamquam explorator' – not as a deserter, but as a scout or spy. Both the epistle and the cited phrase were well known in the seventeenth century, and the latter was often alluded to in connection with literary endeavour, at times apparently feeding into the more general notion of the writer as explorer.[34] Rochester's reference to Seneca's phrase is rather more oblique. Seneca's image of exploring, or scouting through, enemy territory to see what he can abstract for his own advantage is wittily martial and mercenary; in Rochester's lines, it becomes assimilated into a more inclusive and damning image of ambitious poets as explorers and exploitative merchant adventurers. The latter image may even subsume a reference to Milton's Satan.[35] Such implications lend weight to the pejorative tone of Artemiza's shrewd assessment of the failed poetic fortunes of some of her male counterparts. These so-called 'Men of Witt' evince greed, hubris and reckless daring, rather than the alert, self-critical and humorous attitude evidenced by Seneca's epistle, and exemplified by Artemiza herself.

Rochester makes what may be a further allusion to the same epistle later in the poem, where Artemiza offers a penetrating analysis of her own anti-type, that sententious would-be wit, the 'fine Lady'. In noting the latter's not inconsiderable 'Parts', Artemiza remarks sharply that 'such a One was shee, who had turn'd o're / As many Bookes, as Men, lov'd much, reade more' (lines 161–3). Seneca's epistle is largely concerned with warning Lucilius against reading too many books of different kinds, and advises him to concentrate instead on acquiring a thorough knowledge of a few select masterpieces. More-over, Seneca anticipates that his friend might, by way of objection to this advice, indicate a preference for turning over first one book and then another, and comments that it is the sign of an over-nice appetite to pick at too many dishes. Rochester's lines may imply a parallel between the reading habits of the libertine lady and those condemned by the Stoic philosopher: Artemiza's witty linking of the lady's way with books and her way with men stresses again the latter's characteristic quality of 'GIDDINESSE and *Distraction*', as well as hinting at her incapacity to distinguish adequately between people and objects.

The most complex of Rochester's allusions to Seneca's epistle, however, occurs in line 107, and, as already mentioned, appears to be conflated with a second allusion to 'nil admirari', and with the *Leviathan* reference noted earlier. The fact that this line contains a further allusion to the Horace epistle seems to be signalled and emphasised by the triple rhyme 'desire / inquire / admire' of lines 105–7, which repeats the rhyme 'admire / desire' in lines 64–5, where the first allusion to 'nil admirari' occurs. Finally, the triple rhyme appears again with the rhyme words slightly varied in lines 124–6, where a last echo of the allusion may be caught. Such repetition is unlikely to be merely casual (despite Pope's censure of Rochester as having 'very bad versification, sometimes'[36]), and it would seem that Rochester is not only stressing the 'nil admirari' allusion, but is also encouraging the reader to compare and contrast its uses in these passages.

On its first appearance the allusion is employed to endorse Artemiza's strictures on the general lack of wit and moral judgment of fashionable female libertines, since it indicates how the latter, through ignorance or per-versity, misapply a famous Horatian aphorism. On its second appearance, its significance is more complex, as one might expect from the manner in which it is conflated with the allusions to Seneca and to Hobbes, and from its presence in a speech delivered by a perfect exemplar of the female type it has earlier been used to condemn. In fact, the 'fine Lady' compounds the errors of her sisters' misapplication of 'nil admirari', by using it herself, not as they did, to justify their own perverse practice by asserting their claim to wit, but as the basis for lambasting the 'Men of Witt'. Evidently her 'rules' are not only morally and intellectually dubious but are intended for selective and arbitrary application to accord with her own self-interested designs. Thus while she and women of her type pride themselves on having too much wit to 'admire' men, they are illogically outraged at those men who have the temerity to do likewise (*mutatis mutandis*) and who wilfully refuse to settle for 'The perfect Joy of being well deceaved' (line 115). As we have seen, the ironic allusion to Hobbes in lines 105–7 convicts the speaker herself of a basic lack of judgment; Rochester's central conflation in line 107 of the allusion to 'nil admirari' with that to Seneca's 'tamquam explorator' further defines and emphasises this failing. Nevertheless, the attitude of the 'Men of Witt' to women is not thereby condoned. They share the selfish and dispassionate approach to love of the 'fine Lady', though they do not (apparently) seek to justify it by misapplying moral aphorisms, and there is no evidence that they also share that quality of ineffable blindness to their own faults which so distinguishes their female counterpart. The allusions to the moral epistles of Horace and Seneca, however, testify to the fine, but clear, line to be drawn between the alert, ironic, moral-awareness which informs Artemiza's attitude, and the kind of dispassionate, self-interested prudence variously exemplified by the 'fine Lady' and her crew, by the 'Men of Witt', and belatedly, but to chilling effect, by Corinna. Throughout, then, *Artemiza to Chloe* expresses a subtly argued critique of the female condition, which draws much of its efficacy from Rochester's powerfully resonant use of intertextual reference.

Appendix

Chloe to Sabina

My Deare Sabina why should you & I
Inn these soft times be foes to Poetry?
We cannot sure suspect yt ye chast Nine
Should prove as bauds to lead us into sin
Nor need we much those blasts of censure feare
With which ye men of wit so shaken are;
Wee are secure, ye low shrubs of ye plain,
Whilst they, ye tall Oakes, by the Stormes are slain.
Where can a Muse more soft retirement find
Then in a fair white womans gentle mind?   10
Where ye young son of Venus may indite,
And make ye dire Poetick virgin write
As her own forehead smooth, whilst her bright eye
Sends fire & flashes to her poetry.
But I too far am wander'd from the Theme
At which I cheifly in my letter aime;
My Dear Sabina since you left ye town
There is among us a strang faction grown,
A new discover'd crew call'd men of wit,
The silliest rogues yt ever aim'd at it: 20
So vain, so loud, so ungentily ill –
Their wit is froth, whose floods wʰere they swell
Fall like ye headlong cataracts of Nile.
Which neither cherish nor refresh the ground
But make much noise & deafen all around;
Their wickednesse appears more dull to me
Then aged country Parson's Poetry.
Some of this new society are from
That Mistresse of all follies London come
To people here like collonies from Rome.   30
Some from ye Scools & colledges appeare
Where natures unshapt whelps by art & care
Were lickt & form'd each into perfect Beare.
And some are country Squires new come to town
Being happily arriv'd at twenty one
These no acquir'd follies seem to adorne
But are the same rude lumps yt they were born.
Amidst ye many yt infest this place
Up started one extraordinary Asse

Who like ye rest not satisfied yt bare   40
Mien & behaviour should a Fop declare
Gave in a scurrilous & sencelesse Scrole
Under his own hand yt he was a fool.
Twas a lampoon & by Lord Blany writ
An Engine by which fooles sometimes do hit
Because at flocks they allways levell it.
The Oph I hear to forreigne lands is gon
To End ye fool which nature has begun:
So wild geese with ye Season disappeare
To hatch new goslings for ye Ensueing yeare.   50
Let him go on ye Oph to natures Schoole
But sure no care ere can redeem yt soul
Whom God predestinated to be fool.
But Dear Sabina we alas! have found
That bluntest weapons give a cruell wound
Would it not vex a saint thus damn'd to bee
And nere to tast of ye forbidden tree?
The Devil himself shew'd us less cruelty.
We should not much of our hard fate complaine
Had we been nobly in the battle slain   60
Or by ye hand of some fam'd warrior ta'ne
Who like true Venus son had bore his sire
And household gods safe from amidst ye fire:
But to be thus by beardlesse foes undone
Raw puny cocks whose spurs are not yet grown
Sabina for my part for ever more
I am resolv'd to shut up Eden door
Where a strict guard still flameing in their eyes
Shall stop mens passage to yt Paradise.
Mrs Jean Fox.

                              Copy text: Dublin MS 2093, pp. 112–16

10

Pope, Rochester and Horace

JULIAN FERRARO

'Lord Rochester was of a very bad turn of mind, as well as debauched.'
Joseph Spence recorded Pope's less than flattering assessment of Rochester's
character in 1728, and yet, in his own note to the 1744 edition of the *Epistle to
Cobham*, Pope describes Rochester more charitably as 'famous for his Wit
and Extravagancies in the time of Charles the Second'.[1] Pope's recorded
opinions of Rochester's talents as a poet manifest a similarly equivocal
attitude. While his 'observations' from the 1730s are more complimentary –
'Oldham is a very undelicate writer ... Lord Rochester had much more
delicacy and more knowledge of mankind' (I, 473) – they are not without
reservations: 'Rochester has neither so much delicacy nor exactness as Dorset'
(I, 472). Perhaps more telling is the revision of a line of Mulgrave's *Essay
upon Satire*, made by Pope when he published it in his 1723 edition of the
Earl's works. Mulgrave's original line had been the dismissive, 'Rochester I
despise for his mere want of wit', but Pope's revision – 'Last enters Rochester
of sprightly wit' – excises all criticism. Further, it does so in terms borrowed
from Rochester himself; the new version seems prompted by Rochester's
line, 'But I who am of sprightlie vigour full'.[2] Whatever the vagaries of Pope's
recorded opinions of Rochester's verse, his interest in his writing is confirmed in various other ways. The earliest extant manuscript of Pope's poetry
is the poem 'On Silence', written 'in imitation' of Rochester's *Upon Nothinge*,
and his influence continued throughout Pope's career, as evidenced by the
allusions to his verse noted by John Butt in his edition of the *Imitations
of Horace*. Significantly, the copy of the 1696 Tonson edition of Rochester's
Poems (&c.) On Several Occasions is one of the most heavily annotated books
surviving from Pope's library.[3]

13 Autograph manuscript of Alexander Pope for a projected edition
of Horace's *Satires*

The preface of this edition opens with a striking piece of apparent misdirection. Invoking Horace, among the 'Ancients', as the master of occasional verse, the preface goes on to describe Horace's habit of revising his first poetic efforts before offering Rochester as an absolute contrast:

> Amongst the Ancients, *Horace* deservedly bears the Name from 'em all, for Occasional *Poems*; many of which were addressed to *Pollio*, *Mecaenas*, and *Augustus*, the greatest Men, and the best judges, and all his *Poetry* overlook'd by them. This made him of the Temper not to part with a Piece over-hastily; but to bring his Matter to a Review, to cool a little, and think twice before it went out of his hands.
>
> On the Contrary, My Lord of *Rochester* was loose from all Discipline of that kind . . . (sig. A2r)

What then, one is left to ask, is the point of the comparison with Horace in the first place? One purpose it clearly serves is to persuade the reader to conjure Horace, however paradoxically, as a presence behind Rochester's occasional verse. The terms in which this is done seem significant, invoking as they do ideas of patronage and judgment, independence and the business of being a poet in a position to 'Keep [one's] Piece nine years'.

In March 1743, Pope characterised both Dorset and Rochester as 'holiday writers . . . gentlemen that diverted themselves now and then with poetry, rather than as poets' (*Observations*, I, 469). This has been seen as a typical example of the pride of the professional writer asserting itself in opposition to the activities of dilettante amateurs, 'The Mob of Gentlemen who wrote with ease'.[4] However, this opposition is not a straightforward one, at least in terms of the rhetorical strategies by which Pope articulates it. As a successful professional poet in the 1730s, it is from a position 'among the Great' that Pope is able to dismiss 'Scribblers or Peers, alike [as] *Mob*'.[5] Indeed, throughout the 1730s, Pope plays upon his position of independent financial security – 'Un-plac'd, un-pension'd, no Man's Heir, or Slave' – which had been achieved through the success of his translations of Homer, to create a pose of detachment which, ironically, has much in common with the aristocratic opposition of Rochester to Dryden, the successful professional poet of his day.

One of the striking features of Pope's poetry in the 1730s is his creation of a complex satiric persona, drawing on disparate elements of various, particularly Roman, models.[6] This chapter examines the part played in this self-presentation by Pope's reading of the interpretation and appropriation of Horatian satire by Rochester and some of his contemporaries. The significance for Pope's later poetry of Rochester's development of the poetic imitation of a classical model, in terms of an adaptation sustained over the length of a whole poem, has long been recognised.[7] Rochester has also been cited in the debate surrounding the relative merits of Horace and Juvenal as models for late seventeenth- and early eighteenth-century satire.[8] It is in this regard – the question of what precisely is the relationship between Pope and Horace's example at significant points in Pope's verse – that Rochester's particular inflection of Horatian satire becomes so interesting. As Marianne Thormählen points out:

> To most people, the name of Horace immediately suggests suave good taste and decorous irony. It is easily forgotten that Horace the satirist could be both pungent and outspoken – and that his imitator Rochester was able to temper malice and indignation with humour.[9]

Some years ago, in the course of research on Pope's poetical manuscripts, I came across a hitherto overlooked autograph which (among other things) sheds some new light on the importance for Pope of Rochester as an imitator of Horace. It is a dummy for the title-page and list of contents of a projected edition of 'The SATIRES OF HORACE, Translated into ENGLISH VERSE By Mr. POPE and Several other Emin[t] hands', along the lines of Dryden's edition of Persius and Juvenal.[10] The manuscript raises many points of interest and provides an insight into Pope's attitude not only to Horace but also to several of his contemporaries and immediate predecessors. I want to focus on two aspects: first, and briefly, Pope's choice of lines from the first satire of Persius for the epigraph on the title-page; secondly, his choice of Rochester as 'translator' of Horace's *Satires* I.x and II.viii. The epigraph comes from a section of the first satire of which Pope makes interesting use in his published verse. The fragmentary lines on the title-page, 'Omne vafer vitium / Tangit, & admissus', refer to Persius's account of Horace:

> omne vafer vitium ridenti Flaccus amico
> tangit, & admissus circum praecordia ludit
> (Horace, sly dog, worming his way playfully into the vitals of his laughing friend, touches up his every fault.)[11]

At this point in his poem Persius is invoking the distinctive styles of Lucilius and Horace as examples of those who have dared to write satire; examples that confirm Persius's resolution to write satire himself. This chilling image of Horace exploiting the intimacy afforded by laughter to run his fingers over the fleshy embodiments of the exposed vices of his friends provides a striking counterpoint to more prevalent images that characterise him above all as urbane, witty and delicate.

In *One Thousand Seven Hundred and Thirty Eight. A Dialogue Something Like Horace* (1738), Pope cites these lines in a note, highlighting the ironic nature of the presentation of Horace's satiric method in the opening section of that poem. Pope uses Bubo, one of his favourite dunces, to give voice to a subtly distorted version of Persius's view of Horace:

> His sly, polite, insinuating stile
> Could please at Court, and make AUGUSTUS smile.

> (lines 19–20)[12]

Thus, in Bubo's hands, Horace becomes a compromised figure, any scathing effects of his satire vitiated by the very qualities that provided him with access to the Court in the first place.[13] In making this transformation Pope might be said to recall the topos of Rochester's description of Dryden in *An Allusion to Horace*:

> Thô even that Talent merits in some sort,
> That can divert the Rabble and the Court.
>
> (lines 16–17)

This 'borrowing' is symptomatic of the way in which, at important moments in his Horatian poems, Pope comes to Horace through Rochester; and not through Rochester alone but also through the versions of Horace's work embedded, for instance, in the poems by Sir Carr Scroope, printed with Rochester's verse in the edition Pope owned, which testify to the poetical controversies in which Rochester was involved in the 1670s. This subtle invocation of the sometimes vicious, sometimes high-handed, flyting of these young noblemen is an important element in the creation of the distinctive tone of voice which characterises Pope's later satires.

Pope's choice of Rochester as a 'translator' of the 'Tenth Satire of the First Book' and 'Eighth Satire of the Second Book' for his edition of Horace's satires is a striking one. With the exception of Swift and Pope himself, none of the other contributors has more than one poem in the collection, so Pope's projected inclusion of *An Allusion to Horace* and *Satyr.* [*Timon*] is all the more striking.[14] *An Allusion to Horace* is, in some ways at least, an obvious enough choice; *Timon*, however, is altogether more problematic. The title-page of the manuscript says that each 'translation' is to be accompanied by the Latin text of the original poem, something that would have further emphasised the fact that *Timon* – as a loose imitation of Boileau's third satire, itself based loosely on Horace's *Satires*, II.viii – is quite some distance from its Horatian original.[15] It is obviously dangerous to read too much into the choices embodied in this manuscript, given that the edition never materialised; however, the care that Pope has taken over matters such as the imprint and prospective formats does suggest that the project was more than the product of an idle moment. In any event, of two things we can be fairly certain: Pope was well aware of both poems and he thought well enough of them to consider their inclusion in a volume alongside his own.[16]

Although the edition was never produced, Pope's interest in these two poems makes itself felt at significant moments in the *Epistle to Arbuthnot*, the 'Bill of Complaint' in which he offers all he has to say of himself.[17] I want now to focus on some passages from *Timon* and *An Allusion* and look at their relationship to what has been described as one of the most Horatian of Pope's original poems.[18]

In the opening section of *Timon*, the speaker recounts how he was seized in the Mall by a 'dull dining *Sot*' (line 5) – a situation that in fact echoes Horace's *Satires*, I.ix rather than *Satires*, II.viii or Boileau's third satire.[19] Before dragging the reluctant Timon off to the *repas ridicule* which is the subject of the rest of the poem, his prospective host taxes him with the authorship of 'a Libell, of a Sheete or Two':

> Which he admir'd, and prais'd at ev'ry Line,
> At last, it was soe sharpe, it must be mine.
>
> (lines 14, 17–18)

Despite Timon's protestations to the contrary, his host remains convinced of his authorship:

> I vow'd, I was noe more a Witt than he,
> Unpractic'd, and unblest in Poetry:
> A Song to Phillis, I perhaps might make,
> But never Rhym'd but for my Pintles sake;
> I envy'd noe Mans Fortune, nor his Fame,
> Nor ever thought of a Revenge soe tame.
> He knew my Stile (he swore) and twas in vaine
> Thus to deny, the Issue of my Braine.
>
> (lines 19–26)

These last lines have their antecedent not in Boileau's third satire, but in his sixth epistle (lines 69ff): 'Non; á d'autres, dit-il: on connait votre style' (line 74). Unable to dissuade his captor, Timon allows him to persist in his error, with unfortunate consequences:

> Choakt with his flatt'ry I noe answer make,
> But silent leave him to his deare mistake.
> Which he, by this, has spread o're the whole Town,
> And me, with an officious Lye, undone.
> Of a well meaning Foole, I'm most afraid,
> Who sillily repeates, what was well said.
>
> (lines 27–32)

Perhaps the most impressive feature of this passage is the way in which Rochester moves fluidly between various models (rather than sticking to an imitation of a single poem) to create a pose of aristocratic detachment from the literary world at the same time as he concedes that he is to some extent at the mercy of that world. In order to enlist the reader's sympathy with his exasperation, the poet must implicitly concede that the 'well meaning Foole' can damage his reputation. There is, of course, a necessary inconsistency in the position of the aloof figure so persistently importuned by such people – if he were truly aloof and detached from the world of literary opinion there would be no such incidents to make the subject of witty verses (and, presumably, no impulse to write those verses in the first place, nor to share them with readers).

Pope's *Epistle to Arbuthnot* opens with an image of the poet similarly besieged:

> Then from the *Mint* walks forth the Man of Ryme,
> Happy! to catch me, just at Dinner-time.
>
> (lines 14–15)

Here, presumably, it will be Pope, rather than the 'Man of Ryme', who will have to provide what shows every sign of being a *repas ridicule*. Later in the poem, he finds himself victimised, like Timon, by a doltish textual critic:

> (Cries prating *Balbus*) 'something will come out.'
> 'Tis all in vain, deny it as I will.
> 'No, such a Genius never can lye still,'
> And then for mine obligingly mistakes
> The first Lampoon Sir *Will*. or *Bubo* makes.
> Poor guiltless I! and can I chuse but smile,
> When ev'ry Coxcomb knows me by my *Style*?
>
> (lines 276–82)

Here Pope asserts an easy complacency about the consequences of misattribution, although elsewhere in the poem he, again like Timon, sees himself at the mercy of those who apparently wish him well:

> A Fool quite angry is quite innocent;
> Alas! 'tis ten times worse when they *repent*.
>
> (lines 107–8)

While Rochester's disdain for the opinions of the 'Rabble' and his assertion that he 'never Rhym'd but for [his] Pintles sake' should indeed be viewed as the disclaimer of 'a gentleman who must be seen to eschew professionalism',[20] it is also a very effective rhetorical counter to deploy in any attempt to characterise the relationship of the satirist and the 'Town', and the stance that Pope develops in the *Epistle to Arbuthnot* owes a great deal to Rochester's aristocratic filtering of Horace and Boileau.[21] In Rochester, Pope has an English model of the satirist, sometimes urbane and witty, sometimes aggressive and bawdy. What Pope's satire also takes from Rochester's verse is the suggestion of a social superiority to accompany the superiority of poetic ability – although in Pope's case the relationship between the two is causal not casual.

It is not only Rochester from whom Pope borrows in this way. The poems by Sir Carr Scroope – written as part of a running feud with Rochester in the 1670s – seem also to have left their mark on Pope's self-presentation. In particular, there is a striking parallel between a passage from *In Defence of Satyr* (which contemporary scholarship has assigned to Scroope, but which was published in the 1680 edition of Rochester's verse) and the *Epistle to*

Arbuthnot. In the passage in question, an imitation of part of Horace's *Satires*, I.iv (lines 81–5), Scroope mounts a self-defence based on a contrast between his activities and those of Rochester, whom he characterises in the following terms:

> He that can rail at one he calls his *Friend*,
> Or hear him absent wrong'd, and not defend;
> Who for the sake of some ill natur'd Jeast,
> Tells what he shou'd conceal, Invents the rest;
> To fatal *Mid-night* quarrels, can betray,
> His brave *Companion*, and then run away;
> Leaving him to be murder'd in the *Street*,
> Then put it off, with some *Buffoone* Conceit;
> This, this is he, you shou'd beware of all,
> Yet him a pleasant, witty *Man*, you call
> To whet your dull Debauches up, and down,
> You seek him as top *Fidler* of the *Town*.
>
> (lines 48–59)[22]

Pope must surely have had Scroope's version in mind when, in January 1732, he published the following imitation of the same part of Horace's poem, lines that were subsequently incorporated into lines 291–304 of the *Epistle to Arbuthnot*:

> The *Fop*, whose Pride affects a Patron's Name,
> Yet *absent*, wounds an Author's honest Fame;
> That more abusive Fool, who calls me *Friend*
> Yet wants the Honour, injur'd to defend:
> Who spreads a *Tale*, a *Libel* hands about,
> Enjoys the *Jest*, and copies *Scandal* out:
> Who to the *Dean* and *Silver Bell* can swear,
> And sees at *C-n-ns* what was never there:
> Who tells you all I *mean*, and all I *say*;
> And, if he *lies* not, must at least *betray*:
> 'Tis not the *Sober Sat'rist* you should dread,
> But such a *babling Coxcomb* in his Stead.

Here, Pope transforms what for Horace and Scroope is a matter of dishonourable behaviour into a question of malicious literary criticism. What seems significant is the way in which the very particular complaints of a misread professional author are interrelated with the terms in which a Restoration rake chose to upbraid the personal shortcomings of a fellow nobleman. The rather plaintive note struck by Scroope –

> But why am I this *Bug bear* to ye all?
> My *Pen* is dipt in no such bitter Gall
>
> (lines 46–7)

– is replaced by Pope with the bolder self-affirmation of his role as 'Sober Sat'rist'. While Scroope, albeit disingenuously, suggests that satire is a matter of mockery directed at social equals with the object of engendering shared amusement, Pope implicitly takes for himself the role, not so much of professional writer *per se*, but of professional moral and aesthetic arbiter.

Pope seems also to have turned to Scroope for inspiration in the character of Sporus, through which he attacked his own noble adversary, Lord Hervey, in the *Epistle to Arbuthnot*. In the course of this, Pope characterises Sporus as a venomous amphibian in the following terms:

> Whether in florid Impotence he speaks,
> And, as the Prompter breathes, the Puppet squeaks;
> Or at the Ear of *Eve*, familiar Toad,
> Half Froth, half Venom, spits himself abroad,
> In Puns, or Politicks, or Tales, or Lyes,
> Or Spite, or Smut, or Rymes, or Blasphemies.

> (lines 317–22)

In his note to the 1734 edition of the *Epistle to Arbuthnot*, Pope suggests that his description of Sporus 'at the Ear of *Eve*' was suggested by Lord Hervey's and Lady Mary Wortley Montagu's attack upon him in their *Verses on the Imitator of Horace*.[23] However, their poem makes no mention of a toad. This element of the portrait seems to have been drawn from the poem with which Scroope made his final contribution to his war of words with Rochester, a poem entitled, appropriately enough, *Answer By way of Epigram*:

> Raile on poor feeble scribler, speak of mee
> In as bad Terms as the world speaks of Thee,
> Sitt swelling in thy hole like a vex'd Toad,
> And full of pox, and Mallice, spitt abroad.
> Thou canst blast no Mans Fame with thy ill word
> Thy pen is full as harmless as thy sword.[24]

The coincidence of this mixture of venom and impotence is striking, as are the echoes, elsewhere in the portrait of Sporus, of the poem of Rochester's which Scroope's answers: *On The Suppos'd Author of a late Poem in Defence of SATYR*:

> Curse on that silly hour that first inspir'd
> Thy Maddness to pretend to be admir'd,
> To paint thy grizly face, to daunce, to dress,
> And all those awkard follies that express
> Thy Loathsome Love, and filthy Daintiness.

> (lines 16–20)

Here it is Scroope himself who seems to provide a model for Pope's 'painted Child of Dirt that stinks and stings', with his

> Beauty that shocks you, Parts that none will trust,
> Wit that can creep, and Pride that licks the dust.
>
> (lines 310, 332–3)

Rochester's emphasis on Scroope's partial nature also finds echoes in Hervey's 'vile Antithesis' (line 325):

> Halfe witty, and halfe mad, and scarce halfe brave,
> Halfe honest, which is very much a knave;
> Made up of all these halves, thou cans't not pass
> For any thing entirely but an Asse.
>
> (lines 31–4)

Rochester's poem *On Poet Ninny*, another attack on Scroope, embellishes these various themes of impotence, antithesis, and venom:

> Crusht by that just contempt his Follys bring
> On his Crazd Head, the Vermin faine wou'd sting;
> But never Satyr, did soe softly bite,
>
> . . .
>
> And dost at once, a sad Example prove,
> Of harmlesse Malice, and of hoplesse Love.
> All Pride, and Uglinesse! Oh how wee loath,
> A nauseous Creature soe compos'd of both!
>
> (lines 1–3, 8–11)

What seems most interesting in the relationship between these poems by Rochester and Scroope and Pope's 'Bill of Complaint' is not so much the way in which Pope 'borrows' at the level of imagery or turn of phrase, though that is striking enough, but the extent to which the tone echoes that of the earlier poets. In a poem in which the relative social status of the poet and his various enemies becomes increasingly important, the pose of the aristocrat conducting private battles in witty verses, circulated in manuscript amongst a group of cognoscenti, serves at times as a valuable model for the proud professional writer who must deal as effectively with the 'the Great' as with what Rochester in *An Allusion to Horace* calls 'the poor led Poets of the Town' (line 118).

I want, finally, to turn to *An Allusion to Horace*. In the opening section of this poem Rochester's attack on Dryden centres not simply on his 'Rhymes, / . . . stollen, unequal, nay dull', nor the prolixity of his 'loose Volumns', but on the very field of his principal literary endeavour: the theatre, in which his

> false sence
> Hitts the false Judgment of an Audience
> Of clapping fools, assembling a vast Crowd
> Till the throng'd Playhous crack with the dull load.
>
> (lines 1–2, 9, 12–15)[25]

The theatre is the arena in which the professional writer's need for the approval of the public is most brutally dramatised, where the playwright is at the mercy of what Pope describes as 'The many-headed Monster of the Pit: / A sense-less, worth-less, and unhonour'd crowd'.[26]

As we have seen above, the praise that might attach itself to successful performance in this sphere receives a scornful acknowledgment from Rochester:

> Thô even that Talent merits in some sort,
> That can divert the Rabble and the Court.

> (lines 16–17)

This passage from *An Allusion to Horace* was surely in Pope's mind when he came to the description of Codrus in the *Epistle to Arbuthnot*:

> Let Peals of Laughter, *Codrus!* round thee break,
> Thou unconcern'd canst hear the mighty Crack.
> Pit, Box and Gall'ry in convulsions hurl'd,
> Thou stand'st unshook amidst a bursting World.

> (lines 85–8)

The single-mindedness to which Horace refers, in the text to which both Rochester and Pope allude (not *Satires*, I.x but *Odes*, III.iii), is that of the 'iustum et tenacem propositi virum' – the man who is just and firm of purpose.[27] Horace goes on to make it clear that he is describing conduct by which Augustus will achieve deification, and it has been pointed out that Pope has Addison's rendering of these lines from Horace in mind here:

> Should the whole frame of nature round him break,
> In ruine and confusion hurl'd,
> He, unconcern'd, would hear the mighty crack,
> And stand secure amidst a bursting world.[28]

However, Pope re-casts this version in the light of Rochester's, so that the apocalypse is the consequence of the audience's ridicule of a bad playwright. The gesture to Horace also implicates George Augustus in what has become, in the *Epistle to Arbuthnot*, an elaborate conflation of literary, moral and political corruption. What was once an affirmation of the value of individual steadfastness in the face of the opinion of the mob becomes mockery of those in power, who of necessity place themselves at the mercy of the judgment of that mob and are too obtuse to see how they are regarded.

In contradistinction to the talent and aspirations of the laureate playwright, 'that can divert the Rabble', Rochester prescribes the attitude appropriate to a gentleman,

> Scorn all applause the Vile Rout can bestow
> And be content to pleas those few who know,

> (lines 102–3)

before going on to identify himself absolutely with this position:

> I loath the Rabble, 'tis enough for me
> If Sydley, Shadwell, Shepheard, Wicherley,
> Godolphin, Butler, Buckhurst, Buckinghame
> And some few more, whome I omitt to name
> Approve my sence, I count their Censure Fame.
>
> (lines 120–4)

In the *Epistle to Arbuthnot* Pope matches this aristocratic coterie with one equally glittering, designed to emphasise his own complete separation from 'the poor-fed Poets of the Towne':

> [W]hy then publish? *Granville* the polite,
> And knowing *Walsh*, would tell me I could write;
> Well-natur'd *Garth* inflam'd with early praise,
> And *Congreve* lov'd, and *Swift* endur'd my Lays;
> The Courtly *Talbot*, *Somers*, *Sheffield* read,
> Ev'n mitred *Rochester* would nod the head,
> And *St. John*'s self (great *Dryden*'s friends before)
> With open arms receiv'd one Poet more.
> Happy my Studies, when by these approv'd!
> Happier their Author, when by these belov'd!
>
> (lines 135–44)[29]

It is significant that money is nowhere mentioned as a motivation for writing, despite the fact that it was his financial success as a poet which enabled Pope to enjoy the much-vaunted independence of his later career.[30] It is also significant that Pope identifies himself with a very different 'party' from Rochester's while borrowing the terms in which to make that identification. The most striking difference between Pope's aristocratic enthusiasts and those of Rochester is the presence of John Sheffield, Earl of Mulgrave and Duke of Buckingham. There is a Buckingham in Rochester's list, but this is George Villiers (satirised by Pope in the *Epistle to Bathurst*) not Rochester's enemy, Mulgrave.[31] The fact that Atterbury and Bollingbroke are identified as 'great *Dryden*'s friends' further emphasises the complexity of Pope's relationship to Rochester in this context. While he echoes the rhetorical strategy of Rochester's attack on Dryden, he revises, and in some respects reverses, the political, personal and aesthetic allegiances of his model – put simply, Pope's allegiances are with Dryden's party and against Rochester's. Pope's list also mixes writers and lordly patrons to present a more heterogeneous community of supportive readers on whose judgment he is happy to rely.[32] However, while Pope ultimately sides with Dryden, the successful professional poet, he does so in Horatian terms, inflected by the lordly amateur, Rochester.

In October 1735, in a letter to Orrery, Pope quotes from *A Satyre against Reason and Mankind* (line 165): 'You speak of my defending the Bishop's

[Atterbury's] character against Curl, I can hardly defend my own; *The Knaves will all agree to call you Knave*, as my Lord Rochester observ'd, and that is a terrible Majority'.[33] What I hope to have shown in this chapter are some of the ways in which Pope, the proud professional writer, appropriated and transformed elements of the holiday writer's aristocratic self-presentation in his skirmishes with the 'terrible Majority':

> And who unknown defame me, let them be
> Scribblers or Peers, alike are *Mob* to me.[34]

14 *The Palace of Whitehall*, 1680; drawing by George Vertue

11

A *Satyre against Reason and Mankind* from page to stage

BREAN HAMMOND &
PAULINA KEWES

Rochester's *A Satyre against Reason and Mankind*, written in the earlier 1670s, is widely recognised as one of the formative poems of its decade and period.[1] By and large, interest in the poem has centred on its ideas. Editors and critics of *Against Reason and Mankind* have been concerned with establishing the philosophical, intellectual and religious contexts of the poem's inception and reception, and have situated it against native and continental, particularly French, poetic traditions.[2] Our contention is that the Restoration theatre is a context of at least equal importance for the understanding of the poem's literary influences in terms of both subject-matter and language. The broad affinity between Rochester's poetic *oeuvre* and the drama of its time has long been recognised: Dustin Griffin's *Satires against Man*, for example, includes a chapter on 'Rochester and Restoration Drama'. However, Griffin is chiefly interested in the common settings (the park, the watering-places), characters (the rake, the railer, the coquette) and ethical assumptions which Rochester's poetry shares with contemporary plays, both heroic and comedic, and he does not see any one poem as having uniquely strong intertextual links with the drama. We believe that *Against Reason and Mankind* is such a poem. In the decade following its composition, the satire generated several vigorous responses from dramatists, notably John Crowne in *Calisto: or, The Chaste Nimph* and Thomas Shadwell in *The Libertine* and *The History of Timon of Athens, the Man-Hater*. Those reactions have gone largely unnoticed in the critical literature. It is almost as if the flamboyant stage portrayals of Rochester 'the man' – as the glamorous and suave Dorimant in Etherege's *The Man of Mode* (1676), as the viciously immoral Nemours in Lee's *The Princess of Cleve* (*c.* 1681–2), and as the contemptibly hypocritical libertine Florio (and to an extent Artall) in Crowne's *City Politiques* (1682)[3] – have prevented scholars from perceiving the more specific reprises of the ideas and vocabulary of *Against Reason and Mankind* in contemporary plays, Rochester's own adaptation of John Fletcher's *Valentinian* (*c.* 1675–6) among them.

That neglect, admittedly, is understandable. First, although remarkable for its handling of the dialogue form, and its games with the persona of the author-speaker, *Against Reason and Mankind* appears an abstract work, distant from the hustle and bustle of the theatre. In that respect it contrasts sharply with *An Allusion to Horace* and *Satyr.* [*Timon*], two poems brimming with references to plays and playwrights. Second and more important, the dramatic redactions by Crowne and Shadwell of the scandalous creed of *Against Reason and Mankind* may at times appear scarcely distinct from the quite commonplace use of Hobbesian cliches in contemporary plays. Indeed it would be fatuous to deny that the decade's libertinism was steeped in a post-Restoration reading of Hobbes's *Leviathan* (1651).[4] Hobbes's insistence on the subjectivity of judgments about good and evil, for example, has its effect on *Against Reason and Mankind* and resounds through the libertine drama of the time:

> whatsoever is the object of any mans Appetite or Desire; that is it, which for his part he calleth *Good*: And the object of his Hate, and Aversion, *Evill*; And of his Contempt, *Vile* and *Inconsiderable.* For these words of Good, Evill, and Contemptible, are ever used with relation to the person that useth them: There being nothing simply and absolutely so.[5]

What Hobbes has to say about future punishments and rewards, and in general terms his materialist account of human psychology and motivation, could be used to underpin the iconoclastic creed that stage libertines represented. And Hobbes's account of the human race's savage and self-regarding behaviour in the state of nature could be adapted to convey the ferocity of social relations in the modern world.[6] Rochester's poem, however, gave memorable formulation to a complex of ideas drawn from many sources, Montaigne and Boileau as prominent as Hobbes, that were particularly charismatic because they carried the authority of the Earl's own manner of living. As we shall see, specific verbal echoes and borrowings indicate that it was often to *Against Reason and Mankind* rather than to Hobbes that Crowne and Shadwell directly applied. If at times it does seem as if they are writing with a copy of *Leviathan* open on the desk, Rochester's poem has sent them back to the book.

That the impact of *Against Reason and Mankind* – Rochester's best-known and most widely circulated longer poem – upon the plays of the mid- to late 1670s should have been considerable need not surprise us, for in those years the Earl's involvement in theatrical affairs was at its peak; he was an eagerly sought-after patron of the drama, as many as five plays having been dedicated to him between 1672 and 1677.[7] It was his intervention that secured Crowne the commission to supply a masque – *Calisto* – for performance at Court in 1675;[8] it was also the Earl's praise and support that gained Otway's *Don Carlos* a favourable (and bounteous) reception from the king and the Duke of York in 1676.[9] He wrote prologues and epilogues for new plays by Elkanah Settle, Sir Francis Fane and Charles Davenant, and for a revival by an all-female cast of an old play, most likely Beaumont and Fletcher's *The Bloody Brother*.[10] Rochester was not only a sometime patron of a number of professional playwrights (Settle, Lee, Dryden, Crowne, Otway) – even though he ridiculed former favourites in his satires – and a friend of aristocratic amateurs and Court Wits (the Duke of Buckingham, Sir Robert Howard, Sir George Etherege, Sir Francis Fane). He himself tried his hand at playwriting and issued influential versified criticism of recent theatrical offerings (for instance in *An Allusion to Horace* and *Satyr.* [*Timon*]). Besides his revision of Fletcher's *Valentinian* (for which he invited Fane to supply a masque),[11] we have a fragment of a dramatic lament intended for a never-written tragedy, a draft of a comic scene intended for a never-written comedy, and a heroic scene he contributed to Howard's unfinished *The Conquest of China*.[12] And though the story of his coaching Elizabeth Barry to become the period's greatest tragic actress is most likely apocryphal, his long-term liaison with the rising star of the London stage would have brought him into close contact with playhouse affairs.[13]

Rochester's contribution to the Restoration theatrical enterprise in his capacity as patron, critic and amateur playwright, and the fact that several of his satiric verses were inspired by, and responded to, others' plays, ensured that any new poem of his – and especially one so substantial as *Against Reason and Mankind* – would be read with keen interest and attention by his protégés, former protégés and other aspiring dramatists. It is the dramatised polemic to which the poem gave rise that we wish to explore in this discussion. What was the impact of *Against Reason and Mankind* upon the drama in the years immediately following its composition and circulation? How were ideas voiced by Rochester in the poem, and the vocabulary in which he couched them, appropriated, countered or re-formulated in the plays of the 1670s? And how did he render them in his version of Fletcher's *Valentinian*? First, however, we need to read the poem, to emphasise those parts that were most suggestive to contemporary dramatists, those ideas that could be most effectively embodied in stage character and action.

In his rage, misanthropy and condescension toward other mortals, the speaker of *Against Reason and Mankind* resembles a Thersites or an Apemantus (and in 1678 and 1679 respectively, both Apemantus and Thersites would again be on stage, in Shadwell's version of *Timon of Athens* and Dryden's of *Troilus and Cressida*). That rhetorical stance is underlined by the opening of the 'Addition' written sometime between 1675 and 1676:

> All this with Indignation have I hurl'd
> At the pretending part of the proud World,
> Who swoln with selfish Vanity, devise
> False Freedomes, Holy Cheats and formal Lyes,
> Over their fellow Slaves to tyrannize.
>
> (lines 174–8)

The persona's excoriation of the pretentious and the vain – of those philosophers, clerics and courtier-lawyers who terrify the less able with their intellectual bugbears – seems to derive from an ongoing discussion, a continuation perhaps, of one of the 'Genial Nights' amongst the Wits that Dryden describes in his dedication to *The Assignation; or, Love in a Nunnery* (1673), 'where our discourse is neither too serious, nor too light; but always pleasant, and for the most part instructive'.[14] The poem's opening statement is a self-consciously sensational adaptation of the theriophilic tradition as expounded, for instance, in Montaigne's *Apologie de Raymond de Sebonde*. Rochester establishes his basic position – that in conjuring up the 'Ignis fatuus' of deceptive Reason rather than following their 'certain' instincts, humans are inferior to beasts – by means of an impertinent paradox: 'Were I a spirit free to choose'. What would that 'I' be that is doing the choosing, and what kind of a 'Dog, a Monky, or a Bear' would result from the exercise of this election? Would it not be to real dogs, monkeys and bears as Swift's Gulliver is to the Yahoos? Is not the act of choosing a supremely *human* one – indeed, in the Protestant tradition, the defining act of being human? Being witty in the construction of an argument that leads to the abandoning of one's wits is a pervasive feature of this period's wit, upon which John Sitter's comment is illuminating:

> The paradoxical process of asserting a bodily norm by conspicuously intellectual or 'artful' means is part of the game of parody and burlesque, which work only if an author manages to display mastery of the modes 'contained' by the representation. Is a rational argument against rationality, for instance, simply an argument for better rationality?[15]

The question whether Rochester *does* master the modes contained by his poem is certainly one that the reader will pose; and a 'better rationality' is exactly what Rochester's poem will *propose*.

Meanwhile back in the poem, the 'sixth Sense' Reason is being stacked up against the other five; and is pursuing a journey that, through a suppressed allusion to Satan's journey in *Paradise Lost*, is represented as a diabolical departure from the one true path:

> Pathless and dangerous wandring wayes it takes,
> Through Errours fenny boggs and thorny brakes:
> Whilst the misguided follower climbs with pain
> Mountains of whimseys heapt in his own brain;
> Stumbling from thought to thought, falls headlong down
> Into doubts boundless Sea.
>
> (lines 14–19)

Freedom of choice, the exercise of the free will, is surely in the standard Christian account the *product* of rationality and the evidence of the Godhead in us. Here, free choice is pitted *against* rationality, and the latter is redefined as a satanic illusion, a faculty external to its possessor, leading him on schizo-phrenically to darkness and a disillusioned death. Book learning, strikingly rendered in the image of buoyancy bladders, can provide only temporary relief from the 'Sea' of scepticism that debilitates and deluges the rationalist. The satirist's position from line 20 onwards is almost that of a cruel, mocking deity as he looks down upon the 'reasoning Engine', once so animated – albeit by pride, wit and wisdom – now measuring out its length of earth 'hudled in dirt'. If contemporary readers did not take this sneering Olympian voice to be a badge of atheistical libertinism, they would surely hear such a creed announced in lines 33–4: 'His Wisedome did his Happiness destroy, / Ayming to know that World he should enjoy'. 'Wit' consists in the vain attempt to *know* the world rather than experiencing it directly through the pleasure to be gained from sense impressions. It is, at least at this point in the poem, allied to wisdom or knowledge of a Faustian kind. But in the very moment of defining 'wit' as a wasted, prideful attempt to gain an epistemo-logical purchase on the created world, Rochester moves sideways into a socially defined account of *the* wit, of the kind of person who tries to possess such knowledge. This in turn sets up the comparison between wits and whores, and the dialectic between pleasure in them and hatred of them, that brings the world of Restoration comedy into focus but does little to focus the poem itself.

That such a hedonist philosophy caught the attention of Latitudinarians such as Stillingfleet, Barrow and Martin Clifford, whose *A Treatise of Humane Reason* (1674) was the first tract to respond to Rochester in print, is not surprising and is by now well-established.[16] And as Roger Lund suggestively argues, it was as much the witty form in which the argument was cast as the subversive content that drew their attention.[17] The path leading to Jeremy Collier starts out in the reactions of such as Barrow and Glanvill to the Hobbesian account of ridicule and laughter. Rochester's poem inoculates itself against the Latitudinarian cast of mind by embodying it in a 'formal band and beard' (lines 46–71). This *adversarius* figure, who may be Isaac Barrow, is thoroughly sent up, initially by his catching the fag-end of the previous passage (lines 37–44) in which something (he wots not exactly what) is said against 'men of Witt' that provokes him to a Sparkish-like self-advertisement: 'For, I profess, I can be very smart / On witt, which I abhor with all my heart' (lines 52–3). Clearly this foppish, formalistic understanding of wit as a 'gibeing, gingling knack' is not at all what the satirist has been discussing, and the brief alliance of the 'Rev. Formal' with the satirist against wit is rapidly succeeded by a scandalised reaction to the latter's misanthropy. In response to this, the 'formal band and beard' relies upon Reason to take what Pope in *The Dunciad* will call 'the high Priori road', a prideful, speculative journey into the secrets of futurity that human beings are never meant to fathom. The clerical *adversarius* is used by Rochester to line up the distinction between rationality and a better rationality that the poem goes on to draw.

The object of the next verse paragraph (lines 72–111) is to 'right reason', in the punning senses of 'to put reason to rights', to define reason properly, and to demonstrate how to reason properly (or, as one of his real-life adversaries put it, 'To reason Reason out of Countenance').[18] Here, Rochester has in his sights the activities of the group that Louis Althusser once referred to as 'the intellectually semi-retired':[19] those who are in the luxurious position of being paid to think in the abstract, 'modern Cloystred Coxcombs, who / Retire to think, 'cause they have nought to do'. *Caveat lector!* Rochester champions a form of reason that we might more adequately term 'common sense', a form that co-operates with sensory information and appetite, that above all is geared to practical action in the world. What the reader is invited to consider, however, is the relationship between this form of rationality and ethical conduct:

> That Reason which distinguishes by Sense,
> And gives us Rules of Good and Ill from thence:
> That bounds Desires with a reforming Will,
> To keep them more in vigour, not to kill.
> Your Reason hinders, mine helps to enjoy,
> Renewing appetites yours would destroy.
>
> (lines 100–5)

This definition of 'Good and Ill' is prudential rather than moral, in that 'good' and 'ill' is whatever conduces towards, or compromises, the continuing health of the organism. If desires are to be restrained at all, they are to be so only to avoid cloying, not because they may be harmful to the self and others. And it was to this ambiguous issue, more than to any other, that several contemporary dramatists responded, most notably Crowne, Shadwell and Lee, and which Rochester himself took up in his adaptation of Fletcher's *Valentinian*. The second half of *Against Reason and Mankind* reprises the theriophilic arguments of the opening, and it bears upon the crucial central argument in so far as it denies that any altruistic account of human action can be given. For Rochester, any account of moral action is inevitably tinged by altruism, and the effort he makes to banish such an account leads him into the realm of behavioural psychology. Fear is the key to the human psyche: 'virtuous' conduct is simply hypocritical. Recognising this leads to paradoxical formulations worthy of Shaw and Brecht: 'all men would be Cowards if they durst' (line 158). One thinks of Mother Courage boxing her son Schweitzerkäse's ears because he was stupid enough to behave heroically in war. It is this sonorous paradox that Rochester stakes on the bet that no 'just man' can be found to contradict it. The final section describes the types of the just statesman and clergyman who, in the very unlikely event that they could be found, would force him to 'recant [his] paradox to them' and adopt the orthodox morality of the rabble. The concession made in the final couplet, that maybe such exemplars do exist, is one indication of the poem's rhetoricity – and it is partially rescinded by the sceptical inference that, if they do, they are scarcely recognisable as belonging to the human species.

The dramatic responses to *Against Reason and Mankind* fall basically into two categories. To the first category belong those plays which echo, or allude to, particular lines and ideas but which do not purport to offer either a comprehensive endorsement or a rebuttal of the poem's argument. At times a character – for example that of the stage libertine – cites or near-paraphrases a snippet from the satire the same way one would recycle a *bon mot* heard in another company as does Ramble, 'a wild young Gentleman of the Town', in Crowne's *The Countrey Wit* (1675):

> The order of Nature? the order of Coxcombs; the order of Nature is to follow my appetite: am I to eat at Noon, because it is Noon, or because I am hungry? to eat because a Clock strikes, were to feed a Clock, or the Sun, and not my self.[20]

True, Ramble is a professed libertine and uses the appropriated lines to bolster up his rakish credentials but there is little philosophical depth in his hedonist ejaculations and he is more than happy to recant, reform and embrace monogamy and matrimony at the end of the play. Other local resonances from *Against Reason and Mankind* can be found in such plays as Dryden's *Aureng-Zebe* (1676) and *Oedipus* (1678), the latter written in collaboration with Nathaniel Lee.[21] By contrast, John Crowne's masque *Calisto* and Thomas Shadwell's tragedies *The Libertine* and *Timon of Athens* provide more spirited and more sustained retorts to Rochester's *Against Reason and Mankind*, which go beyond mere verbal allusions or repetition of libertine commonplaces.

Calisto: or, The Chaste Nimph, written in the autumn of 1674 and produced at Court in the early months of 1675, was the first answer to, or comment on, Rochester's poem in dramatic form. Crowne was asked to provide the masque on the strength of Rochester's recommendation even though it was Dryden, the then Poet Laureate, who would have been the obvious choice for such a commission. As he tells us in the preface to the printed text of the masque, Crowne had little time allowed him to choose a subject for the piece, and having lighted in the second Book of Ovid's *Metamorphoses* on the story of Calisto – the Arcadian nymph raped and impregnated by Jupiter, transformed into a bear by his jealous wife Juno and later stellified by her lover – he had difficulty in fitting it for the occasion, for the chief roles were to be taken by two teenage daughters of the Duke of York, Princesses Mary and Anne. Forced drastically to alter the Ovidian narrative so as 'to write a clean, decent, and inoffensive Play, on the Story of a Rape',[22] Crowne turned the rape into would-be rape thus fortuitously saving Calisto's chastity. Yet if Jupiter's assault on the nymph's virtue fails, his rhetoric of arbitrary power and appetitive lust prevails, introducing a curious disjunction between the action of the play and its impact upon the audience.[23]

In his characterisation of the God of Gods as a tyrant and a libertine – 'I will be controul'd in no amour; / My Love is arbitrary as my power' (III, p. 36) – who envies mortals their sexual felicity, and who, in order to satisfy his lust, does not shrink from adopting shapes of sundry deities (including female ones such as Diana), men and beasts, Crowne enters into a clever dialogue with his patron's recent pronouncement on the morality (and rationality) of the unrestrained gratification of the senses. He specifically takes up and modifies the Rochesterian account of the relative standing of man and beast, with its theriophilic emphasis on the superiority of animal existence, by introducing a new factor into the equation, a lustful god who easily traverses the 'vertical' scale of creation. For Jupiter, ever catholic in his tastes, both animal and human existence hold irresistible sensual attractions:

> *Jup.* [I]f to Mortals I present Delight,
>   I to the Feast will still my self invite.
> *Mer.* — Yes Yes, we know *Joves* Appetite;   [*Aside.*
>   E're quite abstain from Loves sweet Feasts,
>   Hee'l humbly dine with Birds and Beasts.
> *Jup.* — I still provide with care,
>   We Gods in all Delights should share;
>   Besides the loves by us embrac'd
>   Would kill a poor weak Mortal, but to tast,
>   We know what pleasure Love affords,
>   To Heavy Beasts and Mettled Birds;
>   Here and there at will we fly,
>   Each step of Natures Perch we try;
>   Down to the Beast, and up again
>   To the more fine delights of Man:
>   We every sort of pleasure try;
>   So much advantage has a Deity.
> *Mer.* Nay, if *Jove* Rents the World to Man and Beast,
>   He may preserve the Royalty at least,
>   And freedom take to Hunt in any Grounds;
>   The Pleasures of great *Jove* should have no Bounds.
>
>   (I, pp. 3–4)

Safely sheltered from criticism of the religious who targeted the iconoclasm of *Against Reason and Mankind*, Crowne flaunts the libertine ethics and political despotism of the supreme classical deity. In an inspired parody of the rants of villains in heroic plays, he has Jupiter declare himself a fount of morality to which, however, he himself is superior:

> I cannot erre, what e're my Actions be;
> There's no such thing as good or ill to me.
> No Action is by Nature good or ill;
> All things derive their Natures from my will.
> If Vertue from my will distinct could be,
> Vertue would be a Power Supream to me.
> What no dependency on me will own,
> Makes me a Vassal, and usurps my Throne.
> If so I can revenge me in a Trice,
> Turn all the Ballance, and make Vertue Vice.
>
> (II, pp. 15–16)

While Jupiter's doctrine of absolute sovereignty, which overrides both ethics and law, ultimately derives from Hobbes,[24] his demagogic deployment of it to rationalise his ruthless quest for sexual fulfilment has its source in Rochester's poem.

If amusing in the mouth of a Greek god played by a teenage girl in a Court masque, such moral relativism becomes chilling when professed by a Roman tyrant in a tragedy designed for production at Whitehall by leading professionals.[25] Rochester's Valentinian considers himself above laws human and divine, as he imperiously tells his victim: 'Know I am farre above the faults I doe / And those I doe I'me able to forgive' (IV.iv.87–8). Here the rape is real, Lucina's off-stage shrieks being audible to both other characters and the audience. Yet, like Jupiter's unrelenting pursuit of Calisto, the Emperor's sexual violence is eminently reasonable: he merely seeks to satisfy his appetite in accordance with the dictates of nature:

> Tis nobler like a Lion to invade
> Where appetite directs, and seize my prey
> Than to wait tamely like a begging Dogg
> Till dull consent throws out the scraps of Love.
> I scorne those Gods who seek to cross my wishes
> And will in spite of them be happy – Force
> Of all powers is the most Generous
> For what that gives it freely does bestow
> Without the after Bribe of Gratitude.
> I'le plunge into a Sea of my desires
> And quench my Fever though I drowne my Fame
> And tear up pleasure by the roots – no matter
> Though it never grow againe – what shall ensue
> Let Gods and fates look to it; 'tis their business.
>
> (IV.ii.197–210)

Valentinian's of course is an extreme interpretation of the dictate to follow that 'Reason which distinguishes by Sense, / And gives us Rules of Good and Ill from thence' (*Against Reason and Mankind*, lines 100–1) and we instinctively condemn him as a despot and a reprobate. Yet a powerful reinforcement of his natural creed has already been made much less controversially in III.iii, a scene which, except for the first four lines, radically departs from Fletcher's original.

Rochester rewrites Fletcher's punning and clenching exchange between Lucina's two maidservants, Marcellina and Claudia, in the process staging a contention between artificial virtue (Honour) and natural or rational propensity to fulfil one's sexual appetites (Pleasure). The virtuous Claudia is 'sway'd by Rules not naturall but affected' (III.iii.50) – that is, human-derived – and 'thinke[s] the World / A Dreadfull wildernesse of Savage Beasts' (lines 47–8) – that is, men as bad as, or worse than, beasts – thereby adopting a misanthropic posture ('I hate Mankind for feare of beeing Lov'd' (line 51)). She also launches an attack upon 'cheating witt' which, by 'false wisdome' (lines 71ff), serves to justify vice (note the habitual association of wit and moral corruption). By contrast the frail Marcellina follows the dictates of nature seconded by reason (the better rationality familiar from *Against Reason and Mankind*): 'what Nature prompts us to / And reason seconds why should wee avoyd?' (lines 54–5). Though neither as pompous nor as easily discredited as the 'formal band and beard', Claudia seems to lose the argument. Or, rather, her highly moralistic stance is undermined by the very terms she uses to defend it, for example styling herself 'Honours Martyr' (line 19) and 'the Slave of Vertue' (line 46). For should virtue and honour breed fear and misanthropy? And, if they do, are they worth adhering to?

There are no moral absolutes in the world of Rochester's *Valentinian*. Even Lucina, the victim of rape, is far less obviously 'good' than in Fletcher. And the tyrant's 'poetically just' death at the hands of his rebellious subjects hardly brings about reinstatement of a divinely ordained moral order. Though momentarily overawed by Lucina's husband Maximus who upbraids him for his innumerable sins, treacheries and transgressions – 'Reason noe more, thou troublest mee with Reason' (V.v.163) – Valentinian soon repents of his near-repentance, his end being not only defiant but mischievously sadistic. 'Would the Gods raise Lucina from the grave / And fetter thee but while I might enjoy her / Before thy face', he exclaims, 'I'de ravish her againe' (V.v.240–2). Harold Love's contribution to this collection suggests that the rape scene was identifiably located in Rochester's own lodgings in Whitehall, very close to the Court Theatre where the *play itself* was designed to be performed.[26] Had it been performed, we can imagine the thrill of recognition in the audience. We can imagine, too, that the numerous architectural allusions to Charles's royal palace would have made the fate of the late Roman tyrant appear topical, if not directly applicable to the political situation in England in the mid-1670s. That topicality, as Love points out, would have vanished by the time of the play's eventual production at Court nearly a decade later, in February 1684.

We encounter another unrepentant villain, Don John, in Thomas Shadwell's *The Libertine*, a satirical tragedy which constitutes the most substantial dramatised reply to *Against Reason and Mankind*.[27] The play was premièred in June 1675 at the Dorset Garden Theatre. Though it draws plot elements from various European sources, and in deploying the Don Juan legend is working with very old material, *The Libertine* derives its contemporary energy from an implicit debate with Rochester's stance in the satire. Rochester's poem, as we have seen, recommends a form of rationality that, eschewing recondite subjects favoured by the pseudo-intellectual, directs our practical actions in the world. What is good and what is ill are to be determined entirely by what gratifies and renews our appetites; we are to live according to the immediate dictates of our senses, not according to ethical prescriptions that false rationality abstracts from the flux of everyday living. Rochester's *Against Reason and Mankind* has argued that supposed human 'virtues' are in fact the hypocritical outcomes of a base passion, fear. Animal behaviour is determined by an instinctual need to survive. Reason merely enables humans to devise refined forms of vice beyond the ken of the animal kingdom. Shadwell's *The Libertine* deploys the Don Juan legend to imagine what might be the consequences of trying to live according to his understanding of the Rochesterian code proposed in *Against Reason and Mankind*.

What is at issue is how to define the term 'Nature' and its cognates. The action of Shadwell's play will take the form of a series of situations in which characters act 'naturally' or 'according to Nature'; and it will become apparent that a set of ethical prescriptions not derivable from 'nature' in any simple way, but derivable from religious authority, is absolutely necessary to regulate human conduct. Don John's philosophy expounded in the opening scene carries unmistakably Rochesterian echoes:

> D. *Anto.* By thee, we have got loose from Education,
> And the dull slavery of Pupillage,
> Recover'd all the liberty of Nature,
> Our own strong Reason now can go alone,
> Without the feeble props of splenatick Fools,
> Who contradict our common Mother, Nature.
> D. *John.* Nature gave us our Senses, which we please:
> Nor does Reason war against our Sense.
> By Natures order, Sense should guide our Reason,
> Since to the mind all objects Sense conveys.[28]

In dramatic context there are, however, immediate challenges to the complacency of this position. As the cronies recount their recent conquests, the emphasis on acts that would be widely considered 'unnatural' is hard to miss: Don Lopez has murdered his elder brother for his estate; Don Antonio has impregnated both his sisters; and Don John has plotted the murder of his own father, has murdered Don Pedro for trying to preserve his own sister's chastity, and has ravished scores of women, nuns prominent among them. 'Nature' has therefore prompted these men to act directly contrary to what is 'natural'. All of these crimes are enumerated by Don John's valet, Jacomo, whose dramatic function throughout is to represent a conception of ordinary, unheroic humanity that operates as some kind of a touchstone for 'human nature'. In the opening scene, the jilted Leonora has come in search of Don John, and is apprised by Jacomo of his real nature: 'He owns no Deity, but his voluptuous appetite, whose satisfaction he will compass by Murders, Rapes, Treasons, or ought else' (I, pp. 29–30). Thus brusquely informed, Leonora swoons; and Jacomo considers taking advantage of her while she is unconscious. This crude fantasy is interrupted by her revival, but the point is made that Jacomo is no angel, that he would not let a decent opportunity go to waste – and perhaps many males in the audience would empathise with this. However, Jacomo is subjected to a regime of terror by his master, one of whose pleasures is to make him act *against* his natural predisposition – to fight, when he is a poltroon, and to assist in the commission of crimes that flout the conventional morality to which he subscribes. A dynamic so pronounced as to become almost obsessive in the final act, John's goading of Jacomo goes beyond the comic master–servant stereotype and all the jokes about Jacomo's 'antipathy to Hemp' (II, p. 38), just as Don John himself is well beyond the classification 'rake'.

Female characters in the play also operate to test out the limits of what is 'natural'. In Act II, Leonora's reckoning with Don John makes the point familiar from many of the 1670s sex plays, that 'nature' appears to have invested differently in the two genders. Where she speaks the language of love, vows and constancy, Don John speaks of obeying his constitution and of loving only as long as his natural desires will last. What is in the biological interest of men is not, apparently, in the interest of women. When, in Shadwell's later *Timon of Athens* (1678), Timon is taxed by the equally pathologically constant Evandra with breach of the vows he made to her, he responds that:

> [W]e cannot create our own affections;
> They're mov'd by some invisible active Pow'r,
> And we are only passive, and whatsoever
> Of imperfection follows from th' obedience
> To our desires, we suffer, not commit.

(I, p. 212)

The pop-up appearance to Don John of six women all claiming to be his wives (a device later imitated by Gay in *The Beggar's Opera*) leads to a climax of cartoonish vice in which one of his 'wives' kills herself, an old woman is raped and a sacramental view of marriage is further burlesqued by a mock 'Epithalamium':

> *Since Liberty, Nature for all has design'd,*
> *A pox on the Fool who to one is confin'd.*
> *All Creatures besides,*
> *When they please change their Brides.*
> *All Females they get when they can,*
> *Whilst they nothing but Nature obey,*
> *How happy, how happy are they?*
> *But the silly fond Animal, Man,*
> *Makes laws 'gainst himself, which his Appetites sway;*
> *Poor Fools, how unhappy are they?*

(II, pp. 43–4)

By the end of Act II, the libertine's conception of the natural has been subjected to further pressure. Maria – a woman whose lover Octavio has been killed in Act I and impersonated by Don John – enters cross-dressed. In contrast to Don John's programmatic promiscuity, her commitment to monogamy is so extreme that it has turned her into a bloodthirsty revenger. Arguably, the audience is not much more comfortable with this than with Don John's polygamous permissiveness; and we are to see its effects again later, when Leonora continues to be in thrall to Don John no matter how much she comes to know about his nature and actions. At this point in Act II, Maria's function is further to vex the conception of human nature by introducing the country–city dichotomy, contending that 'barbarous Art' has debauched the innocent natures of all urban dwellers: 'More savage cruelty reigns in Cities, / Than ever yet in Desarts among the / Most venemous Serpents' (II, p. 48). In Act IV this thread is taken up in a pastoral masque, the point of which is to suggest that 'uncorrupted Nature' exists only in the improbable setting of nymphs and shepherds – though their intention to 'geld' Jacomo (the shepherds apprehend him after he has been forced to take part in his master's rape of the nymphs; apparently he lacks Don John's aristocratic fleetness of foot) suggests that these shepherds are not entirely idealised. They also possess some 'georgic' skills! Before Act II ends, the appearance of the Ghost of Don John's father threatening Divine vengeance upon the whole pack of them throws the conception of what is natural into the melting-pot. A legend in which, famously, a stone statue of the murdered Governor of Seville accepts an invitation to supper is one in which, at the very least, what is 'natural' cannot be taken for granted: and in Shadwell's play the super-natural is deployed to interrogate thisworldly philosophies of experience.

Act III is the philosophical heart of the play, where the action responds most directly to Rochester's poem. Fleeing from a Seville that has become too hot for them, our heroes are caught in a storm at sea and later precipitated upon a seemingly strange coast – which is in fact their native land – where they meet with a religious hermit, who is horrified by their demand for whores and is provoked into this discussion:

Herm. Oh Monsters of impiety! are you so lately scap'd the wrath of Heaven, thus to provoke it?

D. Ant. How! by following the Dictates of Nature, who can do otherwise?

D. Lop. All our actions are necessitated, none command their own wills.

Herm. Oh horrid blasphemy! would you lay your dreadful and unheard of Vices upon Heaven? No, ill men, that has given you free-will to do good.

D. Joh. I find thou retir'st here, and never read'st or think'st.

> Can that blind faculty the Will be free
> When it depends upon the Understanding?
> Which argues first before the Will can chuse;
> And the last Dictate of the Judgment sways
> The Will, as in a Balance, the last Weight
> Put in the scale, lifts up the other end,
> And with the same Necessity.

(III, p. 55)

Don John argues that the understanding is programmed by the sense impressions conveyed to it, and thus we do not have free will. So if we are evil, we are so by 'nature', acting as we must according to the sharpness with which sensory imperatives are conveyed to the understanding. To some extent, the irrational behaviour of Leonora and of two local women, Flavia and Clara, appears to bear out Don John's view. The girls are to be married the following day, but they have heard that English women have much more liberty than Spanish, that in England anything goes in sexual mores – and they desire a taste of such 'natural' freedom. The song they sing sets out to vindicate female libertinism:

> *Woman who is by Nature wild,*
> *Dull bearded man incloses;*
> *Of Nature's freedom we're beguil'd*
> *By Laws which man imposes:*
> *Who still himself continues free,*
> *Yet we poor Slaves must fetter'd be.*

(III, p. 60)

But their attempt to follow through on this desire for sexual liberation provokes an orgy of crime culminating in the murder of their father, the death of Maria, and the wounding of their two bridegrooms, such that they are brought to a religious recognition – ''Twas our vile disobedience / Caus'd our poor Fathers death, which Heaven / Will revenge on us' (IV, pp. 73–4) – and they determine to expiate their sins in a religious sanctuary. In the event, they do not spend long enough in the cloister to achieve this because they are smoked out of it like bees in a hive by Don John's gang intent upon their rape. Significantly again in view of this play's attempt to combat vice with pastoral, it is the shepherds who foil the attempt. In what remains of the play, the supernatural machinery of the legend takes over, as Don John's gang are made by the ghost and the statue to celebrate a ritual black mass in the company of the ghosts of all those they have murdered. In the Faustian finale, Don John is haled off to hell still refusing to repent, meeting his death with all the bravado of the villain in a Jacobean tragedy.

Rochester not only recognised *The Libertine* as a reply to *Against Reason and Mankind* but effectively gave it his imprimatur: his self-mocking poetic riposte, *To the Post Boy*, figures the Earl's own imminent damnation in terms that unmistakably recall Don John's brazen end, complete with the prospect of hell, fire and brimstone.[29] Shadwell, however, was not finished yet. In *The Libertine*, he was primarily concerned with staging (and rebutting) the sexual ethics embodied in *Against Reason and Mankind*; in his adaptation of Shakespeare's *Timon of Athens*, which he claimed to have 'Made into a Play', his interest is in the corruption of human nature and the supposed inferiority of men to beasts.

Written at the suggestion of Rochester's friend and political ally, the Duke of Buckingham, to whom it was dedicated, *The History of Timon of Athens, the Man-Hater* (1678) targets the section of *Against Reason and Mankind* in which the speaker renews his onslaught on mankind in rejoinder to the *adversarius*'s vindication of 'Blest glorious Man' (lines 112–73). This is not to say that the poem's libertine creed embodied in the speaker's apology for 'right reason' (lines 72–111) has been forgotten: indeed, Shadwell's most striking alteration of the Shakespearian original is the introduction of Evandra, Timon's loyal and loving mistress, who is abandoned by him for Melissa, a mercenary coquette, but who, in spite of his faithlessness and perjured vows, is the only person to offer support and help when bankruptcy looms by returning the gifts he had bestowed upon her. (Melissa immediately gives him up for Alcibiades whose fortune is now in the ascendant.) One could even argue – perversely – that if Timon had remained true to Evandra, the effect on him of the financial disaster would not have been half so dire. As it is, this good-natured if thoughtless spendthrift and would-be libertine is shocked to discover not only that the erstwhile beneficiaries of his bounty have abandoned him but also that the only person genuinely eager to help him is the woman he had wronged and to whom he had callously expounded his rationale for male sexual freedom:

> *Tim.* Man is not master of his appetites,
> Heav'n sways our mind to Love. (I, p. 210)
> . . .
> Why are not our desires within our power?
> Or why should we be punisht for obeying them?[30]

Evandra's retort to this torrent of ingenious self-justification is telling: 'Your Philosophy is too subtle' (I, p. 212). It certainly is: later on in the play Timon assures her with disarming candour: 'I can love two at once, trust me I can' (II, p. 227).

Shadwell uses Evandra to expose and castigate Timon's libertinism; he uses Apemantus and Timon himself to carry out a scorching attack on human treachery, pride and dishonesty.[31] As in Shakespeare, both Apemantus's and Timon's misanthropic diatribes are pervaded by animal imagery, but Apemantus's speeches have been adjusted to underline thematic correspondence to specific passages in *Against Reason and Mankind*. It is as if the poem's persona had an on-stage deputy:

> *Apem.* When I can find a man that's better than
> A beast, I will fall down and worship him.
>
> (II, p. 222)

Compare *Against Reason and Mankind*:

> If upon Earth there dwell such God-like men,
> I'le here Recant my Paradox to them;
> Adore those Shrines of Virtue, homage pay,
> And with the rabble World, their Laws obey.
>   If such there be, yet grant me this at least,
> Man differs more from Man, than Man from Beast.
>
> (lines 220–5)

And later,

> I fear not man no more than I can love him.
> 'Twere better for us that wild beasts possest
> The Empire of the Earth, they'd use men better,
> Than they do one another. They'd ne're prey
> On man but for necessity of Nature.
> Man undoes man in wantonness and sport,
> Bruits are much honester than he; my dog
> When he fawns on me is no Courtier,
> He is in earnest; but a man shall smile,
> And wish my throat cut.
>
> (III, pp. 231–2)

compared with *Against Reason and Mankind*:

> Be Judge your self, I'le bring it to the test,
> Which is the Basest Creature, Man or Beast.
> Birds feed on birds, Beasts on each other prey,
> But savage Man alone does man betray:
> Prest by necessity they kill for food,
> Man undoes Man to do himself no good.
> With teeth and claws by nature arm'd, they hunt
> Natures allowance to supply their want.
> But Man with smiles, embraces, friendship, praise,
> Inhumanly his fellows life betrayes;
> With voluntary pains works his distress,

> Not through Necessity, but Wantonness.
> For hunger or for Love they fight and teare,
> Whilst wretched man is still in arms for Feare:
> For feare he Arms, and is of arms afraid,
> By fear to fear successively betray'd.
>
> (lines 127–42)

Timon too denounces the 'wicked humane race' ('all such Animals' as 'walk ... upon two legs'), for 'they are not honest, / Those Creatures that are so, walk on all four' (IV, pp. 251–2). Yet in contrast to the persona of *Against Reason and Mankind* (and to Apemantus), Timon, who claims to be as 'savage as a Satyr' (IV, p. 253), is compelled, by Evandra's unceasing solicitude, loyalty and generosity, to recant his paradox and acknowledge that among two-legged beasts 'there is / One woman honest; if they ask me more / I will not grant it' (Act IV, p. 253).

Crowne undercuts the ostensible moral idealism of *Calisto* by imbuing both the masque proper (the story of Jupiter's abortive rape of Calisto) and the pastoral intermezzi of nymphs and shepherds with elements of libertine philosophy and rhetoric extrapolated from *Against Reason and Mankind*; in *The Libertine* and *Timon*, Shadwell grafts elements of libertine comedy (again traceable to Rochester's poem) on to essentially tragic structures,[32] again with a view to literalising and demolishing the precepts put forward by the persona of *Against Reason and Mankind*. The result is a satirical masque and two satirical tragedies respectively. By engaging with its language and topics, all three plays, but especially the two of Shadwell's, strive to question and counter the libertine and misanthropic ethos of *Against Reason and Mankind*. In that attempt they are only partially successful. For although the outcomes of their plots toe the morally correct (and poetically just) line – Jupiter's assault on the nymph is prevented, Don John and his confederates are hauled off to hell, Timon dies a broken man – the imperative to create a figure (or figures) who will embody the satire's creed, and will then be exposed and duly chastised, leads, paradoxically, not to edifying catharsis but to moral ambivalence and generic corruption. To this fact the original audiences were fully alive. The mixed reception of the English Don Juan is a case in point. John Downes, the Duke's Company prompter, recalled that 'it got the Company great Reputation' and that 'The *Libertine* perform'd by Mr. *Betterton* Crown'd the Play';[33] Robert Hooke who saw a performance during the first run was outraged by this 'Atheistical wicked play';[34] Charles Gildon classed it as a 'Comedy', which, he thought, was 'diverting enough';[35] and John Dryden damned it as a 'Farce'.[36]

Our discussion confirms the importance of Rochester's *Against Reason and Mankind* for the libertine debates of the 1670s, especially as they were conducted through the medium of drama. The biographical episodes in which the Earl tried to put libertine beliefs into practice are amongst the best known in Restoration lore: those episodes were strikingly immortalised in the portrayals of Rochester in plays by Etherege, Crowne and Lee. We hope to have demonstrated that *Against Reason and Mankind* prompted Shadwell and Crowne to represent on stage forms of behaviour even more excessive than Rochester's real-life scrapes (if that is an adequate word), searching for a point at which his ethical naturalism would break down, testing it to destruction. Audiences watching representations of behaviour sanctioned by Rochester's arguments would surely reject the premises, though, as we have hinted, the generic complexities that result from such stage experiments do not make it easy to pass moral verdicts. To this extent, the poem is of its time and formative in its time.

The impact of Rochester's *Against Reason and Mankind* (and of his colourful lifestyle) upon the drama did not extend beyond the 1680s. Written as it was for a Court occasion, Crowne's masque was never performed after 1675; by contrast, Shadwell's *The Libertine* and *Timon* proved immensely popular and were regularly revived well into the eighteenth century.[37] It is unlikely, however, that by then many people would have associated the figurations of libertinism in those plays with the person of the Earl or indeed with *Against Reason and Mankind*.[38] Even so, by the eighteenth century the poem seems to have become something of a definitive, if also – paradoxically – a dangerously fluid, statement on 'Man' and 'Reason'. *Against Reason and Mankind* was not only reprinted as a matter of course in successive editions of Rochester's works,[39] but substantial excerpts from it were routinely anthologised under those headings in poetry manuals and dictionaries of quotations such as Edward Bysshe's much-reprinted *The Art of English Poetry* (1702) and his *The British Parnassus* (1714) and Charles Gildon's *The Complete Art of Poetry* (1718). *The Art of English Poetry* prints as many as seventy-two lines from *Against Reason and Mankind* under the heading 'MAN', their tenor being unequivocally misanthropic and cynical.[40] In the Preface to *The British Parnassus* Bysshe professed to 'have carefully avoided to insert any single Line, much less any whole Passage, in this Collection, that was in the former'.[41] Accordingly, under the heading 'MAN', he included twelve lines of the *adversarius*'s apology for 'Bless'd glorious Man . . .', which he had previously excluded from *The Art of English Poetry* (II, 536). But under the heading 'REASON', he now placed a further twenty-five lines from *Against Reason and Mankind*, comprising the persona's scathing debunking of the *adversarius*'s speech (II, 749–50). The impact of such a combination upon the readers of Bysshe's anthologies could hardly have been more ambivalent and contradictory.

In the eighteenth century Rochester's *Against Reason and Mankind* (and his poetic output more generally) influenced verse and prose satire, not drama. In Rochester's poetry can be found some of the most important formal blueprints for eighteenth-century satirical verse; on the level of theme and content, too, he is a model for later writers: the Pope–Swift–Gay circle in particular. The sensational opening statement of *Against Reason and Mankind*, inspired by Montaigne and Plutarch, is echoed in several Scriblerian works. In Book IV of *Gulliver's Travels*, Gulliver's Houyhnhnm 'master' observes that his ability to survive and defend himself in the wild is considerably inferior to that of the average beast. By the end of the fourth voyage the point is thoroughly made that Gulliver is not only *not* an animal, he is less than one.[42] Mortification of human pride is central to this poem's intention, as it is to Scriblerian satire generally. Other lines of *Against Reason and Mankind* bring irresistibly to mind John Gay's fable 'The Man and the Flea':

> And tis this very Reason I despise.
> This supernatural Gift, that makes a mite
> Think hee's the Image of the Infinite;
> Comparing his short life, voyd of all rest,
> To the Eternall, and the ever blest.

(lines 75–9)

In Gay's fable a man, wrought to a pitch of self-congratulation by observing the universe created for his pleasure, is humbled by a flea on his nose.[43] The flea, not the man, is the capstone of the creation. Gay was also drawn to Rochester's Hobbesian account of human beings as the only species who destroy others without any advantage to themselves (lines 129 onwards). An exactly similar account is given by Lockit in *The Beggar's Opera*.[44] Pre-eminently, however, Rochester's poem is a source of inspiration for Alexander Pope.[45] Lines 14 onwards construct a bridge from Milton to his eighteenth-century successors: to Swift's Spider in the *Battle of the Books*, spinning his house out of his own entrails; or to Pope's King of the Dunces, trying to compose in surroundings created by the detritus of his own (de)composition. 'Stumbling from thought to thought' becomes in the *Dunciad* 'Sinking from thought to thought, a vast profound', as Rochester's trip becomes a lead-weighted dive, and the sea changes from the sceptic's doubt to the poet's Sargasso of hopeless images. Joseph Spence records several instances of Pope's attention to Rochester, of his earnestness in comparing him to Oldham and Dorset and in assessing his strengths and weaknesses against those peers:

> Oldham is too rough and coarse. Rochester is the medium between him and the Earl of Dorset. Lord Dorset is the best of all those writers.
> 'What, better than Lord Rochester?'
> Yes; Rochester has neither so much delicacy nor exactness as Dorset. [Instance: his Satire on Man.][46]

If Pope is ambivalent in his verdict, he is no more so than contemporary playwrights were, or than modern readers of Rochester's most significant individual poem continue to be.[47] Stephen Jeffreys is the latest dramatist to put Rochester's life on the stage, in his play *The Libertine*, premièred in 1994. As the lights come up, Rochester walks front stage and, Restoration style, issues a direct challenge to the audience: 'Allow me to be frank at the commencement: you will not like me'.[48] The events of his life unfold and the play closes with Rochester again in direct address to the audience: 'Well. Do you like me now? Do you like me now?' (p. 84). Do we?[49]

12

Rochester and the theatre in the satires

DAVID FARLEY-HILLS

Concepts of acting and being are never far apart in Rochester's thought. Life that is not acting is at best a half life, 'On the Dull Shore of lazy Temperance':

> . . . Thoughts are given for Actions government,
> Where Action ceases, Thought's impertinent.
> Our sphere of Action is Lifes happiness,
> And he who thinks beyond, thinks like an Asse.[1]

Moreover, action in general necessarily implies acting a part to one who believes that human nature dooms us to the constant re-inventing of the self. If 'loves Theatre the Bed'[2] took preference over the boards in Rochester's priorities, it was certainly not to the neglect of the latter. In a letter to Elizabeth Barry, he makes it clear that, while he wishes to see her, he is determined to see the play first: 'Whether you will come to the Duke's Playhouse today, or at least let me come to you when the play is done, I leave to your choice.'[3] He made several attempts to write for the theatre, and he assisted playwrights like Sir Francis Fane, Charles Davenant and Elkanah Settle by writing epilogues, or, in the last example, a prologue, to boost performances of their plays. Throughout most of the 1670s he took an active interest in the major play-wrights of the day. Indeed, from the time in 1672 that Crowne dedicated the *History of Charles VIII* to Rochester, with 'a design to over-aw with Your Name', to Otway's dedication of *Titus and Berenice* to Rochester in 1677, by way of Dryden's dedication of *Marriage A-La-Mode* (1673), Lee's dedication of *Nero* (1675) and Fane's of *Love in the Dark* in the same year, Rochester had become the *arbiter elegantiarum* of the Restoration theatre – and this might well help to account for the upsurge of libertine plays over this period.

15 *Tunbridge Wells* engraved by Johannes Kip (1719). Rochester (or, possibly, his relative Laurence Hyde) subscribed one guinea towards the building of the parish church, dedicated to King Charles that Martyr

In most cases his interest proved a mixed blessing, for he could change rapidly from praise to blame without fear or favour. His judgments, however, are almost always uncannily right. *An Allusion to Horace* is principally about playwrights, and the relative judgments are generally sound. *An Allusion to Horace*, however magisterially, deals mostly in the generalities of literary reputation, whereas in *Satyr. [Timon]* there is a more detailed discussion of dramatic effectiveness. Both poems are concerned that wit, the play of the intellect, should have preference over mere sensation; so, in *An Allusion to Horace*, Lee is pilloried for allowing rhetoric to substitute for intelligence with unintentional comic effect in *Sophonisba*:

> When Leigh makes temperate Scipio fret and Rave,
> And Hannibal a whining amarous slave
> I laugh, and wish the hot-braind fustian foole
> In Busby's hands to be well lasht at school.

(lines 37–40)

Rochester is making a precise point of neo-classical doctrine here (hence the need for Lee to go back to school), for he is pointing to the neo-Aristotelian view (based on *Poetics* IX) that tragedy must be convincing, which explains the preference for historical plots (for what convinces is the possible), but more importantly demands verisimilitude (being convincingly lifelike) and character decorum (depicting a character in accordance with the general reputation of the person, or his or her role). You can depict heroes in love, says Boileau, so long as you do not turn them into whining shepherds:

> Peignez donc, j'y consens, les Heros amoureux;
> Mais ne m'en formez pas des Bergers doucereux.[4]

The main point is one of decorum, that a Scipio should be shown as the exemplar of temperance, that an Aeneas should act with the *pietas* characteristic of Aeneas:

> Que pour ses Dieux Enée ait un respect austere,
> Conservez à chacun son propre caractere.[5]

Drama should deal rationally with the ideas it adumbrates.

Rochester's preference for ideas over the sensational in the theatre is made fully explicit in the epilogue he contributed to Fane's *Love in the Dark* (1675). Here the more conservative repertoire of the King's Company at Drury Lane, where Fane's play is appearing, is contrasted favourably with the elaborate spectacle indulged in by Betterton's company, the rival Duke's Company, at Dorset Garden. Shadwell, whom Rochester praises in *An Allusion to Horace*, comes under attack for the two extravaganzas, *The Tempest* and *Psyche*, produced by the Duke's Company, for their preference for spectacle over sense:

> Now to Machines, and a dull Mask you run,
> We find that Wit's the Monster you would shun.[6]

Turning his attention to the acting, Rochester contrasts the ill discipline of the Duke's Company ('False accent and neglectful Action' (line 24)), and, according to Ellis, of James Nokes in particular, with the legitimate acting of the chief actor of the King's Company, Michael Mohun:[7]

> In Comedy their unweigh'd Action mark,
> There's one is such a dear familiar spark,
> He yawns, as if he were but half awake;
> And fribling for free speaking, does *mistake*.
>
> (lines 20–3)

Ellis's glossary gives 'to stammer' as the meaning of 'fribble', but I have found no good evidence that it could have this meaning in Rochester's time. The *Oxford English Dictionary*, it is true, gives 'to stammer out' as a possible meaning from Middleton's *Mayor of Queenborough* onwards, but none of its three examples before Rochester justifies this definition. The context of the examples in Brome's *Antipodes* (II.i.23) and Middleton's *Mayor of Queenborough* (V.i.368) makes it abundantly clear that the reference is to extemporising, not to stammering, but the third example, from Brome's *A Mad Couple Well Matched*, is rather more problematic: a lady tells the young gallant Bellamy (in fact a woman in disguise), who she thinks is paying court to her, 'I would heare you speake, you have often muttered and fribled some intentions towards me, but I would heare you speake' (II.i.249). The *OED* here presumably regards 'fribbled' as a near synonym for 'muttered', but this seems to assume redundancy: Bellamy does not stammer in the scene, indeed 'he' is rather eloquent (though he does speak *sotto voce* in one extended passage). It seems more likely that 'he' is being accused of being unserious, frivolous, in his declarations of love (the *OED* itself conjectures that the derivation of the word may be from 'frivol', as in 'frivolous'), and it is probable, then, that the semantic range of the word did not extend to 'stammer' in Rochester's time. In Bailey's *Dictionary* (4th edition, 1728), the meaning of 'fribbling' is given simply as 'impertinent, trifling', and I think we should take 'trifling' as the most likely meaning intended by Rochester here. Rochester is accusing the Duke's Company actor of the indiscipline of ad-libbing and the whole company of sloppy, ill-considered presentation ('unweighed action') rather than poor or artificial delivery. Frank Ellis is unlikely to be right to see the contrast as between 'artificial' and 'natural' acting.[8] In any case, Nokes, as a comic actor, might be expected to be more naturalistic (as became comedy) than Mohun, whom Rochester praises principally in tragic roles. Rochester again uses Shakespeare, as he had in *An Allusion to Horace*, as his measure of excellence in his eulogy of Mohun:

> the great *Wonder* of our English Stage.
> Whom Nature seem'd to form for your delight,
> And bid him speak, as she bid *Shakespeare* write.
>
> (lines 31–3)

Rochester ends his epilogue with an interesting comment on the audiences of
the two theatres: the Duke's Theatre is aiming to attract a citizen audience
with these mindless musicals, while Covent Garden appeals to the intelligent,
the 'men of wit'.

Rochester has not been given enough credit for reasserting Shakespeare's
excellence at almost the only time in the history of Shakespearian reception
when there had been some wavering over the relative merits of Jonson, Fletcher
and Shakespeare. Dryden had been the most distinguished waverer, giving
Jonson preference in the essay *Of Dramatic Poesie* and French rhymed tragedy
preference in his own practice, until the conclusive conversion expressed
in the appeal to 'Shakespeare's sacred name' in the prologue to *Aureng-Zebe*
(1676) and the emulation of Shakespearian practice in the subsequent play
All for Love. In *An Allusion to Horace* (1675) Rochester specifically takes Dryden
to task for 'arrogantly' underestimating the merits of the great Jacobean
dramatists (lines 81–6) and singles out Jonson and Shakespeare as models of
excellence in the arts of satire (lines 28–31); it is unlikely that Dryden's *volte
face* is unrelated to this attack on him. Rochester's admiration of Shakespeare
as a satirist is perhaps surprising to a modern reader, but it was not only the
best grounds for praising Shakespeare in an age that prized satire, it also helps
to explain some important features of Rochester's own satires: his delight, for
instance, in allowing the satirised to condemn themselves out of their own
mouths, which is, of course, necessarily a dramatic technique. *A very heroical
epistle in answer to Ephelia* and *An Epistolary Essay, from M.G. to O.B. upon
their mutuall Poems* are the most obvious examples, but the same technique
is used in *Tunbridge Wells, Satyr. [Timon]* and, most successfully of all, *A Letter
from Artemiza in the Towne to Chloe in the Countrey*. The influence of Shakespeare's angriest satire, *Timon of Athens*, in which Shakespeare emulates the
snarling satirist of Elizabethan formal satire, is evident not only in the satire
which bears his name but more obviously and insistently in *A Satyre against
Reason and Mankind*, in *Tunbridge Wells* and in *A Ramble in St. James's Park*.

Sometimes the Shakespearean influence becomes more specific. Frank Ellis
not only finds the occasional Shakespearean echo in *Valentinian* but also makes
the interesting suggestion, in his annotation of the play, that the adaptations
of Fletcher's original are markedly Shakespearean as later defined by Dryden
in his *Heads of an Answer to Rymer* (1677). Ellis describes the relationship as
follows:

> In adapting Fletcher's play Rochester shifts the *object* of imitation from plot to
> character-*plus*-'thoughts' (as Dryden prescribes). He makes the characters lovers:
> 'we are not touched with the sufferings of any sort of men so much as lovers',
> Dryden says. And he shifts the *effect* of imitation from *katharsis* to poetic justice
> (as Dryden also prescribes): 'the suffering of innocence and punishment of the
> offender is of the nature of English [but not of Greek] tragedy') (Dryden 1882–93,
> XV, 382, 390). Dryden supposes that if Aristotle had known Shakespeare, he would
> have changed his theory in these ways.[9]

As the date of Rochester's adaptation of *Valentinian* has been confidently ascribed to 1675–6,[10] we seem to have more evidence here that Dryden's conversion to bardolatry was related to Rochester's advocacy.

Satyr. [*Timon*] is as much concerned with the theatre as *An Allusion to Horace*, and, although the comment is more oblique, as much concerned with the bad taste of the spectators as with the inadequacies of the plays. The criticism is similar to that of the epilogue to *Love in the Dark*, the preference of vulgar audiences for sound over sense. One of the notable things about the discussion of the theatre in *Timon* is its attention to detail, showing Rochester's knowledge of his play texts (or at least his willingness to look them up). Although the poem Rochester is imitating (Boileau's third satire) refers to contemporary French theatre, it is neither so insistent nor as detailed as in *Timon*. As in Boileau's verse, the poem's spokesman is persuaded against his better judgment to dine with a stranger whose vulgarity and that of his wife and of the other guests is the principal target of the satire. The other guests are named as 'Half-Witt and, Huffe, / Kickum, and Ding-Boy' (lines 35–6), names that suggest contemporary stage louts, and anticipate the names Cuffe and Kick, borrowed from Shadwell's *Epsom Wells*, in *Tunbridge Wells*. Their level of sophistication Rochester illustrates in Huffe's reply to a question from the hostess:

> She askt Huffe, if Loves flame he never felt?
> He answered bluntly – 'Doe you thinke I'm Gelt?'
>
> (lines 61–2)

This same level of sensibility is evident in the conversation that follows the lady's departure from table, when 'Some regulate the stage and some the state' (line 112). Half-Witt praises Lord Orrery's *The Tragedy of Mustapha* for the heroic way the two sons of the Turkish Sultan die, before turning to more general praise of Orrery's poetic style, illustrating it by an inaccurate quotation from *The Black Prince*, with the comment:

> There's fine Poetry! you'd sweare 'twere Prose,
> Soe little on the Sense, the Rhymes impose.
>
> (lines 119–20)

By getting the second line of his quotation wrong (Rochester's quotations are more often than not correct in the poem), Half-Witt shows what he means: the sense is so vacuous that it doesn't really matter how you end the couplet so long as it rhymes. The mistake also shows that Half-Witt has completely forgotten the context of the quotation; he has remembered the jingle (or half of it – fair enough for a half-wit) but not the sense. The lines Half-Witt quotes come out as:

> "And which is worse, if any worse can be,
> "He never said one word of it to me.
>
> (lines 117–18)

The actual lines are worth quoting because they have the kind of inspired banality of a William McGonagall. The Black Prince is expressing his disappointment at the defection of the lady he loves:

> Heav'n knows I loved her with so chaste a flame
> As I to marry her did only aim,
> To which at last my Father did consent,
> When she next day but one did marry Kent,
> And which is worse, if any worse can be,
> She for it ne'er excus'd herself to me.

Orrery's lines are a triumph of sound over sense.

Next Ding-Boy chooses to admire Etherege's 'Airy Songs; and soft Lampoones' (line 122), giving as his main reason their lack of grammar, without which, he says, Etherege has managed to write 'Two talking Plays, without one Plott' (line 125). Huffe in his turn admires Settle's *The Empress of Morocco* and quotes three lines from Act 2, two of which consist entirely of exotic (and largely meaningless) names and the other, from an earlier part of the same scene, is given a level of alliteration that successfully puts all sense to rout: '"Whose broad-built-Bulkes, the Boyst'rous Billows, beare' (line 128). Here Huffe's memory is also somewhat at fault, for Settle's actual line is 'Their lofty bulks the foaming billows bear'. But this error simply helps to emphasise by exaggeration Settle's liking for sound effects.

Rochester continues to pick his way through his collection of playbooks. Kickum illustrates his mindlessness in his admiration of three lines from Crowne's *The History of Charles VIII of France* and the host caps the quotations from no less a pen than Dryden's in *The Indian Queen*:

> As if our old world modestly withdrew,
> And here in private had brought forth a new.
>
> (I.i.3–4)

In these two quotations the target is still deficiency of sense in both poet and admirer, but now illustrated by absurdities in the use of metaphor. The host's four lines of admiring exposition neatly damns both commentator and poet:

> There are Two lines! who but he, durst presume
> To make the Old World, a new With-drawing Roome,
> Where of another World, she's brought to Bed?
> What a brave Mid-Wife, is a Laureats Head!
>
> (lines 147–50)

In *An Allusion to Horace*, Satyr. [*Timon*] and the epilogue, interest in the theatre is shown mostly through critical comment. In *Tunbridge Wells* the theatre, and Shadwell's *Epsom Wells* in particular, becomes the measure of the poem's seriousness. At first sight the theatre seems to be less important to *Tunbridge Wells* than to the other poems I have discussed, in that there are few actual references to the theatre: a brief reference to *Love in a Tub*'s Sir Nicholas Cully and his first interpreter, James Nokes, with whom the satirical target is compared, and then, towards the end of the poem, two loutish characters, Cuffe and Kick, are briefly introduced whose names and roles (as readily available studs) derive from Shadwell's *Epsom Wells*. There is, then, no discussion of the theatre here, merely the use of theatrical stereotypes – the solemn fool, the town yob – to place characters who appear at the Wells and whom Rochester wishes to satirise.

The rather casual reference to *Epsom Wells*, however, conceals the importance of Shadwell's play to Rochester's purpose. It is not only that Rochester is alluding to two characters of the play and to the circumstances in which they appear; there are other echoes of the play in the poem's narrative. Ellis, for instance, following R. L. Root, points out that the conversation between the two wives in *Tunbridge Wells* and the poet's comment on them (lines 131–58) reflect the conversation and behaviour of the two merchants' wives, Mrs Bisket and Mrs Fribble, in *Epsom Wells*.[11] In *Tunbridge Wells* both the women (one with her sickly daughter) consider the Wells a good place to become pregnant, which the poet interprets for us as meaning that they intend to take advantage of such 'potent pricks' as the likes of the brawny Cuffe and Kick are willing to provide them (lines 153–4). The theme that the Wells enable women to find fertility through the services of sexual predators is central to *Epsom Wells*. In the first scene Cuffe tells his friend that women come to the Wells 'to procure conception', to which Kick replies: 'that's not from the waters, but something else that shall be nameless' (II.i.469–71).[12] Clearly the merchants' wives agree: in Act 2 Dorothy Fribble tells her neighbours, Mr and Mrs Bisket, of her husband's wish that she should stay at the Wells because 'he longs mightily for a Child' and she promises to use 'all the means I can' to conceive one (II.i.469–71). At the end of the play both Cuffe and Kick and the two women have their expectations realised when Bisket finds his wife in bed with Kick and Fribble finds his in bed with Cuffe (V.i.622, 640). Root sums up aptly: 'This plotline of foolish husbands, wanton wives, and predatory gallants forms the basis for Rochester's treatment of a segment of society at Tunbridge Wells'.[13] But more important still, the whole satire makes use of *Epsom Wells* to establish its satirical stance. Shadwell's play attempts the difficult task attempted by several other Restoration playwrights (including Etherege) of making the nice distinction between the yobbery of louts like Cuffe and Kick and the conduct of the true libertines (the true wits), like the romantic heroes of the play, Bevil and Rains. This theme becomes explicit at one point when Justice Clodpate remarks: 'as for wit, there is such a stir amongst you, who has it, and who has it not, that we honest country gentlemen begin to think there's no such thing'.[14] The distinction is certainly not always obvious: Bevil and Rains drink and whore with as much determination as Cuffe and Kick, though with rather more refinement. The main difference is indeed an aesthetic one, but there are moral implications: Cuffe and Kick are mere stallions, sex machines 'With brawny back and legs and potent prick' (line 154) as Rochester succinctly sums them up. Rains and Bevil on the other hand are capable of something less bestial: a romantic attachment to the heroines Lucia and Caroline which ultimately leads them to a promise of marriage if their 'good behaviour' permits it. Shadwell presents his characters in the Jonsonian manner of *Bartholomew Fair* where the wells provide an opportunity to juxtapose a variety of people at various levels of sophistication to illustrate both their common humanity and their differences. This is another talking play without much of a plot.

Rochester adopts the same structural looseness in *Tunbridge Wells* and spreads his net even wider in smaller compass. It is a commonplace of the criticism of the poem that it suffers from what Ellis calls 'a ramshackle structure';[15] the satirical targets range across the whole of society:

> Here Lords, Knights, Squires, ladyes, and Countesses,
> Channdlers, mum-bacon women, sempstresses
> Were mixt together, nor did they agree,
> More in their humours, then their Quality.

> (lines 94–7)

This is vanity fair, which subsumes distinctions of rank under the overarching disease of their humanity. The splenetic commentator himself does not escape from this same condition, however frantically he tries to escape from each group in turn. He is not by accident named after Shakespeare's mad satirist, and the tradition of destructive satire he represents gives no recourse to an alternative sanity. There is no marriage dance at the end, only a Gulliver-like commentator who seeks the company of horses.

But looseness of structure is not at all the same as a ramshackle structure, for Rochester's purpose stands out most markedly from Shadwell's in bringing his wide range of examples together to illustrate a dogmatic statement about man's absurdity. Shadwell allows his play to drift into sentimental ambiguities: Rains and Bevil hope to 'repair to marriage', as the Woodlys are preparing to celebrate their freedom in divorce; the marital conflicts of the Fribbles and Biskets are only partly resolved by the arrest of Cuffe and Kick, who threaten Justice Clodpate (with some credibility) 'our Party is too strong . . . here in Town', while Clodpate himself, the Justice Overdo of the play, has been tricked into marriage by the unscrupulous Mrs Jilt. The dance at the end is only a weak shadow of Shakespearian benevolence. The looseness of Shadwell's structure represents the diffuseness of his theme: Rochester's poem will have none of this diffuseness nor the benevolence. The couplets, for all their ability to reflect difference, are tight and disciplined, in contrast to Shadwell's easygoing prose, forcing us to see a mad world starkly, and they reveal a maker whose contempt for what he sees and laughs at is not merely temperamental but dogmatic.

Strictly speaking, the dogma is of course that of the satiric spokesman, not the poet's, but I think a comparison with theatrical practice at this time will reinforce my view that the *persona* and the author ultimately merge in this poem. We have already had cause to mention the stage prologue and epilogue as forms with which Rochester was familiar, and these were forms peculiarly characteristic of the Restoration period. A. N. Wiley in his introduction to his collection of prologues and epilogues argues that these forms were of particular importance in the theatre at this time because they acted as a point of mediation between audience and actors when the close physical relationship of stage to auditorium was beginning to give way to the increasing separation of the two.[16] The prologue in particular provided a bridge that an older tradition did not need and later generations learnt to live without. Wiley calculates that while between 1558 and 1642 roughly 21 per cent of plays had prologues and epilogues and a further 16 per cent prologues only, between 1660 and 1700 something like 90 per cent of new plays had prologues.[17] Wiley also remarks on the extension of the range of subjects in prologues over this period, and in particular the satirical use of the prologue. Here we find just that combination of belligerence and mediation that is characteristic of Rochester's satiric voice. Jeremy Treglown has remarked that Rochester can make his major satires 'sound like someone talking',[18] and a colloquial tone is equally characteristic of the contemporary satiric prologue. Take, for instance, this example from Crowne's prologue to *Juliana* (1672), and compare it to Rochester's delightful account of the awkward gallant in *Tunbridge Wells*; Crowne is comparing himself as bashful poet to the inexperienced gallant:

> But you must know he is a modest youth;
> Like country gallant just, whom courtier brings
> To see fine dainty Miss – who plays and sings;
> Approaching to'r, poor gallant falls a mumping,
> Scraping o'legs, and feign he would say something;
> And round about the room he flings and skips,
> Whil'st tongue lies still i' th'scabbard of his lips.[19]

Here, very clearly, is that satirical stance which encompasses even the speaker himself as representative of the poet. This is light-hearted in tone, but the prologue can equally be used for angry satire. I am not sure how far back the biting prologue goes, but John Lacey, whose outspokenness on one occasion caused King Charles to forbid the play he was in, claims in the satiric prologue to *The Rehearsal* (1671) to have reformed the stage by puncturing its pretentiousness; his prologue to his own play *The Old Troop* (1668) attacks the very wits (including the King) who had come to see its first performance. Pepys tells us he returned next day to the King's House specifically 'to hear the prologue', so perhaps he regarded it as a novelty.[20] Later playwrights, Otway in particular, made a speciality of the angry prologue; in the prologue

to his first play, *Alcibiades* (1675), for instance, he pours scorn on the 'would
be Witts' of his audience:

> Hither sometimes those would be Witts repair,
> In quest of you, where if you not appear,
> Cries one – Pugh! Damn me what do we do here?
> Straight up he starts, his Garniture then puts
> In order, so he Cocks, and out he struts,
> To th'Coffee-House, where he about him looks:
> Spies Friend, cries Jack – I've been to Night at th'Dukes:
> The silly Rogues are all undone my Dear.'
> I'gad! not one of sence that I saw there.[21]

As *Alcibiades* was first performed in September 1675, it is possible that Otway
had read *Tunbridge Wells* when he wrote this, but I am not arguing for any
influence either way here, merely that the combination of attack and familiar
address had become well established in the theatre during the years that
Rochester frequented it.

The importance of Rochester's comparison between the stage and 'Love's
theatre, the bed' lies not in the difference but in the similarity. The attacks
on Crowne and Settle, Shadwell and Dryden, as well as Kickum, Ding-Boy,
Half-Witt and Huffe, are complaints that fashionable custom is prevailing over
intelligent use, that form is prevailing over substance, spectacle over thought.
In the same privileging of form, love is becoming a matter of affectation,
of seeming, of ritual formulae rather than a commitment to genuine feeling.
The gauche fop in *Tunbridge Wells* is absurd less because of his ineptitude
than because he assumes love to be a matter of address, not of feeling, and
Artemisa, too, complains that the search for mere sensation usurps the place
of feeling:

> To an exact perfection they have wrought
> The Action *Love*, the Passion is forgott.
> . . .
> Their private wish obeys the publicke Voyce,
> 'Twixt good, and bad Whimsey decides, not Choyce.
>
> (lines 62–3, 66–7)

In *A Ramble*, Corinna affectedly prefers the affectations of her three 'whiffling
fools' to a genuine response to her mountainous sexual appetite. In *Against
Reason and Mankind* the spontaneous feelings of the animal world are contrasted with the malicious whimsies of human conduct.

But there is a further irony. Behind Rochester's apparent pleas for commitment to genuine feeling, there always rises the spectre of the human fatal
love of abstraction. Adam and Eve might live in a world before the Fall where
'Enjoyment waited on desire', but since the Fall we are doomed to take the
word for the thing. The lover in *The Fall* can only offer 'the . . . Tribute of a

heart' and the Disabled Debauchee the pleasure of watching others in action; but these are not special cases. Humans are frequently doomed to imperfect enjoyment, to feelings that lessen as they come on, for, thanks to our consciousness, much human activity takes place at one remove from the feeling that inspires it. Humans are by nature creatures of affectation and pretence. One of Rochester's major achievements as a poet was to find a form to express this 'Greate Negative' at the heart of human experience. And here lies the deeper fascination Rochester must have found in the theatre, whether he was fully aware of it or not, that the feelings it inspires are shadows of our shadows, and the desire for the stage's truth is always, like human love's, infinitely postponed by the abstractions of awareness.

13

Rochester, *The Man of Mode* and Mrs Barry

SIMON HAMPTON

ℭ

Rochester, it is generally agreed, 'blazed out his youth and his health in lavish voluptuousness',[1] his extraordinary creative ability being, arguably, more fully realised in the flesh with numerous well-publicised amours than in the word in a relatively small output of literary works. A dazzling intellect – manifested often in a profound disdain for humanity – and a huge self-destructive energy, combined during his own lifetime to create a legend, both of the man and of his manners. In the world of Charles II's Court, itself characterised by excess and unrestraint, Rochester stands almost alone among his contemporaries as a mythical figure – the intermingled elements of truth, half-truth and rumour which cling tenaciously to a cloudy picture of him making it still notoriously difficult to distinguish fact from fiction. His enigmatic personality is accepted as providing the inspiration for Dorimant in Etherege's *The Man of Mode*, and this chapter discusses Rochester's connection with the Restoration theatre in general, and considers his impact on Etherege's comedy in particular, further arguing that the actress Mrs Barry is likely to have taken the part of Harriet in the opening performances in 1676, before later assuming the role of Mrs Loveit in November 1706, long after her own amour with Rochester was at an end. If this is so, it forms a curious example of life imitating art from a theatrical era which specialised in such curiosities.

The vitality and excitement generated by the Restoration theatre sets it apart from any other period in the history of the English stage. At its best in the 1660s and 1670s, the literature written for it showed a dynamism which was influenced by the gathering spirit of sceptical and intellectual enquiry, turning a cultivated, critical detachment on itself and its own behaviour. It was also an age of unusual freedom concerning sexual relations. A deep vein of sensuality runs through the period, which is at odds with intellectual clarity.

Amphitheatra *filæ et Spectacula Barbara Cæsar:*
Non coeunt Nudi, non Aper, Ursa Leo.
Nos Mites colimus Musas, lenivit Amorœ
Prælia; cum nostro est Incola Marie Venus.
Quosœ ferunt olim Thalamo cepisie, Theatre
Ludentes unà cernat Apollo Deos.

Sold by Will Cademan at the Popes head in the New-Exchange.

W: Shermin

16 The Duke's Theatre in Dorset Garden, designed by
Sir Christopher Wren and opened on 9 November 1671

The dramatists sought to reconcile these qualities, and the greatest works of the time reflect the attempt to bring sensuality and intellect together. This age of enquiry and self-examination brought with it an unease and dis-satisfaction which often broke out into anger and violence. As Jocelyn Powell puts it:

> Restoration society embodied an extreme of a common form of social schizo-phrenia. Idleness was in a sense as brutalising a factor as poverty. The consumption of leisure in thought, reading and conversation had its darker side in riot, atheism and curious forms of nerveless despair. Inigo Jones's fine new church in Covent Garden was as notorious a pick-up place as the playhouse itself.[2]

Writing with the finely honed intellect of the audience in mind, the dra-matists (with Rochester among them) plagiarised French sources, anglicised their plots and characters, and worked these elements into a synthesis which reflected the behaviour and questioning of their own times. During the early, brilliant years from the mid-1660s to the late 1670s, the comedies, in particular, tended to embody a fashionable cynicism that attempted unsuccessfully to rationalise the conundrum of male and female sexuality. Rochester, in his own despairing search for sustained sexual gratification and love in his relationships, defines in *The Imperfect Enjoyment* the problem for the age:

> Thou Treacherous, base Deserter of my Flame,
> False to my passion, fatall to my Fame,
> Through what mistaken Magick doest thou prove
> So true to Lewdness, so untrue to Love?

(lines 46–9)

The atmosphere within the theatre was intimate and volatile. The audience – especially during the 1660s and the early 1670s – was composed of members of the Court and the aristocracy, supplemented by wealthy citizens, and, while they jostled with orange wenches and prostitutes, openly selling their wares, they expected to interrupt the play with examples of their improvised wit. Such contributions punctuated the text and became an integral part of performance, for whilst the interruptions may have appeared to be casual and off-hand, they combined with the intellectual capacity of the audience to form a critical detachment which has been described by Jocelyn Powell as pre-Brechtian.[3] Rochester attended, of course, with his circle of Court friends including Buckingham, Sedley and Savile, but – with limited evidence – it is difficult to assess his participation in the life and fashions of the pit with any degree of accuracy. That he was interested in the theatre is certain. He adapted Fletcher's tragedy *Valentinian* for the stage (performed Monday 11 February 1684) and he is credited with having, at least, a hand in the satirically obscene *Sodom*, which may have been published in 1684.[4] He wrote a prologue for Settle's *The Empress of Morocco* (spring 1673) and an epilogue for Sir Francis

Fane's *Love in the Dark* (performed at the King's Theatre in 1675). There, Rochester customarily criticises the sophisticated stage machinery of the rival Duke's Theatre, and launches an attack on spectacular scenic effects in general and on Shadwell in particular (an attack which is, incidentally, inconsistent with his judgment of that dramatist in *An Allusion to Horace*, written during the winter of 1675–6):

> As Charms are Nonsense, Nonsence seems a Charm,
> Which hearers of all Judgment does disarm;
> For Songs and Scenes, a double Audience bring,
> And Doggrel takes, which two-ey'd Cyclops sing.
>
> . . .
>
> Players turn Puppets now at your desire,
> In their Mouth's Nonsense, in their Tails a Wire,
> They fly through Clouds of Clouts, and showers of Fire.
>
> (lines 1–4, 10–12)

Rochester is also credited with having written an epilogue for Davenant's *Circe* (1676), a 'Scaen' for Sir Robert Howard's *The Conquest of China* (which the author planned but never wrote) and a delightful opening, 'Mr Dainty's Chamber', which beautifully complements the opening to *The Man of Mode*.[5] He was patron at one time to, amongst others, Dryden (whom he dubbed 'Poet Squab'). Rochester, in his privileged and, at times, desultory manner, believed the Muses should be invoked for genuine inspiration; Dryden was forced to earn his living by his pen. It seems to have been a strained relationship and the two fell out, exchanging insults in print, although Dryden's spiteful description of the Earl, 'this Rhyming Judge of the Twelve-penny Gallery, this Legitimate Son of *Sternhold*', who is unable to write his name, lacks any real foundation in fact, and is therefore some of Dryden's least effective criticism.[6] Rochester seems to have been on friendlier terms with another of Dryden's enemies, Shadwell, and with Wycherley, whom he genuinely respected: Shadwell for his development of Jonsonian 'humours' in a new age, Wycherley for his brilliant and satiric mannered comedy. He also knew Crowne and Settle, Aphra Behn, Otway and Lee and Nell Gwyn. He is alleged to have rehearsed the great Mrs Barry after her apparent failure on the stage, thereafter commencing an affair with her which produced a child, and he may have been similarly involved with Barry's colleague and rival, Mrs Boutel (or Bowtell).[7] His lodgings were, at one time, in Arbor House, Portugal Row, which was adjacent to the King's Theatre, Lincoln's Inn Fields; later, some time after 1675, he had moved to Whitehall, and in a letter, reportedly, to Mrs Barry he says, 'They are at present pulling down some part of my lodging, which will not permit me to see you there'.[8] So, intellectually and physically, he was at the centre of London's fashionable society, which embraced the theatre as one of its essential recreations.

Rochester's charismatic appearance at the theatre – especially in the late 1660s and early 1670s – was always worthy of comment. When John Dennis looked back at the Restoration from the vantage point of the early eighteenth century, he cited the powerful influence of men of rank like Rochester, who, as part of an audience, could effectively sway public opinion when it came to the verdict on a new play. Naming Rochester in the company of the Duke of Buckingham, the Earl of Dorset, Sir John Denham and Edmund Waller, Dennis goes on to say '[when] these or the majority of them Declared themselves upon any new Dramatick performance, the Town fell Immediately in with them, as the rest of the pack does with the eager cry of the staunch and the Trusty Beagles'.[9] Pepys, attending *Heraclius* on 4 February 1666/7, is more interested in celebrity spotting:

> the house being very full, and great company; among others, Mrs Steward, very fine, with her locks done up with puffs . . . and several other great ladies, had their hair so . . . Here I saw my Lord Rochester and his lady, Mrs Mallet, who hath after all this ado married him; and, as I hear some say in the pit, it is a great act of charity; for he hath no estate.[10]

Rochester seems to have had an ambivalent attitude towards the people sitting around him in the theatre. While enjoying the intellectual reward offered a pit *habitué* in orchestrating his own ripostes to energise with a particular text or characterisation, to become an active part of the performance, he was also pleased to ridicule what quickly became a scrabbling for true wit and sense amongst the audience:

> 'Tis therefore not enough when your false sence
> Hitts the false Judgment of an Audience
> Of clapping fools, assembling a vast Crowd
> Till the throng'd Playhous crack with the dull load.
> Thô even that Talent merits in some sort,
> That can divert the Rabble and the Court.
>
> (*An Allusion to Horace*, lines 12–17)

Picking out an individual would-be wit, he turns a cynical eye on this character:

> The Second was a *Grays Inn Wit*,
> A great Inhabiter of the *Pit*;
> Where *Critick-like*, he sits and squints,
> Steals Pocket-Handkerchiefs, and hints,
> From's *Neighbor*, and the *Comedy*.
>
> (*A Ramble in St. James's Park*, lines 63–7)

This criticism sits well with Bellinda's speech to Mrs Loveit in *The Man of Mode*:

I was yesterday at a play with 'em where I was fain to show 'em the living as the man at Westminster does the dead. That is Mrs Such-a-one, admired for her beauty; this is Mr. Such-a-one, cried up for his wit; that is sparkish Mr Such-a-one, who keeps reverend Mrs Such-a-one; and there sits fine Mrs Such-a-one, who was lately cast off by my Lord Such-a-one.[11]

Clearly, Rochester considered Etherege to be a poet of the front rank. Referring to the influence of Shakespeare and Jonson – a potent influence for the dramatists of the Restoration – he notes Etherege's debt to them:

> Whome refin'd Etheridge coppys not att all,
> But is himself a sheer Originall.
>
> (*An Allusion to Horace*, lines 32–3)

And this judgment is confirmed in *A Session of the Poets*, by the hand which wrote admiringly:

> But Apollo had got gentle George in his eye;
> And frankly confessed, of all men that writ
> There's none had more fancy, sense, judgment and wit.
>
> (lines 16–18)[12]

Given such regard for the man and his work, it is unlikely that Rochester would have condoned Etherege's 'long seven years silence', brought about by 'th' crying sin idleness' (lines 19, 20). Etherege (1634/5–91) was a boon companion of not only Rochester (with whom he was involved in the notorious brawl at Epsom in the summer of 1676) but other wits like Buckingham and Sedley.[13] Despite his genius and the privileged connections he enjoyed with the Court, he produced only three comedies. His first play, *The Comical Revenge, or, Love in a Tub*, was produced at Lincoln's Inn Fields in March, 1664; there was a strong cast, led by Betterton and Smith, and Downes records enthusiastically: 'The clean and well performance of this Comedy, got the Company more Reputation and profit than any preceding Comedy; the Company taking in a Months time at it 1000*l*.[14] This was followed by Etherege's second comedy, *She Wou'd if She Cou'd*, in which were drawn scenes in the Mulberry Garden, the New Exchange and New Spring Garden. Its first performance took place at Lincoln's Inn Fields on 6 February 1668, but it met with little success, Pepys recording that it was a 'silly' play, 'there being nothing in the world good in it, and few people pleased in it'.[15] Shadwell, himself a dramatist who suffered from actors who were under-rehearsed in their parts, refers to *She Wou'd if She Cou'd* as a play initially received with such critical prejudice that it was only the influence of the Court Wits – with Rochester, of course, among them – that prolonged its life. Idleness, or disappointment perhaps now conspired together, and for the next seven years, Etherege produced no work for the stage. When, at length, he wrote his last play, *The Man of Mode, or, S*ʳ *Fopling Flutter*, a sparkling comedy of manners, it was received with 'Extraordinary Success; all agreeing it to be true Comedy, and the characters drawn to the Life'.[16] It was first produced at the Dorset Garden Theatre on 11 March 1676, and Summers records: 'Dorimant was generally recognised to be Rochester. Sir Fopling represented Sir George Hewett. It is disputed whether Etherege drew himself in Medley.'[17] As the Restoration theatre regularly took notorious or famous figures from life to be represented on the stage, just how certain is it that Rochester was the model and inspiration for Dorimant?

> *Emil.* He's a very well bred man.
> *Bell.* But strangely ill natur'd.
> *Emil.* Then he's a very Witty man.
> *Bell.* But a man of no principles.
>
> (*The Man of Mode* II.ii.26–9)

The twentieth-century voice of Graham Greene seems convinced of the connection between the man and the playhouse creation, opening Chapter VII of his biography of the poet: 'Rochester's character as a lover was drawn by Sir George Etherege in *Sir Fopling Flutter* or *The Man of Mode* ... It was generally agreed that the hero, Dorimant, represented Etherege's friend.'[18] Greene is conveying the apparent certainty expressed by the critic John Dennis, writing in 1722, and by St Evremond. Dennis makes a persuasive case for such a pairing – citing the esteem in which Waller was held by both Rochester and Dorimant:

> Waller by nature for the Bayes design'd
> With force, and fire, and fancy unconfin'd
> In Panegericks does excell Mankind.
> He best can turn, inforce, and soften things
> To prais great Conquerors or to flatter Kings.
>
> (*An Allusion to Horace*, lines 54–8)

Downes records 'that it was unanimously agreed that he [Dorimant] had in him several of [Rochester's] qualities' and St Evremond considers, somewhat fulsomely, that in Dorimant Etherege had given us Rochester with his vices 'burnished to shine like perfections'. In the song he wrote for the play, Sir Carr Scroope (then presumably on friendly terms with Rochester) 'gave an attractive portrayal of "the charming Strephon," who, like Dorimant ... is modeled upon Rochester'.[19] It is indeed an attractive portrait:

> As Amoret with Phillis sat
> One evening on the plain,
> And saw the charming Strephon wait
> To tell the nymph his pain.
>
> (*The Man of Mode*, V.ii.73–6)

The other leading characters were probably modelled on other famous people of the day: Medley, according to Dennis, was based on Sir Fleetwood Sheppard, although another credible possibility is Sir Charles Sedley; Sir Fopling has traditionally been identified as the famous fop Beau Hewitt. Dryden, who wrote the epilogue, follows standard procedure to protect the satirist by claiming that no portrayal of living individuals is intended:

> none Sir Fopling him, or him, can call:
> He's knight o' the shire and represents ye all.
>
> (*The Man of Mode*, epilogue, lines 15–16)

John Dennis believed the play to be 'an agreeable Representation of the Persons of Condition of both Sexes, both in Court and Town',[20] so, when the curtain flew up on this original piece, the audience, knowing of Rochester's libertine reputation and of his relationship with Mrs Barry, must have awaited the opening with keen excitement. Dorimant was played by the famous actor Betterton, who had been awarded the bays by the writer of *A Session of the Poets*:

> Apollo quite tired with their tedious harangue,
> Finds at last Tom Betterton, face in the gang,
> And since poets without the kind players may hang
> By his own sacred light he solemnly swore
> That in search of a laureate he'd look out no more.
> A general murmur ran quite through the hall,
> To think that the bays to an actor should fall.
>
> (lines 88–94)

When considering *The Man of Mode* at its première on that March Saturday, it is important to try and define certain elements which must have been crucial to its dynamics in performance: certain elements of life that would have informed the fiction on the stage. First, the evidence would seem to confirm that Rochester – often in the company of Etherege at this time (for example, the escapade at Epsom) – was indeed the model on which the character of Dorimant is based. It seems reasonable to assume therefore that both men would look forward to the first performance; both men would be intrigued to see how effectively Etherege's portraits of well-known men and their manners were received by the audience. At this time, however, Rochester was seemingly out of favour at Court, first smashing the King's sundial in the Privy Garden in June 1675, and then falling out with the Duchess of Portsmouth, although this was a quarrel which had begun in 1674 when he had written an obscene poem about her relationship with Charles II. It was, according to Wilson, 'the winter of Rochester's discontent', and somewhere during this period, 1675–6 (although it is a particularly difficult time in which to establish the Earl's movements with any degree of certainty), it is thought that he assumed the role of a quack doctor in Tower Hill, where he 'took asylum and shelter under the disguise of an Italian Mountebank, and vouchsafed the appellative of Doctor Alexander Bendo'. Bendo cut an imposing figure seemingly, dressed 'in an old overgrown Green Gown which he religiously wore in Memory of Rabelais his Master ... lyned through with exotick furs of divers colours, an Antique cap, a great Reverend Beard, and a Magnificent false Medal sett round with glittering Pearl, rubies and Diamonds'.[21] While it is merely fanciful to think that Rochester may have attended the play as Bendo, it seems unthinkable that he would have missed the performance altogether, a performance carrying with it such social and literary significance. Characteristically throwing caution to the winds, it is likely that he watched the play.

Second, it is true that Rochester had an affair with the enigmatic Mrs Barry. This is verified in a letter to him from his friend at Court, Henry Savile, dated 17 December 1677: 'the greatest newes I can send you from hence is what the King told mee last night, that your Lp has a daughter borne by the body of Mrs Barry of which I give your honour joy'. Then, in mild rebuke, Savile continues, 'I doubt she dos not lye in in much state for a friend and protectrice of hers in the Mall was much lamenting her poverty very lately not without some gentle reflexions on your Lps want either of generosity or bowells toward a lady who had not refused you the full enjoyment of all her charms'.[22] But in his comedy of power and conquest, Etherege has captured this strain of the libertine in Dorimant: '"For Mrs. Loveit." What a dull, insipid thing is a billet-doux written in cold blood, after the heat of the business is over!' (*The Man of Mode*, I, 3–5). But, as far as Rochester and Mrs Barry are concerned, it is difficult to trace with any accuracy the course which their relationship took both before and after the birth of the child known as 'Little Barry', and whether their *amour* around the time of the performance was strong enough to have informed audience appreciation of the libertine figure of Rochester–Dorimant and his treatment of his three principal women: Mrs Loveit, Bellinda and Harriet. The letters from Rochester, and supposedly to Barry, make no mention of her by name, and, although when read in apparent chronological order, they do tell of a liaison which moves from the idyllic, through an irritated jealousy to bitterness, there is no certain evidence that they are to her. Rochester, after all, was connected, in fact and fiction, with numerous women, among them, for example, Mrs Boutel, a leading actress in the King's company who had recently created the role of Margery Pinchwife in *The Country Wife* (1675). Greene refers to her as a mistress of Rochester four times, citing as his source Tom Davies's *Memoirs of Nell Gwyn* which are reprinted in Davies's edition of Downes's *Roscius Anglicanus* (1789): 'It noways appear that Lord Rochester was ever enamoured of her [Gwyn]. Mrs Barry was his passion, and Mrs Boutel antecedently to Mrs Barry, at the time when Mrs Gwyn trod the stage.'[23]

There is an incident recounted first in Curll's *The History of the English Stage*, and later in *The London Stage*, where Boutel and Barry were involved in an on-stage battle for supremacy, conceivably, but not very likely, sparked by their reciprocal jealousy over Rochester. The main problem in assigning the letters to Barry, or to another actress, lies, as Prinz first pointed out, in their specific lack of information regarding plays, performers or criticism of performance.[24] Barry had begun her career in 1675, playing the supporting role of a maid, Draxilla, in Otway's *Alcibiades*, and, if Colley Cibber is correct, she made no significant impact upon her debut on either audience or players: 'There was, it seems, so little hope of Mrs. Barry at her first setting out, that she was, at the end of the first year, discharg'd the company among others that were thought to be a useless expence to it.'[25] It seems reasonable in the light of her subsequent rise to stardom that the letters between an influential Court figure and a struggling actress should contain signs of encouragement (as well as of passion) in a specifically theatrical context. It is possible that there was agreement between the two of them that most professional business be excluded from their correspondence, but there is, perhaps, reference to Rochester trying to secure a part in *Abdelazar* for Barry, in two letters tentatively dated early summer 1676: firstly when he refers to 'my endeavours', which Treglown feels could relate to getting her a part in a play, and, secondly in the following letter which would seem to record the success his 'endeavours' had so far enjoyed: 'In the meantime I can give you no account of your business as yet but of my own part, which I am sure will not be agreeable without others who I am confident will give full satisfaction in a very short time to all your desires'. Another letter, tentatively dated around the time of performance of *The Man of Mode*, 'late Spring, 1676, when Rochester came out of exile', begins in effusive apology: 'If there be yet alive within you the least memory of me (which I can hope only because [all] of the life that remains with me is the dear remembrance of you' but soon moves to effrontery: 'It seems, till I am capable of greater merit, you resolve to keep me from the vanity of pretending any [service to you] at all'.[26]

The letter is signed 'Your restless servant', and it may represent evidence of Rochester's stormy relationship with Barry at this time, although it is equally possible that the two may have been experiencing a period of comparative peace together. However, of crucial importance to the performance of the play is: did Mrs Barry act in it, and, if so, which part did she take? There is tantalising report here, but no certainty. The redoubtable Downes provides a cast list which ascribes to Barry the part of Dorimant's discarded mistress, Mrs Loveit, but doubt about this was first expressed by J. H. Wilson, who felt that Loveit was more likely to have been played by the more experienced and mature Mrs Mary Lee. This judgment was followed by *The London Stage*, although it has since been challenged, first by Hume in *Theatre History Studies* (1985) and then by Milhous and Hume in the 1987 edition of *Roscius Anglicanus*.

Hume argues that 'Loveit was a more important role than we might expect for an inexperienced actress, but Barry could well have been thrust into it by the temporary unavailability of another performer'.[27] This could be true, of course, but there is at least one omission in Downes's casting which could throw further light on the matter: no actress is down to play Harriet, an important part. Harriet is young and attractive, and, as Dale Underwood says, 'She is almost as fond of and quite as skilled at dissembling as he [Dorimant]; and she is far from immune to the pleasure of conquest and power. She has, that is, some of the nature and most of the art of the hero . . . She has something of Loveit's intensity but with a greater self-control.'[28] Besides, each of the first seven roles recorded as being played by Barry – that is, in 1675–6 and into 1677, when she took on her first breeches part in Aphra Behn's *The Rover* – have her as the 'young girl' type. As Elizabeth Howe says, 'In no comedy of this period did Barry play a discarded mistress: she was invariably cast as virgin or wife'.[29] Barry was eighteen years old in 1676, and, if the original intention had been to include her in the cast, it seems far more appropriate to her age and experience that she spoke Harriet's words: 'pardon my want of art. I have not learnt those softnesses and languishings which now in faces are so much in fashion' (*The Man of Mode*, IV.i.105–7). Dorimant's lines are meant to be directed towards an attractive yet ageing woman: 'I am honest in my inclinations and would not, wer't not to avoid offense, make a lady a little in years believe I think her young, wilfully mistake art for nature, and seem as fond of a thing I am weary of as when I doted on't in earnest' (II.ii.187–91).

It is tempting to think there may be a clue to the identity of the actress who first played Harriet as it is drawn by Etherege. Medley refers to Harriet as having:

> a fine, easy, clean shape; light brown hair in abundance; her features regular; her complexion clear and lively; large, wanton eyes; but above all, a mouth that has made me kiss it a thousand times in imagination – teeth white and even, and pretty, pouting lips, with a little moisture ever hanging on them . . . Then she's as wild as you would wish her, and has a demureness in her looks that makes it so surprising. (I, 126–31)

This portrait is clearly at odds with the description of Mrs Barry cited by Pinto and others taken from the 1889 edition of Cibber's *Apology*, edited by R. W. Lowe, with a significant addendum by the strolling player Anthony Aston, who was performing for the first time in 1722. Aston's picture of 'a fine creature [but] not handsome, her mouth op'ning most on the Right Side, which she strove to draw t'other way, and, at times, composing her Face, as if sitting to have her Picture drawn. [She was] middle siz'd and had darkish Hair, light Eyes, dark Eye-brows and was indifferently plump', is of an older, more mature person, a picture he may have received from Cibber himself, who began acting for the United Company in 1690.[30] Because there is no independent evidence to corroborate Aston, this description of Barry should be approached with caution.

Etherege's drawing of Harriet is more likely to be an idealised picture of a particular type – in this case, the sprightly, exuberant and young leading lady – the part being written to accommodate a succession of youthful and pretty actresses over the years. As with the portraiture of the time, there is a conventional treatment of the subject: a depiction of features and facial texture which, to take the portrait of Rochester attributed to Jacob Huysmans, tends to concentrate on social expectation: a clear linear description of a full mouth, an aquiline nose and rounded eyes. Such characteristics also define portraits of Charles II and of Nell Gwyn: there is a common denomination and an expectation of shape that rules out much variation. So it is not surprising in Aphra Behn's *The Rover* that Hellena (a part Barry is known to have played in May 1677, also at Dorset Garden) refers to herself as being 'well Shap't', 'clean limb'd' and 'sweet breath'd' (I.45–6). Later, when she removes her vizard and Willmore (played by Betterton) sees her face for the first time, he exclaims: 'By heaven, I never saw so much beauty! Oh the charms of those sprightly black eyes! That strangely fair face full of smiles and dimples! Those soft round melting cherry lips and small white teeth!' (*The Rover*, III.i.190–5).[31]

That the descriptions of these two female characters seem to concur represents no substantial evidence that both parts were written with Mrs Barry in mind, but Elizabeth Howe's convincing argument, especially when referring to revivals of the plays in the early 1700s, makes the idea far more tenable. Referring to *The Man of Mode* with Barry as Mrs Loveit in recorded performances in November 1706 and April 1708, Howe states

> [there was] also in April, 1708, incidentally ... a revival of *The Rover* in which Barry played another discarded mistress, Angellica Bianca. Since Barry played the heroine of the latter in 1677, it would seem natural that she played also the heroine of *The Man of Mode* at that time.[32]

Another report that surrounds Rochester and Barry at this time is his alleged coaching of the actress. It is first reported in Cibber's *Apology* that 'There was, it seems, so little hope of Mrs Barry at her first setting out, that she was at the end of her first year discharg'd the Company, among others that were thought to be a useless Expence to it'. This report is enlarged in Curll's *History of the English Stage*, where Barry was 'Three times ... rejected', before Rochester intervened and under his personal tutelage trained her for the stage. The title-page of Curll's *History* proclaims the work to be not his but Betterton's, and it seems likely that he compiled it with reference to the actor's papers, and with some assistance from the antiquarian William Oldys. If Betterton's papers were consulted, the results ought to inspire confidence, as the actor must have known Barry very well, but, irritatingly, Curll does not indicate which of the points he makes are validated by Betterton. Consequently he, too, is to be approached with caution. Writing more than sixty years after Rochester's death, and with no independent corroboration, he tells how Rochester 'entered into a Wager, that by proper instruction, in less than six Months he would engage she should be the finest Player on the Stage'. He is supposed to have instructed her in two roles: the 'Little Gipsy' in *The Rover*, which is known to have been a success, and Isabella in Orrery's *Mustapha*, of which there is no authoritative record of her performance. Cibber, whose *Apology* was published in 1740 (a year earlier than Curll's *History*), makes no mention of Rochester, but does, though, refer to the difficulty Barry was experiencing at the time: 'I take it for granted that the Objection to Mrs Barry at that time, must have been a defective Ear, or some unskilful Dissonance, in her manner of pronouncing'.[33] Curll attributes Barry's triumphant return to the stage to Rochester appealing to her 'very good Understanding' and insisting she 'enter into the Nature of such Sentiment, perfectly changing herself as it were into the Person, not merely by the proper Stress or Sounding of the Voice, but feeling really, and being in the Humour, the Person she represented, was supposed to be in'.[34] Davies, in *Dramatic Miscellanies* (1785, 3 vols) repeats the story; J. H. Wilson is frankly sceptical whether such extensive rehearsals existed at all; and Pinto, after sounding the right note in questioning what 'truth there may be in the details of the story', proceeds with detailed analysis of the rehearsals, according to Rochester the directorial insight of a Stanislavsky in his approach to the art of acting in the Restoration theatre, 'It shows him as a champion of individualism and realism in the theatre as he was in poetry'.[35]

If indeed Rochester did coach Mrs Barry, as Curll insists, then he was at least partially responsible for helping to develop one of the most formidable female acting talents known to the English stage, for, as Cibber testifies:

> [Mrs Barry] had a Presence of elevated Dignity, her Mien and Motion superb, and gracefully majestick; her Voice full, clear, and strong, so that no Violence of Passion could be too much for her: And when Distress, or Tenderness possess'd her, she subsided into the most affecting Melody, and Softness. In the Art of exciting Pity, she had a Power beyond all the Actresses I have yet seen, or what your Imagination can conceive.[36]

It is known that Cibber had a tendency towards effusive flattery, but it is also true to say that he recognised real talent when he saw it on the stage. As he defines Barry's style of tragic acting and of her artistic achievement in that genre, it is really a standard not to be emulated again until the mature emergence of 'the tragic muse', Mrs Siddons who, like Barry, suffered initial failure on the London stage and a temporary rejection from it in 1775–6, although Siddons, unlike Barry, after her services were dispensed with 'was compelled to spend the following six years practising her art in the provinces, chiefly at York and Bath'.[37]

As for Rochester – part man, part myth – his involvement with, arguably, the greatest actress of the Restoration and her rise to fame is, typically, lacking in substantiated evidence, and it is still unclear just how far he helped to influence her career and how much of a sustained interest he took in developing her stage presence and in promoting the art of acting in general. Despite her fame and success though, and her reputedly genteel upbringing with Lady Davenant, Mrs Barry was effectively a servant, albeit one who was much in demand.

In the play world of *The Man of Mode*, Dorimant's *ennui* with a discarded mistress, 'after the heat of the business is over', is all too evident, but so too is his liking and care for Handy and others from the lower orders. Act I.i is a private scene, in which Dorimant, clothed in 'gown and slippers', quibbles and trades insults with his servants, frank and unaffected:

> *Dorimant.* Is the coach at the door?
> *Handy.* You did not bid me send for it.
> *Dorimant.* Eternal blockhead!
>
> > [Handy offers to go out.
>
> > Hey, sot!
> *Handy.* Did you call me, sir?
> *Dorimant.* I hope you have no just exception to the name, sir?
> *Handy.* I have sense, sir.
> *Dorimant.* Not so much as a fly in winter.
>
> > (*The Man of Mode*, I.i. 559–64)

Dorimant's manner reflects, in the words of Bishop Burnet, 'that openness of heart and hand which sometimes makes a libertine so amiable'.[38] Aside from the humour and Handy's ironic tone here, there is, beneath the surface of Dorimant's badinage, a genuine affection for his man, which, by implication informs Rochester's relationship with his own servants. Two further pieces of evidence point to Rochester caring not only deeply for Mrs Barry but also for their child. The first refers to a time after Rochester's death when his niece, the poet Anne Wharton, was looking after the child, and this is not necessarily the child 'Elizabeth Clerke' mentioned in Rochester's will; the second is a reference in a letter from the Wharton family to Mrs Barry, again after the Earl's death, indicating that the two parties were still in contact.[39] Did Rochester really discard his famous mistress, and follow Dorimant's treatment of Mrs Loveit, or was his lot to pursue Mrs Barry, as the theatrical character chased Harriet?

14

Was Lucina betrayed at Whitehall?

Harold Love

Both Fletcher in the original *Valentinian* and Rochester in the adaptation which he retitled *Lucina's Rape* are creating versions of the Roman past. Putting it as succinctly as possible, I would say that Rochester's version is the more Roman according to the neo-classical construction of Romanness, but that Fletcher's is more faithful to the historical sources.[1] I suspect also that Fletcher was aware, in a way Rochester was not, that he was dealing with the terminal collapse of the Roman world, and that the central conflict of the drama was one between the values of an unregainable heroic past and encroaching barbarism. Rochester's very different concern is with an idealised, timeless Rome whose reigning ethos, though necessarily cast in an imperial mould, is still that of selfless, republican virtue. There is little sense that we are on the brink of an historical abyss. Things may have sagged a bit under Valentinian but Maximus and the army will prop them up again, whereas, in Fletcher, Maximus is simply the next corpse on the conveyor belt. What Rochester has done is to quarry an acceptable neo-classical tragedy – which is to say a tragedy whose real substance is ethical and psychological allegory[2] – out of Fletcher's messier, more circumstantial but much more plausible version of the collapse of the Western empire. The Romanness of Rochester's play is the Romanness of Plutarch and Livy: that of Fletcher's play anticipates the seamier pages of Gibbon, but is also closer to the England both of his time and of Rochester's.

And yet Rochester does make his own kind of connections with England. This is done firstly through *Lucina's Rape* being a play about a court, and secondly by making the palace of Valentinian subtly suggestive of the palace of Whitehall. We are told of the Emperor's 'closet' (II.ii.176), 'the garden gate' (II.ii.173), the 'Councell dore' (III.iii.127); 'the old Hall' (IV.ii.190), the 'great

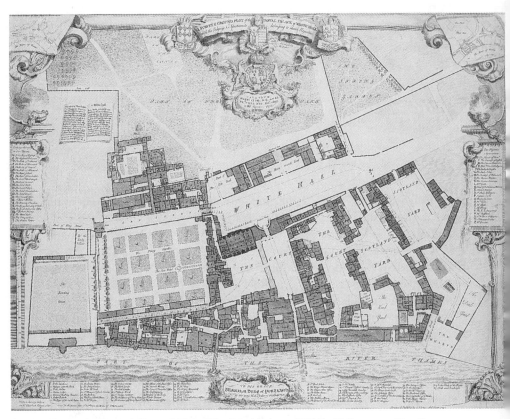

17 *A Survey & Ground Plot of the Royal Palace of White Hall* engraved by George Vertue, 1747. This is based on Greatorex's 1670 survey, and Rochester's lodgings, between the Privy Garden and the Stone Gallery, are marked by a gothic letter 'I'

Chamber' (IV.ii.4), the 'Lobby' (IV.ii.18) and a staircase leading to the royal apartments (IV.ii.78). There are galleries, both public and private, and an 'Appartment . . . That lies upon the Garden' (III.ii.52–3) that is so close to the public gallery that a crime committed in it might be overheard there.[3] All of these locations had counterparts at Whitehall. Fletcher, on the other hand, is not much interested in the architecture of Valentinian's palace, though he conveys a strong sense of the human activities taking place within it. He sees it as a busy, bustling place, in which flunkeys and officials talk and move at a dash, in which discourse shifts rapidly from register to register, and in which grand set pieces like the poisoning of Valentinian or the coronation feast of Maximus are given a pageant-like character which is absent from Rochester's version. Rochester takes over something of Fletcher's rapid comings and goings, especially when the pimps are on stage, but the great events of his play are private not public occasions, and when he introduces a masque it is in order to explore subjectivity, not, as with Fletcher, to display the vulnerability of power.

A memorable image from Rochester's version is that of Æcius roaming through the palace in search of someone to kill him; but the building is deserted – its life is lived in withdrawn spaces, not in its public rooms. Rochester is interested, in a way Fletcher is not, in the enclosures and inner chambers of the palace – the scenes of these intimate, secluded actions. One reason for this must be that in his own life as a courtier he knew them thoroughly.

Fletcher also makes one or two possible connections with Whitehall; but this would have been because Whitehall, and its sister residences around England, were the only palaces he knew, whereas Rochester's generation of educated English males must have had some understanding of what the palace of a Roman emperor was really like. If they were more deeply learned than Rochester himself, this understanding might have embraced the actual literary and archaeological knowledge (such as it then was) of the palace of Domitian or of Hadrian's villa. But Rochester, while on the grand tour, had at least seen genuine Roman ruins, and must have had a clear sense of the monumentality and simplicity of Roman public architecture. He had also seen some of the new generation of neo-classical European palaces which were to culminate in Versailles. In addition, he would have been constantly exposed to the idealised version of ancient architecture that was universal in classicising book illustrations: these presented enormous Parthenon-like buildings with pillars and arcades. Finally, there was the stock scenery used for classical palaces in plays: usually rows of wings in the shape of pillars framing a hall in deep perspective. Even in the case of a somewhat dubious, late emperor like Valentinian III, the instructed imagination must have offered something not unlike a grander version of the Queen's House at Greenwich or the New Exchange. So the fact that Rochester's version of Valentinian's palace is not monumental, classical and unified but a collection of mysteriously linked intimate spaces indicates conscious contrivance.

It should be unnecessary for me to say that the palace of Whitehall was not classical, was not unified and was not even monumental; in fact it was a post-medieval mess. Though Inigo Jones in the reign of Charles I had begun to reconstruct it on neo-classical principles, and had got as far as giving it the Banqueting Hall, the palace in Rochester's time was essentially 'a heap of houses', a vast interlocking fabric of separate and semi-separate structures containing overall about two thousand rooms.[4] If one looks at the ground plan of 1670 prepared by Ralph Greatorex, one sees that it was peppered with tiny courtyards and passageways; Hendrick Danckerts's well-known view from the Park tells the same story (plates 5 and 6). What we are shown looks like and is the roofs of a cramped medieval town: a forest of chimney pots. We should remember too that this already complex structure was far from stable; construction and demolition were always in progress. There can have been few days during the reign of Charles II on which one would not have been aware, distantly or nearby, of the noise of hammers and saws, or of builders' carts clattering over cobbles. Some of this construction was completely transient: the Duchess of Portsmouth had her lodgings torn down and re-built three times before they satisfied her, new favourites demanded apartments, or administrative innovations required office space, and new structures were squeezed in accordingly. It was not until James II's time that anything was done to counteract this. James demolished the major east–west range in order to replace it with an Italian baroque Catholic chapel and a French baroque Queen's palace; but the rest of the palace was still in its older state when all except the Banqueting Hall was gutted by fire in 1698.

One's sense on entering Whitehall, then, cannot have been one of experiencing a grand and harmonious construction with clear pathways to one's goals, but more like entering a warren. This is one of the points made in *Lucina's Rape*. When Lucina arrives in Valentinian's palace she finds herself disoriented:

> *Lucin.* But is my Lord not gone yet, doe you say Sir?
> *Chyl.* Hee is not Madam and must take this kindly,
>   Exceeding kindly of yee, wond'rous kindly,
>   You come soe far to visit him – I'le guide you.
> *Lucin.* Whither?
> *Chyl.*   Why to my Lord.
> *Lucin.*   Is it impossible
>   To finde him in this place without a guide
>   For I would willingly not trouble you?

(IV.ii.65–71)

It is a place of mystery. Space, as we learn, is one of the factors that is being used to entrap Lucina: she is to be deceived about her destination until she is unwittingly brought to the room that Valentinian has decided on as the scene of the crime in 'the Appartment . . . That lies upon the Garden' (III.ii.52–3).

Although Whitehall was a warren, it was a warren which had fixed points of reference in its central garden, called 'the privy garden', and two intersecting galleries which were the eastern and northern boundaries of the garden respectively. So let us orientate ourselves with regard to these. The palace lay on the western bank of the Thames at a point where it runs roughly north–south. Parallel to the river, and therefore also running north–south, was a long two-storeyed gallery: its lower storey was known as the Stone Gallery and its upper storey as the Long Gallery or the Matted Gallery. In the reign of Charles II these were public galleries, in the sense that respectable visitors to the Court had free access to them. Pepys refers to them several times as places in which to have long conversations or simply indulge in energetic exercise when it was too wet to walk in the Park. Security was casual: on the one occasion when he was asked to identify himself he regarded this as something quite exceptional.[5]

At its northern end, the Long Gallery intersected with another second-floor gallery running east–west, which is to say on an axis from the river to Whitehall. In the reign of Charles II this was the Privy Gallery, to which the public were not admitted except by special invitation. The King's and Queen's lodgings and the principal council and reception rooms were accessed from this gallery, and the Duchess of Portsmouth's lodgings were just outside its entrance, at the end of the Long Gallery. The Privy Garden, lying, as mentioned, within the right angle formed by these two galleries, was planted in squares with pathways between them. If one thinks of these two ranges – the north–south and the east–west – framing the garden, and of the garden's western boundary being a street which was a continuation of Whitehall and its southern boundary the orchard and the bowling green, one should have a fair idea of the southern section of the palace complex. The other two things to bear in mind are that the area between the north–south gallery and the river was heavily built over with offices, kitchens and courtiers' lodgings, and that on the western side of the gallery four buildings extruded into the garden.

Let us look in *Lucina's Rape* for references to the public areas of the Court. One of the most striking comes in Lycias's imaginary account of tumult on the rumour of civil war – a passage that, like most of those quoted in this chapter, is one of Rochester's additions to Fletcher:

> In all Obedient hast I went to Court
> Where busy crowds confus'dly did resort:
> Newes from the Camp it seemes was then arriv'd
> Of Tumults rays'd and civill Warres contriv'd.
> The Emperour frighted from his Bed does call
> Grave Senators to Counsell, In the Hall.
> Throngs of ill favour'd faces fill'd with Scarres
> Wait for employments praying hard for warres;

> At Councell dore attend with faire pretence
> In knavish decency and Reverence
> Banquers, who with officious diligence,
> Lend money to supply the present need
> At treble use, that greater may succeed,
> Soe Publique wants will private plenty breed.
>
> (III.iii.119–32)

This seems a lot more English to me than Roman. At Whitehall, sights such as these must have accompanied the outbreak of the Third Dutch War on 17 March 1672. The area described is called the Hall but seems from its function to correspond to the public galleries of the palace, rather than either of its known halls. A later reference to the galleries is more specific. The Emperor is arranging details of his crime with Lycinius:

> *Emp.* Where are the Masquers that shoud Dance to Night?
> *Lycini.* In the old Hall Sir going now to practice.
> *Emp.* About it straight, 'twill serve to draw away
>   Those listning Fooles who trace it in the Gallery;
>   And if (be chance) odd noises shoud bee heard,
>   As womens shrieks or soe, say tis a play
>   Is practicing within.
> *Lycini.*   The Rape of Lucrece
>   Or some such merry pranck – it shall bee done Sir.
>
> (IV.ii.189–96)

Here it is very clear what Valentinian is saying. Sightseers and courtiers have gathered in the Gallery – clearly here the public gallery, corresponding to the Long or the Stone Galleries at Whitehall. The masquers on the other hand are practising in the 'old Hall'. In terms of Whitehall this would be Wolsey's original hall of 1528; and it is very appropriate that the rehearsal would be taking place there because it was now the Court theatre. It was first altered for this purpose in 1665 by the provision of proper dressing rooms and a tier of seating at the south end.[6] During the winter of 1674–5 the Old Hall was in use for the prolonged rehearsals for John Crowne's Court masque, *Calisto*, with further structural changes made in this connection, including a new ceiling to improve acoustics. When *Valentinian* itself was performed at Court, after Rochester's death, it was done as a matter of course in the Old Hall.

The relationship of the spaces in Valentinian's palace is also right for Whitehall. The Old Hall stood a little to the north of the intersection of the two galleries. The sound of music would easily cover that distance and perform the function proposed by Valentinian of drawing away those who were killing time in the Long and Stone Galleries. The other piece of information we have been given is that the sound of screams in the 'Apartment . . . that lies upon the Garden' might be heard in the Gallery. This would also hold true of Whitehall, as we shall see.

With this information in mind we can begin to follow Lucina into the palace. Her arrival is revealed to us in the conversation of the pimps:

> *Licini.* How now –
> *Chyl.*   She's come –
> *Balb.*   Then Il'e to the Emperour –
> > > *Exit Balbus*
>
> *Chyl.* Is the musick plac't well?
> *Lycin.*   Excellent.
> *Chyl.* Lycinius you and Proculus receive them
>   In the great Chamber at her entrance.
>
> > > (IV.ii.1–4)

Lucina has entered the palace but has not yet reached the 'great Chamber'; instead she finds herself in a ground floor public gallery similar to the Stone Gallery at Whitehall. This is made clear by her conversation with Chylax:

> *Chyl.* My only trouble Madam is my fear
>   I'me too unworthy of so great an Honour;
>   But here you're in the publique Gallery
>   Where the Emperour must pass – unless you'd see him.
> *Luci.* Blesse me Sir, no – pray lead mee any whither.
>   My Lord cannot be long before he find mee.
>
> > > (IV.ii.72–7)

The suggestion that the Emperor might suddenly appear in the public gallery is knowingly false on this occasion; but it was not unusual for Charles II to walk in the galleries. Pepys records one such occasion which is quite suggestive of the ambience of the place in the early Restoration years.[7] The next step for a visitor to the palace would be to ascend to the first-floor galleries by a staircase, known as the Adam and Eve staircase because of the gilt paintings of 1607 by John de Critz with which it was decorated. Lucina does the same:

> *Lycin.* She's coming up the Staires: now the Musick,
>   And as that softens her Love will grow warme
>   Till she melts downe, then Cesar lays his stamp.
>   Burn those perfumes there!
>
> > > (IV.ii.78–81)

Having arrived this far, Lucina is greeted by Phorba and Ardelia. As part of the plan Lucina's two waiting women are to be separated from her:

> Tis necessary that her shee companions
> Bee cut off in the Lobby by the women
> They'd break the business else.
>
> > > (IV.ii.17–19)

('Lobby' is taken over from Fletcher.) Phorba and Ardelia initially set out to reassure Lucina. When she asks where Maximus is Phorba replies:

> *Phor.* We'll lead you to him hee's i'th Gallery.
> *Ard.* We'll shew you all the Court too.
>
> (IV.ii.126–7)

In fact Maximus is not in the Court at all; but, if he was, one of the galleries would be the most likely place. The separation of Lucina from her women is accomplished very quickly in stage time. Only a couple of speeches after the women's joint exit, the Emperor drags in Lucina, who is now alone with him. At the end of their exchange he pretends she is to be taken to Maximus, though in reality she is being taken to the place appointed for the crime. 'I dare not do it here' is his comment (IV.ii.171), which would be appropriate enough if he was in a public gallery. Before he follows her, he has the conversation about the maskers already quoted and gives Chylax the excuse he is to use if shrieks from the apartment should be heard in the gallery.

The place where the crime is to be committed has already been described to us in III.ii where the Emperor orders:

> *Emp.* . . . . You see the Appartment made very fine
> That lies upon the Garden: Masques and Musick
> With the best speed you can, and all your Arts
> Serve to the highest, for my Masterpiece
> Is now on foot –
>
> (lines 52–6)

The apartment that lies upon the garden is Rochester's addition to Fletcher, and is not present in any of the other sources for the story. The vital question here is whether it may be another reference to a recognisable part of Whitehall. I have suggested that the scene just mentioned takes place in a space modelled on the Long Gallery. We have seen that the Emperor is worried that sounds from the crime will be heard from there, and that he is relieved that music from the Old Hall, which is also nearby, will draw away those who might otherwise linger in the gallery: we are therefore looking for an apartment that is adjacent to the public gallery and open to the royal garden. At Whitehall this would indicate an apartment in the Privy Garden extending westward from the Stone Gallery (i.e., the ground floor to the Long or Matted Gallery) or southward from the Privy Gallery. To the best of my knowledge there was no such apartment on the garden side of the Privy Gallery in Rochester's time: the royal apartments, like the gallery itself, were on the first floor and the ground floor was given over to offices. The famous back stairs from the royal apartments led down to the Stone Gallery.

But in 1670 there were four apartments on the garden side of the Stone Gallery. The one which is of particular interest is the northernmost one, which is to say the one nearest to the staircase and the royal lodgings. As it happens, we know quite a lot about this structure. The contract for rebuilding it in 1675 is cited in the *Survey of London* from the Works accounts in the Public Record Office: it was to consist of two storeys and a garret floor and 'to correspond in hight and uniformitie of his Matie's Elaboratory'; it was also to have 'a Celler and other conveniencies ... but soe that a light may be preserved into ye stone Gallery'; and in the following year more land was appropriated from the garden to give it a staircase. I cannot imagine that this was an internal staircase, since it would have one already; but would suggest that it was to give direct access to the Long Gallery. The point about this particular building that makes it of interest is its occupant: this was in fact Rochester's apartment at Court. Or perhaps I should say his new apartment, as the records make clear that it was to replace his earlier apartment which had stood nearby.[8] Once again the indication is that we are being told not about an imaginary palace in fifth-century Rome but about a very specific palace in England. The rape of Lucina is to take place in Rochester's own bedroom.

What are we to make of all this? One point to bear in mind is that when the play was performed in the theatre the scenery would not have represented Whitehall, but would have been the conventional Roman interiors described earlier. We are dealing with a verbal game not a visual one. But the references I have cited are insistent enough, I think, for the courtiers in the audience to appreciate their drift, especially if they were seeing the play in the Court Theatre rather than one of the public theatres. At the very least we might use them as a claim to say that Rochester was thinking of the Court Theatre as his primary venue for performance. This Court Theatre was a fully equipped playhouse which charged for admission and had contracted out the right to sell oranges during performances: its only differences from the public theatres were the right to screen its clientele, and that performances were sporadic not continual. It was undoubtedly the best place to see plays in London in the 1670s; and Rochester must have been there very often around the time he was writing *Lucina's Rape*, observing and assisting with the interminable rehearsals for *Calisto*, which was first performed in February 1675.

It would be easy to go on from this to play interpretative games with the fact that the scene of rape seems also to have been the scene of writing; but it is more interesting to enquire why Rochester should have thought fit to adapt this particular play of Fletcher in this particular way at this particular time. Here we have to speculate a little. Such revisions were a good way of learning how to write an original play: that may well have been Rochester's long-term ambition. Quite a number of other amateur writers of the time had undertaken such adaptations, including Rochester's close friend and patron, Buckingham, who had revised another Fletcher play, *The Chances*; but I am going to suggest that in Rochester's case there was also a political motive. It is not easy to date just when he performed his adaptation; but, if we can go by the King's Company cast list that appears in two of the early manuscripts, it can be no later than 1676, but possibly up to a year or two earlier. This brings us close to the sharp change in royal policy that saw the abandonment by Charles II of the comprehending policies of the Cabal ministry (which had led in March 1672 to the Declaration of Indulgence), and the movement towards the pro-French and pro-Anglican policies put into place by Danby.

We need to remember that Buckingham was one of the casualties of this change. Not only was he dismissed in January 1674 from the King's inner council, but he also lost most of his major appointments, among them those of Master of the Horse and Vice-Chancellor of Cambridge; eventually he was despatched for a long holiday in the Tower. There can be little doubt that Rochester, along with Rochester's other close friends, Dorset and Sedley, sympathised with Buckingham's stand from an anti-Yorkist and anti-Danby position.[9] (On Buckingham's eventual release from the Tower, he moved straight into Rochester's apartment at Court.) In other words, they remained loyal servants of Charles but were opposed to the political aspirations of his brother, and of his chief minister who were themselves opposed to each other – James seeking toleration for Catholics while Danby fought to protect the Church of England from both Catholics and Dissenters. The Buckingham faction was part of the coalition that in the course of time brought down Danby and, with the help of the Popish Plot, came close to having York denied the succession, but which in the end was overthrown by its own extremism. Effectively they were anticipating what was soon to become known as the Whig position: thus the choice of a play dealing with the abuses of a corrupt court and a sex-mad despot, and offering opportunities for anti-court polemic, was an appropriate one for a writer who, while still close to the King, was developing opposition sympathies. It is also a play in which, as a result of Rochester's omitting Fletcher's last act, regicide is not punished.

This is not to say that the character of Valentinian is meant as a portrait of Charles II or of James, though there might be a kind of veiled hint of what things would be like if James ever became king. What Valentinian and Charles had in common was an insatiable appetite for sex; but Charles was not, as far as is known, a sadist or a rapist, nor was he bisexual: Valentinian was all three of these things. But there are places in the play where Rochester is able situationally to comment on Charles, one example being where Valentinian is described by Maximus:

> Yet even his errours have their good effects
> For the same Gentle temper which inclines
> His minde to softness do's his heart defend
> From savage thought of Cruelty and Blood
> Which through the Streets of Rome in streams did flow
> From hearts of Senators under the Reignes
> Of our severer warlike Emperours,
> Whilst under this, scarcely a Criminall
> Meets the hard sentence of the dooming Law
> And the whole World dissolv'd into a peace
> Owes its security to this mans pleasures.

(I.i.90–100)

This was a very commonly expressed view of the character of Charles II: his mercy towards criminals was notoriously shown in his pardoning of Thomas Blood in 1671 for his attempt to steal the crown jewels. Lines 469–74 of the same scene seem to hint at Charles II's attitude towards the Earl of Clarendon whom he dismissed from office and drove into exile in November 1667,[10] but the lines spoken by the Emperor over the body of Æcius must surely be directed at Charles's reliance in the mid-1670s on Danby:

> Ah what a Lamentable Wretch is hee
> Who urg'd by feare or sloth yields up his pow'r
> To hope protection from his favourite,
> Wallowing in Ease, and Vice, feels noe contempt
> But weares the empty name of Prince with scorne
> And lives a poore Led Pageant to his Slave?

(V.v.82–7)

We are still getting used to the idea that Rochester may have been the author of the anti-Danby satire *An Allusion to Tacitus* ('The Freeborne English Generous and wise'), but it is interesting to note the similarity in tone between the passage I have just quoted and that poem:

> What King wou'd change to be a Catiline,
> Break his own laws, stake an unquestion'd throne,
> Conspire with vassals to Usurp his own?
> Tis rather some base favourites vile pretence
> To Tyrannize at the wrong'd kings expence.[11]

Yet Rochester does not wish to attack Charles, or Danby, frontally. How could he when he was a serving member of the royal household? What he does is introduce a series of subtle architectural references to Whitehall which amplify the play's otherwise muted allusions to national politics.

As we have seen, these allusions were designed to work in a special venue before a special audience. They also belong to a particular moment in national and Court affairs. Robert D. Hume, in questioning a political reading by Curtis Price of Part 1 of Davenant's *The Siege of Rhodes*, observes that an interpretation possible in 1656 would have been 'no longer pertinent' when that work was revived with its second part in 1661. He concludes, 'Authorial allegory dates just as fast: the more specific and detailed the more evanescent'.[12] So it was to be with Rochester. When *Lucina's Rape* finally reached the stage in 1684, the attendant circumstances had changed, as had the text itself, following a professional rewriting that restored several features of Fletcher's version, including his title.[13] The new *Valentinian* allowed for extensive use of music and dance which, together with strong performances by Betterton and Barry and the broad comedy of the pimps' scenes, made it a popular repertory piece but inevitably de-emphasised the allusions which have been the subject of the present chapter. It was in this form that the play was seen by Charles II at the Court Theatre on 11 February. He is unlikely to have known which parts of the dialogue were by Rochester and which by Fletcher, and was no doubt able to accommodate the dramatic action to the familiar genre of 'usurper' plays in which the errant autocrat was to be identified with Cromwell. Less easy to explain is that the play was given on 16 May 1687 in the same venue before James II, whose own crown was to be snatched from him in the following year. James was no less a whoremonger than his brother, and would have been singularly dull had he failed to perceive that the play contained important lessons for monarchs in his perilous position. Perhaps whoever arranged the performance was trying to teach him such a lesson; but it was hardly Rochester's subtly mediated one.

15

Rochester's 'death-bed repentance'

(from a sermon preached at a 350th anniversary service on
30 April 1997 in All Saints Church, Spelsbury, Oxon.)

RICHARD HARRIES

Lord Rochester's death-bed repentance caused a sensation at the time and
was much quoted by churchmen in the eighteenth and nineteenth centuries.[1]
There were those even then who were sceptical or scornful of it and there is
a tendency in some modern circles to disparage it;[2] I believe that Rochester's
conversion was powerful and authentic, and I suggest some reasons for this.
First, his mother was religious. One way or another her influence on him was
inescapable: for most of Rochester's life he was in revolt against much of
what his mother stood for, and it makes entire psychological sense to think
that in the end he capitulated to her values. This does not mean that what
she believed was true or even desirable, but it is easy to understand how he
could come, after a life of rebellion, to believe what she believed. Secondly,
Rochester's fierce satire against the society of his time bears all the marks of
a disillusioned idealism. Satire, however scurrilous or scatological, gets its
energy not only from the views it attacks but from the sense of corresponding virtues which are betrayed. There is a desperation about both Rochester's
life and his poetry which speaks of disillusionment and betrayed ideals. This
peeps through occasionally as a positive in his recognition of genuine love,
despite his own infidelities and praise of inconstancy, but, more than this,
the violence of his criticisms indicates the power of an ideal that still held
him. Taking these two points together, the influence of his mother as a kind
of female superego and the disillusionment, it is not surprising that Rochester
was often wracked by guilt and gave expression to feelings of bitter remorse.
He went through periods of feeling bad, really bad about himself.

Thirdly, Rochester had both an appetite for life and a fundamental
honesty. He had, wrote Burnet, 'a violent love of pleasure and a disposition
to extravagant Mirth';[3] he was wholehearted in a world in which most of us

A

LETTER

TO

Dr. BURNET,

From the Right Honourable the

Earl of Rochefter,

As he lay on His

DEATH-BED,

AT

𝕳𝖎𝖘 𝕳𝖔𝖓𝖔𝖚𝖗𝖘 𝕷𝖔𝖉𝖌𝖊

IN

Woodftock-Park.

Printed from the Original, wrote with his own Hand,
June 25. 1680. at Twelve at Night.

LONDON,
Printed for *Richard Bentley* in *Ruffel-ftreet* near
Covent-garden. 1680.

(1)

A

LETTER

TO

𝕯𝖗. 𝕭𝖀𝕽𝕹𝕰𝕿,

From the Right Honourable the

Earl of Rochefter.

My moft Honoured
Dr. Burnet,

MY Spirits and Body decay fo equally
together, that I fhall write You a
a Letter as weak as I am in Perfon.
I begin to value Churchmen above all Men
in the World, and You above all the Churchmen I know in it. If God be yet pleafed to
fpare me longer in this World, I hope in
Your Converfation to be exalted to that degree of Piety, that the World may fee how
much I abhor what I fo long lov'd, and how
much I glory in Repentance in God's Service.
Beftow

(2)

Beftow Your Prayers upon me, That God
would fpare me (if it be his good will) to fhew
a true Repentance, and amendment of Life
for the time to come ; or elfe, if the Lord
pleafeth to put an end to my Worldly Being
now, That he would mercifully accept of my
Death-bed Repentance, and perform that Pro-
mife he hath been pleafed to make, *That at
what time foever a finner doth repent, he would
receive him.* Put up thefe Prayers (*moft dear
Doctor*) to Almighty God, for Your moft
obedient and languifhing Servant,

ROCHESTER.

FINIS.

18 *A Letter to Dr. Burnet . . .* 1680

are halfhearted, an extremist in a world where most of us tend to be moder-
ate, controlling our excesses and hedging our bets, and he was honest in
a world where most people dissemble in one way or another. Rochester's
voracious appetite for life and his transparency are attractive qualities, and
they are also part of what made it possible for him to embrace eternal life.
The Argentinian writer Borges has a poem on the Penitent Thief in which
he writes:

> O friends, the innocence of this friend
> Of Jesus! That simplicity which made him,
> From the disgrace of punishment, ask for
> And be granted Paradise.
> Was what drove him time
> And again to sin and to bloody crime.[4]

I suspect that Rochester had something of that directness.

Fourthly, Gilbert Burnet's account rings true. It is not just that he stresses
he could not possibly lie before God: he indicates quite clearly what he
remembers and what he doesn't, what he elaborates and what he reports
verbatim. Basically, he admits to not being able to remember his own arguments in the conversation with Rochester and says that he has extended
them on paper; he also says he left out some of the elaboration of Rochester's
wit but presents the nub of Rochester's objections in his own words. Those
objections come across with great force. A number of times Rochester is
recorded as saying that Burnet's understanding of religion is a 'fancy', or a
'contrivance' (in other words the product of human imagination and very
often one which is self-serving). On another occasion, when Burnet has set
out his argument in defence of a particular aspect of religion, Rochester
replies to the effect that that is all very well but the fact is he can't believe
it. At another point when Burnet is trying to distinguish between religious
experience based on rational and moral principle by sane people and that
which is simply the result of deluded imagination, he gives the example
of people being able to tell whether they are asleep or awake, dreaming
or actually acting something out. Then, as Burnet puts it, 'All this he said he
did not understand, and that it was to assert or beg the thing in Question,
which he could not comprehend'.[5] Again, while Rochester tells Burnet
about how guilty he feels, he honestly admits that he has no sense of sinning
against God, simply a sense of remorse about what he has done to other
people and himself. All this rings true. Finally, Burnet makes it clear that
Rochester remained unconvinced by all the arguments put forward in favour
of revealed religion. His conversion, when it came about, was not directly
as a result of Burnet but through the priest who preached at Rochester's
funeral, Parsons, and it was not the result of rational reflection but of hearing Scripture read.[6]

Rochester was an attractive person, good to look at and enormous fun to be with. It is not difficult to understand why he was a favourite at the Court of Charles II and why Charles was endlessly forgiving of him. He was also an alcoholic, a libertine, who took women as freely as he took wine, and a bitter mocker of conventional morality. Yet he did also have some qualities of conventional goodness. Despite his sexual unfaithfulness to his wife, he clearly cared for her, wrote to her very regularly and felt guilty when he behaved badly towards her.[7] As already mentioned, he had a directness and honesty about him. If, as St Irenaeus said, 'The glory of God is man fully alive', then Rochester was certainly alive.[8] Burnet puts this well in his description:

> his Conversation was easie and obliging; He had a strange Vivacity of thought, and vigour of expression: His Wit had a subtility and sublimity both, that were scarce imitable. His Style was clear and strong: When he used Figures they were very lively, and yet far enough out of the Common Road. (p. 7)

Women loved him and it is not difficult to think of Christ loving him, the Christ who said to the penitent thief on the cross, 'Today shalt thou be with me in paradise' (Luke 23.43).[9] Jesus told parables about the shepherd who left ninety-nine sheep in order to scour the countryside for the one who was lost, and about the prodigal son who was joyfully welcomed back home by his father; both were referred to at Rochester's funeral, for, as Jesus said, 'joy shall be in heaven over one sinner that repenteth, more than over ninety and nine just persons, which need no repentance' (Luke 15.7). Rochester was one of those who sinned boldly and who repented boldly, and he stands in contrast to those who are small-minded in their sinning and mean-minded in their repentance. It is understandable that churchmen in the past should have exulted in the conversion of Rochester; it is, however, more edifying to see what lessons we might learn from his life and death today.

Dr Johnson in his essay on Rochester wrote: 'He lost all sense of religious restraint; and, finding it not convenient to admit the authority of laws which he was resolved not to obey, sheltered his wickedness behind infidelity'.[10] Burnet made something of the same point as well, and it was not difficult to do, for Rochester said quite honestly that he objected to religion, amongst other things, because it put restraints on his desire for women and alcohol.[11] That, though, was only one of his objections to religion and he was quite open about it: he did not use his lack of belief as a cover or excuse for it, and his lack of belief had substance behind it. So one of the points that we might take from his life is the importance of weighing seriously the arguments and objections to the Christian faith, for some of Rochester's objections are as valid today as they were then. Burnet was in my view a skilled apologist for the faith and a sensitive pastor to Rochester; he cared about Christian truth and wanted Rochester to believe. Not all his arguments are convincing, but the point is that he was seriously and thoughtfully engaged. This is vital, not as mere propaganda, which is always counterproductive, but sincerely in the interest of truth: Rochester raised not just questions and difficulties about the faith but objections to it on both intellectual and moral grounds. Those moral objections need to be taken particularly seriously. A second point is that one of the major reasons for Rochester's disbelief was what he perceived as the hypocrisy of the Church. In *A Satyre against Reason and Mankind* he castigates clergy who 'hunt good Livings, but abhor good Lives';[12] he enlarged on this point to Burnet, who wrote:

> He upon that told me plainly, There was nothing that gave him, and many others, a more secret encouragement in their ill ways, then that those who pretended to believe, lived so that they could not be thought to be in earnest, when they said it: For he was sure Religion was either a meer Contrivance, or the most important thing that could be: So that if he once believed, he would set himself in great earnest to live suitably to it. The aspirings that he had observed at Court, of some of the Clergy, with the servile ways they took to attain to Preferment, and the Animosities among those of several Parties, about trifles, made him often think they suspected the things were not true, which in their Sermons and Discourses they so earnestly recommended. Of this he had gathered many Instances; I knew some of them were Mistakes and Calumnies; Yet I could not deny but something of them might be too true.[13]

In the end it is not intellectual arguments but the profound moral appeal of Christianity or moral revulsion against Christian practice or certain aspects of Christian doctrine that sways people. Burnet recognised this when he referred to the character of Christ. Rochester had been putting forward various objections to the faith and Burnet countered this first by saying that one had to see the Christian faith as a whole, including the great benefits it had brought to the human condition, and secondly one should focus upon Jesus himself:

> Interest appears in all Humane Contrivances: Our Saviour plainly had none; He avoided Applause, withdrew Himself from the Offers of a Crown: He submitted to Poverty and Reproach, and much Contradiction in his Life, and to a most ignominious and painful Death.[14]

It is highly significant that Rochester's final conversion to the faith was brought about by the reading of Isaiah 53, the suffering servant passage, with its sublime picture of a servant of God bruised and battered for human redemption, again which was mentioned at Rochester's funeral. Rochester had said to Mr Parsons:

> That as he heard it read, he felt an inward force upon him, which did so enlighten his Mind, and convince him, that he could resist it no longer: For the words had an authority which did shoot like Raies or Beams in his Mind; So that he was not only convinced by the Reasonings he had about it, which satisfied his Understanding, but by a power which did so effectually constrain him, that he did ever after as firmly believe in his Saviour, as if he had seen him in the Clouds.[15]

As Burnet reminded Rochester, a true turning away from egotism to the beauty of God's love is a rational and calmly principled activity, seriously done and seriously sustained. Rochester was a remarkable sinner who repented and, I believe, genuinely turned away from self-interest to move his life in accord with the music of God.

A
SERMON

PREACH'D at the

FUNERAL

Of the Right Honourable

JOHN Earl of *Rochester*,

WHO

Died at WOODSTOCK-PARK, *July* 26, 1680.

AND WAS

Buried at SPILSBURY in *Oxfordshire*, *August* 9.

By *THOMAS PARSONS*, M. A.
Chaplain to the Right Honourable ANNE
Countess-Dowager of *Rochester*.

---

*I say unto you, that likewise joy shall be in Heaven over one Sinner
that repenteth, more than over ninety and nine just persons that
need no Repentance.* LUKE XV. 7.

The THIRTEENTH EDITION.

❧ All the leud and profane Poems and Libels of the late Lord
ROCHESTER having been (contrary to his dying Request, and
in Defiance of Religion, Government, and common Decency)
publish'd to the World, and (for the easier and surer Propaga-
tion of Vice) in Penny-Books, and cry'd about the Streets of
this City, without any Offence taken at them; 'tis humbly
hop'd that this short Discourse, which gives a true Account
of the Death and Repentance of that Noble Lord, may likewise (for the Sake of his Name) find a favourable Reception
among some Persons.

LONDON:

Printed for THOMAS ASTLEY, at the ROSE in
St. *Paul's Church-Yard*, 1728.

Price 4 *d*, or £ 1 : 10 *s*. ℔ Hundred,

19 Title-page of *A Sermon Preach'd at the Funeral of the Right Honourable
John Earl of Rochester . . . 1728*. Within fifty years of Rochester's death,
the sermon had reached its thirteenth edition

20 Portrait of Elizabeth, Countess of Rochester (d. 1681)

NOTES

Short references used in the notes

1680   *Poems on Several Occasions by the Right Honourable, the E. of R—* (London, 1680)

1685   *Poems on several Occasions. Written by a late Person of Honour* (London, 1685)

1691   *Poems, etc. on Several Occasions: With Valentinian; A Tragedy. Written by the Right Honourable John Late Earl of Rochester* (London, 1691)

Burnet   Gilbert Burnet, *Some Passages of the Life and Death of the Right Honourable John, Earl of Rochester* (London, 1680)

Chernaik   Warren Chernaik, *Sexual Freedom in Restoration Literature* (Cambridge and New York, 1995)

Critical Heritage   Rochester: The Critical Heritage, edited by David Farley-Hills (London, 1972)

Greene   Graham Greene, *Lord Rochester's Monkey: being the Life of John Wilmot, Second Earl of Rochester* (London, Sydney and Toronto, 1974)

Griffin   Dustin Griffin, *Satires against Man: The Poems of Rochester* (Berkeley, Los Angeles and London, 1973)

Letters   The Letters of John Wilmot Earl of Rochester, edited by Jeremy Treglown (Oxford, 1980)

Rochester 1968   *The Complete Poems of John Wilmot, Earl of Rochester*, edited by David M. Vieth (New Haven and London, 1968)

Rochester 1984   *The Poems of John Wilmot Earl of Rochester*, edited by Keith Walker (Oxford, 1984)

Rochester 1993   *Rochester: Complete Poems and Plays*, edited by Paddy Lyons (London and Rutland, Vermont, 1993)

Rochester 1994   *John Wilmot, Earl of Rochester: The Complete Works*, edited by Frank H. Ellis (Harmondsworth, 1994)

Rochester 1999   *The Works of John Wilmot Earl of Rochester*, edited by Harold Love (Oxford, 1999)

Spirit of Wit   Spirit of Wit: Reconsiderations of Rochester, edited by Jeremy Treglown (Oxford, 1982)

Thormählen   Marianne Thormählen, *Rochester: The Poems in Context* (Cambridge, 1993)

1   Introductory

1 Greene, pp. 9, 10. The preface was written shortly before the biography was published.

2 Alexander Pope, *An Essay on Criticism*, line 298.

3 John Sheffield, Earl of Mulgrave, *An Essay upon Poetry* (1682), quoted in *Critical Heritage*, pp. 42–3.

4 See Rochester, *Valentinian: A Tragedy* (1685), sigs a1r–c1v; 'They call whatever is not Common, nice' (*A Letter from Artemiza in the Towne to Chloe in the Countrey*, line 59); Samuel Pepys, letter to Will Hewer, 4 November 1680, quoted in *Critical Heritage*, p. 7.

5 *Critical Heritage*, pp. 94–104, 137–60, 161, 177; Samuel Johnson, *The Lives of the English Poets; and a Criticism of their Works*, 3 vols (Dublin, 1779), I, 428.

6 *The Dictionary of National Biography*, vol. LXII (London, 1900), pp. 63–7 (p. 66).

7 Edmund Gosse, 'Rochester' in *The English Poets*, 5 vols, edited by T. H. Ward (London, 1880), II, 424–5 (p. 425).

8 In 1989, for example, the present writer asked the then Dean of Wesminster, The Very Reverend Michael Mayne, whether he would consider allowing a memorial to Rochester in Westminster Abbey; he declined specifically on the basis of the inappropriateness of honouring in the Abbey someone whose work was described in the *DNB* as 'licentious' (personal letter dated 24 January 1989).

9 *The Cambridge History of English Literature*, 8, edited by A. W. Ward and A. R. Waller (Cambridge, 1912), pp. 198–221 (p. 206). See also *Critical Heritage*, pp. 2, 25.

10 *Collected Works of John Wilmot Earl of Rochester*, edited by John Hayward (London, 1926); *Poems by John Wilmot Earl of Rochester*, edited by Vivian de Sola Pinto (London, 1953); *The Complete Poems of John Wilmot, Earl of Rochester*, edited by David M. Vieth (New Haven and London, 1968); *The Poems of John Wilmot Earl of Rochester*, edited by Keith Walker (Oxford, 1984); *John Wilmot, Earl of Rochester: The Complete Works*, edited by Frank H. Ellis (Harmondsworth, 1994); *The Works of John Wilmot Earl of Rochester*, edited by Harold Love (Oxford, 1999).

11 Unless otherwise indicated, reference to *The Imperfect Enjoyment* in this chapter and those that follow is to the poem beginning 'Naked she lay clasp'd in my loving Armes'.

12 David M. Vieth, *Rochester Studies, 1925–1982: An Annotated Bibliography* (New York and London, 1984)

13 See *Critical Heritage*.

14 David Brooks, *Lyrics and Satires of John Wilmot Earl of Rochester* (Sydney, 1980), p. 10.

15 Johannes Prinz, *John Wilmot Earl of Rochester: His Life and Writings* (Leipzig, 1927), pp. 241, 113; Oliver Elton, *The English Muse: A Sketch* (London, 1933), p. 252; Rochester 1968, p. xxxix.

16 *Letters*, pp. 2–3.

17 C. F. Main, 'The Right Vein of Rochester's *Satyr*' in *Essays in Literary History Presented to J. Milton French*, edited by Rudolf Kirk and C. F. Main (New Brunswick, 1960), pp. 93–112 (p. 110).

18 F. R. Leavis, *Revaluation: Tradition and Development in English Poetry* (London, 1936; Harmondsworth, 1964), p. 36; Shakespeare, *As You Like It*, V.iv.79–80.

19 Isobel Grundy, 'Restoration and Eighteenth Century (1660–1780)' in *An Outline of English Literature*, edited by Pat Rogers, 2nd edition (Oxford, 1998), pp. 200–49 (p. 205).

20 Griffin, p. 306; *Rochester Studies 1925–1982*, p. xviii; Peter Beal, *English Literature and History*, Sotheby's Sale Catalogue (London, 18 December 1995), p. 44.

21 *Letters*, p. 67.

22 See Ken Robinson, 'The Art of Violence in Rochester's Satire' in *English Satire and the Satiric Tradition*, edited by Claude Rawson (Oxford, 1984), 93–108 (p. 94).

23 E. A. J. Honigmann, *Myriad-minded Shakespeare: Essays on the Tragedies, Problem Comedies and Shakespeare the Man*, 2nd edition (London, 1998), pp. 1–3.

24 *The Penguin Book of Restoration Verse*, edited by Harold Love (Harmondsworth, 1968), p. 368.

2 'I loath the Rabble': friendship, love and hate in Rochester

1 Aristotle, *Rhetoric*, IV.4, translated by Terence Irwin, in *Other Selves: Philosophers on Friendship*, edited by Michael Pakaluk (Indianapolis and Cambridge, 1991), p. 72.

2 Cicero, *De Amicitia*, translated by Frank Copley, in *Other Selves*, p. 98. Cf. Aristotle, *Nichomachean Ethics, ibid.*, pp. 33–4; and Irving Singer, *The Nature of Love: Plato to Luther*, 2nd edition (Chicago and London, 1984), p. 90.

3 Chernaik, p. 67.

4 *Letters*, p. 117.

5 *Song* ('How perfect Cloris, and how free'), lines 7, 27, 29–32.

6 *Letters*, p. 67; *Satire* ('What vaine unnecessary things are men'), lines 33–4. For further discussion, see Chernaik pp. 73–4, 216–17.

7 *Letters*, p. 67; Francis Bacon, *The Essays*, edited by John Pitcher (Harmondsworth, 1985), p. 142; Cicero, *De Amicitia, Other Selves*, p. 112.

8 *Letters*, pp. 66–7.

9 *Upon his Drinking a Bowl*, line 23; *Letters*, p. 67.

10 Thomas Hobbes, *Leviathan*, edited by Michael Oakeshott (Oxford, 1960), Ch. XIII, p. 81.

11 Bacon, *Essays*, 'Of Love', pp. 88–9; 'Of Friendship', p. 141.

12 Harold Weber, '"Drudging in fair Aurelia's womb": Constructing Homosexual Economies in Rochester's Poetry', *The Eighteenth Century: Theory and Interpretation*, 33 (1992), 99–117, esp. 111.

13 *A Ramble in Saint James's Park*, lines 92, 119–20; *Song* ('Quoth the *Dutchess* of *Cleveland*'), line 11.

14 Lines 3–4, 11–12. The poem and its authorship are discussed at length in Chernaik, pp. 70–2. For an account of *A Ramble in St. James's Park*, see *ibid.*, pp. 74–8.

15 *Letters*, pp. 122, 132; Bacon, *Essays*, p. 142.

16 *Letters*, pp. 187, 189. For another instance of Rochester acting on Nell Gwyn's behalf, serving as her trustee and 'to advise her' in a claim for Irish property worth £800 a year, see *ibid.*, p. 144. On Savile's 'disgrace', the result of voting with the Whig opposition, see *ibid.*, pp. 182, 188–9.

17 Montaigne, 'Of Friendship' (Essay 28), translated by Donald. M. Frame, *Other Selves*, p. 195; Aristotle, *Nicomachean Ethics, ibid.*, p. 67.

18 *Letters*, pp. 108–9; *Against Reason and Mankind*, lines 175–6.

19 *Paradise Lost*, VII, 26–8.

20 *Letters*, pp. 108, 158, 243; *An Allusion to Horace*, line 17.

21 *Letters*, p. 243.

22 *Letters*, p. 119.

23 *Artemiza to Chloe*, lines 38–40; *Against Reason and Mankind*, lines 94, 100–1; Hobbes, *Leviathan*, Chapter VI, p. 32. The influence of Hobbes on Rochester and on Restoration libertinism is discussed in Chernaik, pp. 22–51.

24 *Tunbridge Wells*, lines 35, 40, 84–5, 100; Thormählen, pp. 241–2; see also the account of the poem in David Farley-Hills, *Rochester's Poetry* (London, 1978), pp. 192–3.

25 Lines 100–3. Cf. *Satires*, I.x, lines 72–4, 81–90, in Horace, *Satires, Epistles and Ars Poetica*, edited by H. Rushton Fairclough, Loeb Classical Library (Cambridge, Mass., and London, 1955).

26 *Timon*, line 175; *A Ramble in St. James's Park*, lines 155–7.

3   Dissolver of reason: Rochester and the nature of love

1 Thormählen, p. 83.

2 On Milton, see Gale H. Carrithers, Jr, and James D. Hardy, Jr, *Milton and the Hermeneutic Journey* (Baton Rouge and London, 1994), pp. 30, 44–6. Among present-day theorists on love, see, for instance, Reuben Fine, *The Meaning of Love in Human Experience* (New York, 1985), p. 274, and Vincent Brümmer, *The Model of Love: A Study in Philosophical Theology* (Cambridge, 1993), pp. 206, 240–1.

3 Robert A. Johnson, *The Psychology of Romantic Love* (London, 1983), pp. 191–2.

4 *The School of Love: The Evolution of the Stuart Love Lyric* (Princeton, 1964).

5 See Griffin, pp. 11–12, 18–19, and Thormählen, pp. 42, 100, 106. Pages 42–3 in the latter book deal with the lyric 'To this Moment a Rebell', where security and truth are expressly connected with a gorgeous girl who seems to possess every charm the speaker could want; her very perfections, however, are too overwhelming, and he apparently gets no further than teetering on the brink.

6 Thormählen, pp. 106–10.

7 See Warren Chernaik above, p. 9.

8 See Barton's 'John Wilmot, Earl of Rochester', Chatterton Lecture read on 18 January 1967, *Proceedings of the British Academy*, 53 (1968), pp. 67–8, and Chernaik, pp. 79, 112–15.

9 See, for instance, David Farley-Hills, *Rochester's Poetry* (London, 1978), pp. 78–80.

10 *Confessions*, VIII.7.

11 See 'John Wilmot', pp. 57–8.

12 The poem is reprinted in Rochester 1999, p. 29.

13 'John Wilmot', p. 57.

14 See Rochester 1953, p. 220.

15 See, for instance, Griffin, pp. 10–20; Reba Wilcoxon, 'Rochester's Philosophical Premises: a Case for Consistency', *Eighteenth-Century Studies*, 8 (winter 1974–5), 183–201 (p. 198); Thormählen, pp. 1, 5; and Edward Burns's excellent introduction to *Reading Rochester* (Liverpool, 1995), pp. 1–5.

16 Harold Love kindly drew my attention to the existence of a final stanza in the Harbin manuscript (it is not reproduced in Keith Walker's collated edition) which explicitly identifies the lady with God and the lovers' tribulations with purgatory: 'God does not Heav'n afford untill / In purgatory we / Have felt the utmost pains of Hell – / Then why the Devill shou'd she' (Rochester 1999, p. 29).

17 A more comprehensive discussion of this poem and its seventeenth-century context is found in my article 'Rochester and *The Fall*: the Roots of Discontent', *English Studies*, 69.5 (October 1988), 396–409.

18 Frank Ellis quotes Rochester's alleged rejection of the idea of the fall of man from Burnet, most easily accessible in *Critical Heritage*, p. 65. Ellis suggests that '[t]his fact may switch the tone of the poem from tragi-comic to straight comic' (Rochester 1994, p. 355).

19 Cf. Ronald Berman's contention that *The Fall* parodies the Christian vision of bliss in 'Rochester and the Defeat of the Senses', *The Kenyon Review*, 26.2 (spring 1964), 357. David M. Vieth has noted an 'analogy to religious experience' and religious metaphors, bliss among them, in 'Absent from thee' and 'An Age in her Embraces pas'd'; see '"Pleased with the contradiction and the sin": the Perverse Artistry of Rochester's Lyrics', *Tennessee Studies in Literature*, 25 (1980), 35–56 (pp. 43–7).

20 'The Sense of Nothing', in *Spirit of Wit*, p. 24.

21 I have analysed the social dimension of this poem at some length in 'Rochester and Jealousy: Consistent Inconsistencies', *The Durham University Journal*, 80.2 (n.s. 49.2, June 1988), 213–18.

22 See, for instance, *The Imperfect Enjoyment*, lines 10, 15.

23 Thormählen, p. 101.

24 See, for example, Thomas K. Pasch, 'Concentricity, Christian Myth, and the Self-incriminating Narrator in Rochester's '*A Ramble in St. James's Park*', *Essays in Literature* 6 (spring 1979), 21–8, and Reba Wilcoxon, 'The Rhetoric of Sex in Rochester's Burlesque', *Papers on Language and Literature*, 12.3 (summer 1976), 273–84.

25 *Critical Heritage*, p. 64.

26 *Ibid.*, p. 65.

27 See Martin S. Bergmann, *The Anatomy of Loving: The Story of Man's Quest to Know What Love Is* (New York, 1987), pp. 129–36.

28 See Carrithers and Hardy, *Milton*, pp. 44–8.

29 See n. 26 (p. 124 in Bergmann's book).

30 *The Natural History of Love* (London, 1960), p. 219.

31 Larry Carver conceives Rochester's stance in respect of religion differently, but his article 'Rascal Before the Lord: Rochester's Religious Rhetoric' contains much valuable discussion on the prevalence of Christian notions in Rochester's poetry. First published in *Essays in Literature*, 9 (fall 1982), 155–69, it was reprinted by David M. Vieth in his collection of essays on Rochester, *John Wilmot, Earl of Rochester: Critical Essays* (New York and London, 1988).

32 *Critical Heritage*, p. 77.

4 Rochester and Falstaff

1 *Letters*, p. 193: letter from Rochester to Henry Savile, dated 18–25 June 1678; Rochester 1994, p. 268.

2 *Letters*, pp. 67, 159.

3 Quotations from Shakespeare are from *The Complete Works*, edited by Peter Alexander (London and Glasgow, 1951). Shakespeare's *1 Henry IV* was performed on 2 November 1667, when Pepys praised the way Cartwright played Falstaff's soliloquy on honour. It was performed again in January 1668 and on 18 September in the same year. William van Lennep plausibly presumes that in the two latter cases *1 Henry IV* and not *2 Henry IV* is meant (*The London Stage, 1660–1800: Part I, 1660–1700*, edited by William van Lennep *et al.* (Carbondale, 1965), pp. 122, 127, 146.

4 *Letters*, p. 96.

5 'He knew my style, he swore', in *Spirit of Wit*, pp. 75–91 (p. 79).

6 Of Shakespeare's Falstaff plays, only *1 Henry IV* and *The Merry Wives of Windsor* are known to have been performed on the Restoration stage in Rochester's lifetime. *Merry Wives* was performed on 25 September 1661, 14 August 1667 and 17 December 1675 (*The London Stage, Part I*, pp. 40, 11, 241). Shakespeare's *Henry V*, with its account of Falstaff's death, was not performed, while the Earl of Orrery's *Henry V* (not an adaptation of Shakespeare) has no low company and no allusion to Falstaff.

7 *The Poems of Charles Sackville Sixth Earl of Dorset*, edited by Brice Harris (New York and London, 1979), pp. 8–9; *Letters of Sir George Etherege*, edited by Frederick Bracher (Berkeley, Los Angeles and London, 1974), p. 157: letter from Etherege to Henry Guy dated 3 November 1687.

8 *Letters*, p. 194: the letter is dated 25 June 1678.

9 A. J. Smith, *The Metaphysics of Love* (Cambridge, 1985), p. 244.

10 Walter Kaiser, *Praisers of Folly: Erasmus, Rabelais, Shakespeare* (London, 1964), chapters 16–17. See also *1 Henry IV*, V.iv.2.

11 There is a useful summary in Rochester 1994, p. 269.

12 *Letters*, pp. 195, 198–9.

13 *Letters*, p. 232.

14 'Affairs of State', in *Spirit of Wit*, pp. 92–110 (p. 106).

15 *Letters*, pp. 66–7.

16 *Letters*, pp. 193, 202.

17 *Rollo, Duke of Normandy* was performed on Thursday 6 December 1660, Wednesday 17 April 1667, Monday 9 November 1674 and Monday 19 April 1675 (*The London Stage, Part I*, pp. 22, 106, 223, 231).

18 *Letters*, pp. 202–3.

19 *Spirit of Wit*, p. 26.

20 Thormählen, pp. 70, 72.

21 *The Metaphysics of Love*, p. 249.

22 'Libertinism and Sexual Politics', in *Spirit of Wit*, pp. 133–65 (pp. 155–9).

23 David Farley-Hills, *The Benevolence of Laughter* (London, 1974), pp. 137–8.

24 The Hartwell manuscript, on which Harold Love bases his reading (Rochester 1999), separates the third stanza into two equal parts; the presence of a recurring refrain would seem to indicate, however, that the poem was conceived in terms of three stanzas.

25 *Spirit of Wit*, p. 158.

26 As n. 21 above.

27 Rochester 1994, p. xiii.

28 *The Poems of John Dryden*, edited by James Kinsley, 4 vols (Oxford, 1958), II.852.

5 Rochester's homoeroticism

1 See Paul Hammond, *Love Between Men in English Literature* (Basingstoke, 1996), pp. 1–9.

2 Alan Bray, *Homosexuality in Renaissance England* (London, 1982).

3 Michel Foucault, *Histoire de la sexualité: I: La volonté de savoir* (Paris, 1976), p. 134.

4 For examples see Paul Hammond, 'Marvell's Sexuality', *The Seventeenth Century* 11 (1996), 87–123, and 'Titus Oates and "Sodomy"' in *Culture and Society in Britain 1660–1800*, edited by Jeremy Black (Manchester, 1997), pp. 85–101.

5 Hammond, *Love Between Men in English Literature*, especially pp. 88–9.

6 Hammond, 'Marvell's Sexuality'.

7 Eve Kosofsky Sedgwick, *Between Men: English Literature and Male Homosocial Desire* (New York, 1985).

8 *Letters*, p. 157.

9 *Rochesteriana: Being Some Anecdotes Concerning John Wilmot Earl of Rochester*, edited by Johannes Prinz (Leipzig, 1926), p. 15.

10 *Letters*, pp. 157–8.

11 For example, when writing on 16 January 1680 from Paris to his brother, George Savile, about the imminent arrival there of George's eighteen-year-old son, Henry Savile says:

> My nephew's coming over is the very best news I have heard since he went hence; his chamber shall be ready and clean sheets, with a promise to you that his priveledges in my house shall be only of that kind, and I will never force upon him any of those cruel enemys that come out of the cellar; but, as I know every young man must have a vice, I will not curb him in his inclinations to the sex; and be no otherwise a spy upon him or them, but to examine that all his tackling be sound, and to find good workmen to repair the breaches that may unfortunately happen; and truly I think I owe so much to the stallion of our family, abstracted from the personal kindness I have for him. (*Savile Correspondence: Letters to and from Henry Savile, Esq.*, edited by William Durrant Cooper, Camden Society Publications 71 (1858), pp. 132–3)

Here Savile's promise to examine his nephew's 'tackling' is jocularly offered in the interests of ensuring the continuity of the male line. Savile himself is not known to have married. In an earlier letter he had told his brother:

> As for the pleasures that you tell me there are to be had in these parts, I confess they would be very great ones to one that was not of my humour ... as for ladyes, the fairest cannot tempt me, for I am as rightly cut out for a batchelor as ever was man, and therefore I am much obliged to nature that made me a younger brother. (p. 2)

The tone and implications of this comment are, at this distance, irretrievable.

12 *Familiar Letters: Written by the Right Honourable John late Earl of Rochester, And several other Persons of Honour and Quality*, 2 vols (London, 1697), I, 41–2.

13 For contemporary poems on William's homosexuality see *Poems on Affairs of State*, edited by George deF. Lord *et al.*, 7 vols (New Haven, 1963–75), vol. 5; and Paul Hammond, 'Titus Oates and "Sodomy"', p. 97.

14 French propaganda had spread allegations about William's homosexuality in 1673 (Stephen B. Baxter, *William III* (London, 1966), p. 111). Savile wrote to his brother in 1677: 'Here is Monsr Bentinck, a chief favourite to the Prince of Orange, come over yesterday to his Maj^{ty}, but his business not publickly known' (*Savile Correspondence*, p. 59). The word 'favourite' in this period could, but need not, include a sexual implication: nothing untoward is being committed to paper here.

15 'deserving [the penal colony of] Gyara and prison': a quotation from Juvenal, *Satires*, I.73.

16 *Familiar Letters*, I, 9–10.

17 Treglown suggests that Baptiste may subsequently have tried to blackmail Rochester on the basis of his homosexual interests, but this is no more than conjecture (*Letters*, p. 243). One would like to know more about what prompted the letter from Rochester to Savile concerning the need to 'distinguish from' or 'comply with' certain pages and grooms of the King's Bedchamber (*Letters*, p. 113).

18 See Hammond, 'Titus Oates and "Sodomy"', pp. 89, 100.

19 The following discussion draws on and amplifies some portions of my essay 'Censorship in the Manuscript Transmission of Restoration Poetry' in *Literature and Censorship*, edited by Nigel Smith (Cambridge, 1993) pp. 39–62.

20 Pages 60–1. I quote from the facsimile of the Huntington Library copy published as *Rochester's Poems on Several Occasions*, edited by James Thorpe (Princeton, 1950). A later reprint of this edition is reproduced as figure 6.

21 Peter Beal, *Index of English Literary Manuscripts, Volume II: 1625–1700, Part 2: Lee–Wycherley* (London, 1993) pp. 269–70. See also Rochester 1999, pp. 533–4.

22 See Michael Brennan and Paul Hammond, 'The Badminton Manuscript: A New Miscellany of Restoration Verse', *English Manuscript Studies 1100–1700*, 5 (1995), 171–207.

23 The two leaves preceding *Love to a Woman* in MS Danchin have been torn out, so the context which that MS provides for this poem cannot be precisely established (Pierre Danchin, 'A Late Seventeenth-century Miscellany: a Facsimile Edition of a Manuscript Collection of Poems, largely by John Wilmot, Earl of Rochester', *Cahiers Elisabéthains*, 22 (1982), 51–86).

24 *Poems on several Occasions. Written by a late Person of Honour* (London, 1685).

25 *1685*, p. 49.

26 *Poems, etc. On Several Occasions: With Valentinian; A Tragedy. Written by the Right Honourable John Late Earl of Rochester* (London, 1691).

27 David Vieth, 'An Unsuspected Cancel in Tonson's 1691 "Rochester"', *Papers of the Bibliographical Society of America*, 55 (1961), 130–3, p. 131 n. 2. The cancel is reproduced as figure 6.

28 It is placed in *1691*, quite fittingly, alongside other love songs, coming between 'While on those lovely looks I gaze' and 'To this moment a rebel I throw down my arms'.

29 *1680*.

30 MS Danchin.

31 Nottingham University Library MS Portland PwV 40, p. 66.

32 Nottingham University Library MS Portland PwV 40, p. 66.

33 *1680*, p. 34.

34 MS Tyrrell-Fisher, MS Rutland and Bodleian MS Eng. Misc. e. 536 omit the stanza completely. In MS Tyrrell-Fisher the poem is dated 15 February 1673, so this text comes from a point close to the poem's composition, not from a later milieu. Bodleian Library MS Eng. Poet. e. 4 has the stanza number but omits the stanza itself. Six other manuscripts omit the lines as part of a larger excision, so that cannot be attributed specifically to sensitivity about homosexual sex. For information about variant readings see Rochester 1999, pp. 538–41.

35 Thus Thormählen, p. 22.

36 The exceptions are Nottingham University Library MS Portland PwV 40, p. 211, which agrees with *1680*, and National Library of Ireland MS 2093, which replaces 'fucked' with 'kiss'd'.

37 For example *1680*, pp. 30, 72, 75.

38 Bodleian Library MS Don. b. 8, p. 410.

39 *1680*, p. 29.

40 The exceptions are Nottingham University Library MS Portland PwV 40, p. 204, which once again agrees with *1680*, and Bodleian MS Add. B 106, which may derive from a printed text.

41 Keith Walker and David Vieth both take *1680* as their copy-text here, but both emend 'boy' to 'man' on the strength of the MS evidence. I disagree with the suggestion (Thormählen, p. 21) that the editors should have retained 'boy'. For the textual, grammatical and sexual complexities of the readings at this point see Rochester 1999, pp. 353–4.

42 *1685*, p. 29.

43 There has been disagreement about the exact source of Rochester's poem (see Thormählen, pp. 16–19), but its ultimate origin lies in the two poems which modern scholars now print as nos 4 and 5 of the *Anacreontea* (see *Greek Lyric: Volume II*, edited by David A. Campbell, Loeb Library (Cambridge, Mass., 1988)). The Greek originals were first printed by Henri Estienne in *Anacreontis Teii Odae* (Paris, 1554), with a Latin translation. Such parallel texts continued to be available through the seventeenth century, and Rochester probably used an edition such as *Anacreontis et Sapphonis Carmina. Notas & Animaduersiones addidit Tanaqvillvs Faber* (Saumur, 1660). He was said by contemporaries to be proficient in the classical languages, but he seems to have also consulted Ronsard's adaptation, and possibly Stanley's.

44 *1680*, p. 57.

45 *Anacreontea* IV.12–21: 'Put vines on for me with bunches of grapes on them and Bacchants picking them; put a wine-press and men treading it, the satyrs laughing, Loves all in gold, Cythere laughing together with handsome Lyaeus, Love and Aphrodite' (Loeb translation).

46 *Anacreontea* V.16–19: 'Under a spreading leafy vine covered with bunches of grapes add handsome youths, unless Phoebus is playing there' (Loeb translation).

47 'An Ode of Anacreon Paraphras'd: The Cup', lines 42–57, in *The Poems of John Oldham*, edited by Harold F. Brooks with the collaboration of Raman Selden (Oxford, 1987), p. 217.

48 Nathaniel Lee, *The Princess of Cleve*, III.i.129–33; cited from *The Works of Nathaniel Lee*, edited by Thomas B. Stroup and Arthur L. Cooke, 2 vols (New Brunswick, 1955). The allusion is noted in Rochester 1994, p. 336.

49 Act I scene i and Act II scene iii.

50 Bodleian MSS Eng. Misc. e. 536 and Rawl. Poet 173, the latter perhaps copied from *1691*. For other variants see Rochester 1999, pp. 366, 534.

51 Thormählen, pp. 22–3.

52 *1680*, p. 60.

53 *1685*, p. 48.

54 Huntington MS HA 12525; quoted from Rochester 1984, p. 311.

55 See Hammond, 'Censorship in the Manuscript Transmission of Restoration Poetry'.

56 Hammond, *Love Between Men in English Literature*, pp. 93–4.

57 However, I offer no opinion as to the authorship of *Sodom*.

58 *Valentinian: A Tragedy. As 'tis Alter'd by the late Earl of Rochester* (London, 1685), p. 19.

59 In the production which was planned to take place circa 1675–6 it was intended that Lycias would be played by Thomas Clark and Valentinian by Charles Hart (*The London Stage 1660–1800: Part 1: 1660–1700*, edited by William Van Lennep (Carbondale, 1965), p. 238). There is an intriguing echo in this casting of the roles which they took in Lee's *The Rival Queens* in 1677, when Hart played Alexander and Clark played Hephestion; even more intriguing is the fact that Hart and Clark also played Antony and Dolabella in *All for Love*, which makes one wonder how that relationship was portrayed on stage (*London Stage*, pp. 255, 265).

60 *Valentinian: A Tragedy*, pp. 74–5.

6 Love in the ayre: Rochester's songs and their music

1 Samuel Johnson, *The Lives of the English Poets; and a Criticism of their Works*, 3 vols (Dublin, 1779), I, 428–9.

2 *Boswell's Life of Johnson*, edited by George Birkbeck Hill, 6 vols (London, 1889), III, 191. For the background to *The English Poets*, see the letter from Edward Dilley to Boswell (26 September 1777) reprinted in *Johnson: The Critical Heritage*, edited by James T. Boulton (London, 1971), p. 251.

3 The other poems omitted are *To Love* ('Oh! Love how cold and slow') and 'Impia blasphemi sileant convitia vulgi'. 'What Cruel pains' is placed after 'Phillis, be gentler, I advice', and added are 'Too late, alas, I must confess', 'Since the Sons of the Muses' (by Settle), *An Allusion to Horace* and *Verses to Sir Carr Scroope*.

4 *Letters*, p. 31.

5 See *Critical Heritage*, p. 193.

6 See *Critical Heritage*, pp. 195, 15; Maynard Mack, *Collected in Himself: Essays Critical and Biographical on Pope and Some of His Contemporaries* (Newark, London and Toronto, [1982]), pp. 394–5, 437–8.

7 Burnet, p. 25.

8 Burnet, pp. 47–8.

9 David Vieth, 'A Textual Paradox: Rochester's *To a Lady in a Letter*', *Papers of the Bibliographical Society of America*, 54 (1960), 147–62, p. 147; Rochester 1984, p. 249. See also Rochester 1994, p. 393.

10 For Rochester's characteristic use of a single word to alter the focus of a poem, see, for example, Anne Righter [Barton], 'John Wilmot, Earl of Rochester', *Proceedings of the British Academy*, 53 (1967), 47–69 (p. 62) and Ken Robinson, 'The Art of Violence in Rochester's Satire' in *English Satire and the Satiric Tradition*, edited by Claude Rawson (Oxford, 1984), 93–108 (p. 94).

11 *Letters*, p. 31; Vieth, 'A Textual Paradox: Rochester's *To a Lady in a Letter*', p. 159.

12 See Thormählen, p. 309; Johnson, I, 428.

13 See *Critical Heritage*, p. 40. Aphra Behn echoes this view in her elegy *On the Death of the late Earl of Rochester* (*ibid.*, pp. 101–4).

14 See *Critical Heritage*, pp. 94–131.

15 *Ibid.*, p. 94.

16 *Ibid.*, pp. 94–101.

17 Oldham also satirised Rochester in the so-called *Satyr against Vertue* and *A Dithrambique on Drinking*, but it is in *Bion* that he makes a serious comment on Rochester's poetry (as Paul Hammond has pointed out to me, it is positioned in *Some New Pieces* immediately after his 'Praise of Homer'). For Oldham's 'unresolved engagement with Rochester', see Paul Hammond, 'Censorship in the Manuscript Transmission of Restoration Poetry' in *Literature and Censorship*, edited by Nigel Smith (Cambridge, 1993). See also *John Oldham: Selected Poems*, edited by Ken Robinson (Newcastle upon Tyne, 1980), p. 10, and *The Poems of John Oldham*, edited by Harold F. Brooks with the collaboration of Raman Selden (Oxford, 1987), pp. xlii–v.

18 See John Dryden, *Of Dramatic Poesy and Other Critical Essays*, edited by G. Watson, 2 vols (London, 1962), I, 7.

19 David M. Vieth, *Attribution in Restoration Poetry: A Study of Rochester's Poems of 1680* (New Haven and London, 1963), pp. 56–100. The link between the manuscripts points to the operation of a scriptorium; see Harold Love, *Scribal Publication in Seventeenth-century England* (Oxford, 1993), pp. 259–65.

20 See Michael Brennan and Paul Hammond, 'The Badminton Manuscript: A New Miscellany of Restoration Verse', *English Manuscript Studies 1100–1700*, 5 (1995), 171–207; *The Gyldenstolpe Manuscript Miscellany of Poems by John Wilmot, Earl of Rochester, and other Restoration Authors*, edited by Bror Danielsson and David M. Vieth (Stockholm, 1967); Thynne Papers, Longleat House, vol. XXVII, Harbin MS. I am grateful to Keith Walker for supplying me with a copy of his transcript of the Harbin MS.

21 *Selected Lyrics and Satires of John Wilmot 2nd Earl of Rochester*, edited by Ronald Duncan (London, 1948), pp. 25–6.

22 See Rochester 1994, p. 307 and *passim*.

23 See Harold Love, 'The Scribal Transmission of Rochester's Songs', *Bibliographical Society of Australia and New Zealand Bulletin*, 20 (1996), 161–80 (pp. 165, 177). Relatively little attention has been paid to the lyrics *per se*, but one of the most perceptive studies is Vieth's ' "Pleased with the contradiction and the sin": the Perverse Artistry of Rochester's Lyrics', *Tennessee Studies in Literature*, 25 (1980), 35–56; see also the same author's *Rochester Studies, 1925–1982: An Annotated Bibliography* (New York and London, 1984), refs 129–50.

24 These have been collated, along with twelve related poems and elegies, in *Songs to Phillis: A Performing Edition of the Early Settings of Poems by the Earl of Rochester (1647–80)*, edited by Steven Devine and Nicholas Fisher (Huntingdon, 1999).

25 See Claude M. Simpson, *The British Broadside Ballad and its Music* (New Jersey, 1966), pp. 19–20.

26 Robert Graves, *The Greek Myths*, 2 vols, revised edition (Harmondsworth, 1960), I, 356–7. See also Paul Hammond's observation concerning memorial reconstruction in 'Censorship in the Manuscript Transmission of Restoration Poetry', pp. 49, 54–5.

27 *Of Dramatic Poesy*, II, 40–1; compare with Dryden's less peevish view of his role when he prepared for 'the Artful Hands of Mr. *Purcel*' the libretto for *King Arthur* (1691):

> But the Numbers of Poetry and Vocal Musick, are sometimes so contrary, that in many places I have been oblig'd to cramp my Verses, and make them rugged to the Reader, that they may be harmonious to the Hearer. (*John Dryden, Dramatic Works*, edited by Montague Summers, 6 vols (London, 1931–2), VI, 242).

28 See the useful index to *Music for London Entertainment 1660–1800, Series A, Vol. I: The Theater of Music*, introduced by Robert Spencer (Tunbridge Wells, 1983).

29 Ian Spink, *English Song: Dowland to Purcell* (London, 1974), p. 184.

30 Useful sources for the scarce information about many of the composers are *The New Grove Dictionary of Music and Musicians*, 20 vols, edited by Stanley Sadie (London, 1980); *A Biographical Dictionary of Actors, Actresses, Musicians, Dancers, Managers & Other Stage Personnel in London, 1660–1800*, 16 vols, edited by Philip H. Highfill, Kalman A. Burnim and Edward A. Langhaus (Carbondale, 1973–93); and Ian Spink, *Restoration Cathedral Music 1660–1714* (Oxford, 1995).

31 Rochester 1984, p. 140. Eleven settings of Rochester's songs have been recorded on a fine CD by The Consort of Musicke (*Charming Strephon*, Etcetera, KTC 1211).

32 See diary entry for 1 October 1667. A modern critic has observed, 'Louis Grabu is perhaps the most derided figure in English musical history' (see Peter Holman, *Four and Twenty Fiddlers: The Violin at the English Court 1540–1690* (Oxford, 1993), p. 296).

33 The early settings illustrate the changing transmission of songs from manuscript, broadsides and printed collections to printed song-sheets (such as the anonymous engraved setting of 'As Cloris full of Harmless thoughts' (British Library Huntington MS 1601)) and printed collections. In terms of the music, as Adrian Partington kindly demonstrated at his piano to me, the seventeenth-century settings evidence a clearly definable English style – 'fresh and direct, lyrical and "airy"' – but by the middle of the eighteenth century, primarily under the influence of Italian music, the settings generally contain a smoothness and simplicity calculated to cause no distress to the ear. For a summary of the seventeenth-century English style, see Stanley Sadie in *Music for London Entertainment 1660–1800, Series A, Vol. 5a: Choice Ayres, Songs and Dialogues* (London, 1989), p. vii.

34 *Of Dramatic Poesy*, II, 37. See also Peter Holman, *Four and Twenty Fiddlers*, pp. 282–304.

35 See *Critical Heritage*, pp. 198ff.

36 Folger MS W.b.515.

7   Lord Rochester's monkey (again)

1 Richard Bentley, *The Folly of Atheism* (1692), p. 27; 'The Eighth Satire of Monsieur Boileau, Imitated', lines 11–15, in *The Poems of John Oldham*, edited by Harold F. Brooks with the collaboration of Raman Selden (Oxford, 1987), p. 162.

2 Thomas Rymer, in *The Works of John Earl of Rochester*, 1714, sig. [A5].

3 The text is taken from *Valentinian: A Tragedy. As 'tis Alter'd by the late Earl of Rochester* (London, 1685), p. 59.

4 *Letters*, pp. 193–4, letter dated 18–25 June 1678. Rochester's letters are quoted from this edition.

5 Hans-Joachim Zimmermann, 'Simia laureatus: Lord Rochester Crowning a Monkey' in *Functions of Literature: Essays presented to Erwin Wolff on his Sixtieth Birthday*, edited by Ulrich Broich et al. (Tübingen, 1984), pp. 147–72.

6 *The Diary of Samuel Pepys*, edited by Robert Latham and William Matthews, 11 vols (London, 1970–83), 5, 254 (26 August 1664). The Warwick Castle portrait is reproduced, notably, on the covers of Greene and Rochester 1993; the version now in the

National Portrait Gallery is reproduced on the dust jacket of Griffin, and facing p. 59 in Vivian de Sola Pinto's *Enthusiast in Wit: A Portrait of John Wilmot Earl of Rochester (1647–1680)* (London, 1962).

7 C. H. Collins Baker, *Catalogue of the Principal Pictures in the Royal Collection at Windsor Castle* (London, 1937), p. 174.

8 *The Diary of Samuel Pepys*, 6, 170 (26 July 1665).

9 The painting, the property of the Duke of Buccleuch of Drumlanrig Castle, is reproduced in Gervase Jackson-Stops, *The Treasure Houses of Britain: Five Hundred Years of Private Patronage and Art Collecting* (New Haven and London, 1985), p. 156.

10 *Rake Rochester* (London, 1955), p. 125.

11 Greene, p. 37.

12 *Letters*, p. 96 (conjectural date '1674–5'). The text is corrected from BL MS Harleian 7003, ff. 228–9.

13 Harold Love, 'Shadwell, Rochester and the Crisis of Amateurism' in *Thomas Shadwell Reconsider'd: Essays in Criticism*, edited by Judith Bailey Slagle, *Restoration: Studies in English Literary Culture, 1660–1700*, 20 (1996), 127.

14 The complex mass of allusions to Rochester in this preface is very well explicated in David M. Vieth's edition of *All for Love* (Lincoln, Neb., 1972).

15 *Letters*, pp. 119–20.

16 *On The Suppos'd Author of A late Poem in Defence of Satyr*, lines 1–10.

8   The missing foot of *Upon Nothing*, and other mysteries of creation

1 John Lennard, *The Poetry Handbook* (Oxford, 1996), p. 184.

2 All quotations are taken from the broadside version illustrated in figure 11.

3 Sir William Temple, 'Of Poetry' (1690), in *Critical Essays of the Seventeenth Century*, edited by J. E. Spingarn, 3 vols (Oxford, 1908–9), III, 73–109 (p. 74).

4 Thomas Hobbes, *De Corpore* (English version 1656), I.ii.6, in *The Complete Works of Thomas Hobbes*, edited by Sir William Molesworth, 10 vols (London, 1839), vol. I.

5 G. S. Kirk, J. E. Raven, M. Schofield, *The Presocratic Philosophers*, 2nd edition (Cambridge, 1983), p. 245.

6 George Puttenham, *The Arte of English Poesie* (1589) in *Elizabethan Critical Essays*, edited by G. Gregory Smith, 2 vols (Oxford, 1904), II, 1–193 (p. 3).

7 Sir John Harington, *A Preface, or rather a Briefe Apologie of Poetrie* (1591), in Smith, II, 194–222 (p. 204).

8 Thomas Hobbes, *Answer to Davenant's Preface to* Gondibert (1650), in Spingarn, II, 54–6 (p. 55); Sir Philip Sidney, *An Apology for Poetry* (1595), edited by Geoffrey Shepherd (Manchester, 1973), p. 103.

9 *Ben Jonson*, edited by Ian Donaldson (Oxford, 1985), p. 603.

10 Francis Bacon, *The Advancement of Learning* (1605), in Spingarn, I, 1–9 (p. 5).

11 Sir William Alexander, *Anacrisis* (1634), in Spingarn, I, 180–9 (p. 185); and Sir William Davenant, *Preface to* Gondibert (1650), in Spingarn, II, 1–53 (p. 10).

12 *Ben Jonson*, p. 587; John Dryden, *Of Dramatic Poesy, and other Critical Essays*, edited by George Watson, 2 vols (London, 1962), II, 236.

13 *Ben Jonson*, p. 596.

14 Robert Wolseley, *Preface to* Valentinian (1685), in Spingarn, III, 1–31 (p. 27).

15 Thomas Hobbes, *Preface to Homer* (1675), in Spingarn, II, 67–76 (p. 69).

16 Hobbes (1650), p. 57.

17 Samuel Daniel, *A Defence of Ryme* (1603?), in Smith, II, 356–84 (p. 366).

18 George Chapman, *Preface to Homer* (1610–16?), in Spingarn, I, 67–81 (p. 79).

19 Davenant, p. 19.

20 David Farley-Hills, *Rochester's Poetry* (London, 1978), p. 178.

21 Griffin, p. 279.

22 Paul Baines, 'From "Nothing" to "Silence": Rochester and Pope' in *Reading Rochester*, edited by Edward Burns (Liverpool, 1995), pp. 137–65 (p. 149).

23 Dryden, II, 237, 247.

24 Puttenham, p. 3.

25 Sidney, p. 133.

26 Daniel, p. 365.

27 *Ben Jonson,* p. 603; Sidney, pp. 133, 103.

28 Thomas Campion, *Observations on the Art of English Poesie* (1602), in Smith, II, 327–55 (p. 329).

29 Sidney, pp. 103, 142.

30 Daniel, p. 366.

31 Dryden, I, 2.

32 For a useful summary of this issue, see under 'Creation' in *A Dictionary of Biblical Interpretation*, edited by R. Coggins and J. Houlden (London, 1990).

33 'It is more unthinkable that matter exist in actuality without form than an accident without a subject', St Thomas Aquinas, *Summa Theologica*, translated and edited by T. Gilby (London, 1964–80), X, 66.1.

34 See Plato, *Timaeus and Critias*, translated and edited by H. D. P. Lee (Harmondsworth, 1971), pp. 21–2.

35 *Romeo and Juliet*, I.ii.174–6.

36 *Donne: The Complete English Poems*, edited by C. Patrides, revised by R. Hamilton (London, 1994), p. 40.

37 *Spenser: Poetical Works*, edited by J. C. Smith and E. De Selincourt (Oxford, 1912): *Faerie Queene*, III.vi.36–7.

38 Harington, p. 201.

39 Thomas Rymer, *Preface to* Rapin (1674), in Spingarn, II, 163–80 (p. 175).

40 *The Twickenham Edition of the Poems of Alexander Pope*, edited by John Butt and others, 11 vols (London, 1939–69): *An Essay on Criticism*, line 365.

41 Kirk, Raven and Schofield, p. 249.

42 *Senec. Troas. Act. 2. Chor. Thus English'd by a Person of Honour.*

43 *De Corpore*, II.viii.24.

44 See *Davideis*, in *Abraham Cowley, Poems*, edited by A. R. Waller (Cambridge, 1905), p. 251.

45 Daniel, p. 384; the *mise en page*, however, is not reproduced in Gregory Smith.

46 See *Oxford English Dictionary*, where its first sense (as used by Wycliffe) is given as 'Empty, vacant', and its second sense as 'Void of any real worth, usefulness, or significance'.

47 Rosalie Colie, *Paradoxica Epidemica* (Princeton, 1966), p. 229; Henry Fielding, 'On Nothing', in *A Book of English Essays (1600–1900)*, edited by S. Makower and B. Blackwell (Oxford, 1912), pp. 78–90 (p. 90).

48 See above, p. 91.

9 *Artemiza to Chloe*: Rochester's 'female' epistle

1 *A Satyrical Epistle to the Female Author of a Poem called Sylvia's Revenge Etc.* (London, 1691), p. 19. For details of Gould's attack on the 'Female Author', see F. Nussbaum, *The Brink of All We Hate: English Satires on Women 1660–1750* (Lexington, 1984), pp. 34–7.

2 *Kissing the Rod: An Anthology of Seventeenth-century Women's Verse*, edited by G. Greer *et al.* (London, 1988), pp. 287–8. The second extract was omitted from the first published version of the elegy in 1685.

3 *Kissing the Rod*, pp. 249–50.

4 There is a copy of *Chloe to Sabina* (reproduced at the end of this paper in an appendix) in the National Library of Ireland, Dublin MS 2093, pp. 112–16, where it is attributed to Mrs Jean Fox (as yet unidentified, though perhaps the Fox attacked as an 'Irish whore' in Rochester's lampoon, 'To longe the Wise Commons have been in debate', lines 6–7). For details of Dublin MS 2093, see Peter Beal, *Index of Literary Manuscripts*, 2, pt 2 (London, 1993), p. 232. *Chloe to Sabina* follows closely after *Artemiza to Chloe* in the Dublin MS, there being only one intervening poem, also attributed to Rochester ('This Bee alone of all his race': see Rochester 1999, pp. 282–4), which may indicate that the scribe recognised a link between the two verse epistles. However, while I have suggested that Fox's poem responds to *Artemiza to Chloe*, the reverse cannot be ruled out, given the uncertain date of *Chloe to Sabina*. *An Epistle to Artemisia. On Fame* is printed in Mary Leapor, *Poems Upon Several Occasions*, vol. 2 (London, 1751), pp. 43–54; *Cloe to Artimesa* is unascribed in *A New Miscellany of Original Poems Translations and Imitations By the Most Eminent Hands* (London, 1720), p. 123, though the compiler, A[nthony] H[ammond], lays claim to 'the pieces which appear without any name' ('Preface', sigs Ar–Av).

5 Other contemporary spellings of Artemiza are: Artemisia, Artemisa, Artimesa, Artemise.

6 H. D. Weinbrot, '"The Swelling Volume": the Apocalyptic Satire of Rochester's *Letter from Artemisia In The Town To Chloe In The Country*', *Studies in the Literary Imagination* 5 (1972), 19–37 (p. 33 and n. 10); Ben Jonson, *The Works*, edited by C. H. Herford, and Percy and Evelyn Simpson (Oxford, 1941), 7, 308. Jonson also quotes what (according to Herodotus) was Xerxes' comment on Artemisia's courage at Salamis: '"Viri quidem extiterunt mihi feminae, feminae autem viri"'. *La Cléopâtre*, first published 1646–8, was translated by Robert Loveday as *Hymen's Praeludia, Or Loves Master-Piece Being That so much admired Romance entituled Cleopatra*, twelve parts (London, 1665).

7 B. Everett, 'The Sense of Nothing' in *Spirit of Wit*, p. 29; C. Fabricant, 'The Writer as Hero and Whore: Rochester's *Letter From Artemisia To Chloe*', *Essays in Literature*, West Illinois University 3 (1976), 158.

8 E. Rothstein, *Restoration and Eighteenth-Century Poetry 1660–1780* (London, 1981), p. 33.

9 *Ibid.*

10 See Fabricant, 'The Writer as Hero and Whore', 157.

11 Noted by Everett in *Spirit of Wit*, pp. 29–30.

12 Rothstein, *Restoration and Eighteenth-century Poetry*, p. 33; Everett, *Spirit of Wit*, p. 29.

13 Pliny, *Natural History*, with an English translation in ten volumes by W. H. S. Jones, Loeb Library (Cambridge, Mass., 1956), VII, Book 25, XXXVI, 73, p. 189; John Gerard, *The Herball or General Historie of Plantes. Very Much enlarged and Amended by Thomas Johnson* (London, 1636), p. 1104.

14 See *Critical Heritage*, p. 54; *Letters*, p. 142.

15 'An Account of the Life and Writings of Mr Abraham Cowley' in *The Works of Abraham Cowley*, 3 vols (London, 1707), 1, xxvii–xxviii; *Plantarum Libri duo* (1662); *Poemata Latina. In quibus Continentur, Sex Libri Plantarum* (London, 1668).

16 Cowley, *Poemata Latina*, p. 60, n. 1 and *The Works*, 3, sig. P7r.

17 'Non immerito in hoc conventu praesidet Artemisia (quam honoris puto, causa quidam matrem herbarum appellant)', Cowley, *Poemata Latina*, p. 67, note to line 5.

18 Cowley, *The Works*, 3, sigs P4v–P5r, P7r.

19 Cf. Wycherley to Shadwell: 'I wou'd turn o're the Leafe, but know / My Muse has tyr'd her self and you /And so Adieu', *The Works of Thomas Shadwell*, edited by Montague Summers, 5 vols (London, 1927), 5, 232. Noted also Thormählen, p. 137, n. 63.

20 'I.e. such Medicines as bring away dead Children, or cause Abortion', Cowley, *The Works*, 3, p. 323, note*.

21 'Etherege's *Man of Mode* and Rochester's *Artemisia to Chloe*', *Notes and Queries*, New Series, 5 (1958), 473–4.

22 Griffin, p. 139.

23 Cowley, *The Works*, 3, sig. Qv. Artemisia was often administered in sweet wine (see Pliny, *Natural History*, vol. 7, Book 25 LXXXI, 130, p. 229; and vol. 7, Book 26 XLIX, 81, p. 325).

24 Perhaps, also, a biblical allusion. Cf. that in line 17, noted by Walker in Rochester 1984, p. 278; and that in line 260, noted by Fabricant, 'The Writer as Hero and Whore', 162, and by Weinbrot, 'The Swelling Volume', 34.

25 First noted by P. C. Davies, 'Rochester and Boileau: a Reconsideration', *Comparative Literature*, 21 (1969), 354.

26 *The Poems of Sir Philip Sidney*, edited by William A. Ringler, Jr (Oxford, 1962), p. 201. We have no other evidence to suggest Rochester knew Sidney's works. There were twelve editions of *Astrophil and Stella* between 1599 and 1739.

27 T. Hobbes, *Leviathan*, edited by C. B. Macpherson (Harmondsworth, 1968), pp. 135 and 137. Cited by Walker in Rochester 1984, p. 280, note to line 168.

28 Hobbes, *Leviathan*, p. 139.

29 Weinbrot, 'The Swelling Volume', 27.

30 Hobbes, *Leviathan*, p. 139.

31 Weinbrot, 'The Swelling Volume', 33.

32 Only two modern scholars have noted its presence: C. Rawson, 'Rochester's Systems of Excess', *The Times Literary Supplement* (29 March 1985), 336; and Frank H. Ellis

(Rochester 1994), p. 347, note to line 64. Pope's reference in his Imitation of Horace *Epistles*, I.vi to 'Wilmot' and the '"cordial drop"' (lines 126–7), suggests that he recognised Rochester's appropriation of 'nil admirari'.

33 *John Wilmot, Earl of Rochester: Selected Poems*, edited by Paul Hammond (Bristol, 1982), p. 102, note to lines 7–10.

34 The epistles were also included in summarised form in Sir Roger L'Estrange's *Seneca's Morals By Way of abstract* . . . (London, 1678), which ran to many editions, and see, for instance, the prologue to Behn's first play, *The Forc'd Marriage, or the Jealous Bridegroom* (London, 1671), where the speaker remarks of the new female playwright:

> Today one of their party ventures out,
> Not with design to conquer, but to Scout:
> Discourage but this first attempt, and then,
> They'le hardly dare to sally out again. (lines 23–6)

35 For Satan as a merchant adventurer, see *Paradise Lost*, 2, 629–43 (*The Poems of John Milton*, edited by John Carey and Alastair Fowler (London, 1968)). See, too, Book 10, where the fallen angels await the return of 'their great adventurer from the search / Of foreign worlds' (lines 440–1). Rochester evidently knew *Paradise Lost* (see *Letters*, p. 202, n.).

36 Recorded by Joseph Spence, *Observations, Anecdotes, and Characters of Books and Men*, edited by James M. Osborn, 2 vols (Oxford, 1966), I, 202, para. 471.

10   Pope, Rochester and Horace

1 Joseph Spence, *Observations, Anecdotes, and Characters of Books and Men*, edited by James M. Osborn, 2 vols (Oxford, 1966), I, 470. The date is conjectural.

2 *An Epistolary Essay*, line 71. There is of course a further irony in this 'borrowing': Since the publication of David M. Vieth's *Attribution in Restoration Poetry* (New Haven and London, 1962), scholars have, more or less unanimously, accepted Vieth's suggestion that Mulgrave is the 'persona speaker' of *An Epistolary Essay*, which thus amounts to a 'satirical self-exposé'. For pertinent recent discussion of the poem, see Thormählen, pp. 338–44.

3 Preserved in the Berg Collection of the New York Public Library (pressmark (Pope)-A). There are over fifty separate entries in Pope's hand. See Maynard Mack, *Collected in Himself: Essays Critical and Biographical on Pope and Some of His Contemporaries* (Newark, London and Toronto, 1982), pp. 437–8.

4 See *Critical Heritage*, p. 14, and Griffin, p. 258. Compare Pope's opinion of Crashaw, expressed in a letter to Cromwell of 1710: 'I take this Poet to have writ like a Gentleman, that is, at leisure hours, and more to keep out of idleness, than to establish a reputation: so that nothing regular or just can be expected from him', *The Correspondence of Alexander Pope*, edited by George Sherburn, 5 vols (Oxford, 1956), I, 109.

5 *The First Satire of the Second Book of Horace, Imitated*, lines 140 and 133 (*The Twickenham Edition of the Poems of Alexander Pope*, edited by John Butt and others, 11 vols (London, 1939–69), IV, 19). All quotations from Pope are from this edition.

6 For discussion of Pope's use of various classical models, see, for example, Howard Erskine-Hill, *The Augustan Idea in English Literature* (London, 1984) and Howard Weinbrot, *Alexander Pope and the Traditions of Formal Verse Satire* (Princeton, 1982).

7 See, for instance, Griffin, *passim*, and Michael Phillips, 'The Composition of Pope's *Imitation of Horace, Satire II. i*' in *Alexander Pope, Essays for the Tercentenary*, edited by Colin Nicholson (Aberdeen, 1988), pp. 172–4. See also Harold Brooks, 'The "Imitation" in English Poetry', *Review of English Studies*, 25 (1949), 124–40.

8 Howard Weinbrot identifies Rochester's satire with that of Juvenal, leaving unanswered the problem of why it was that Rochester chose to write imitations of Horace's poems rather than Juvenal's. See *Alexander Pope and the Traditions of Formal Verse Satire*, pp. 101–4.

9 Thormählen, p. 310.

10 The manuscript is in the collection of the Pierpont Morgan Library (MA 3719). It consists of one half of one folio sheet, measuring approximately 20 cm by 16 cm, folded and torn to make a duodecimo booklet with text on four pages. Of some interest is the specificity of the projected imprint, 'Printed for J. Knapton L. Gilliver, & R. Dodsley', which would suggest a possible date for the manuscript early in 1738 (in this year Pope used both J. Knapton and Dodsley, together with Lawton Gilliver for an edition of his imitations of Horace (Reginald Harven Griffith, *Alexander Pope, a Bibliography* (Austin, 1922–7)). While pressure of space precludes further detailed comment on the manuscript, one striking detail requires some mention: the suggestion that Pope produced four imitations in addition to those published in his name – *Satire I, i, Satire II, iii* and *iv*, and *Epistle I, xx* – and that he had a hand in a further four – *Satire I, ii* and *iv*, and *Epistle I, ii* and *iii*.

11 *Juvenal and Persius*, translated by G. C. Ramsay, *Loeb Classical Library* (Cambridge, Mass., 1940), pp. 328–9.

12 In the lines that follow he even becomes a prototype of the arch Tory bug-bear, Walpole:

> An artful Manager, that crept between
> His Friend and Shame, and was a kind of *Screen*.

As the *Twickenham* editors point out, the account of Horace to which Pope gives expression in the text of his poem owes a good deal to Dryden's translation of this section of the first *Satire* of Persius, in which Horace 'with a sly insinuating Grace, / Laugh'd at his Friend, and look'd him in the Face' (lines 231–4, *The Poems of John Dryden*, edited by James Kinsley, 4 vols (Oxford, 1958), II, 748–9). However, he pointedly stops short of rendering the next couplet, in which Dryden more closely translates the lines of Persius that Pope quotes in his note:

> Wou'd raise a Blush, where secret Vice he found;
> And tickle, while he gently prob'd the Wound. (lines 235–6)

See *Twickenham Edition*, 11 vols (London, 1939–69), IV, 299.

13 For more detailed discussion of this passage, see Erskine-Hill, *The Augustan Idea*, pp. 345–6, and Weinbrot, *Alexander Pope and the Traditions of Formal Verse Satire*, pp. 311–12. Weinbrot, ignoring the debt that the passage owes to Persius, does not see any irony in Pope's presentation of Horace at this point.

14 The preface to Pope's copy of Rochester's poems announces it as 'a Collection of such Pieces only, as may be received in a vertuous Court, and not unbecome the Cabinet of the Severest Matron' (sig. A5v); neither *Timon* nor *An Allusion* seem to have met these criteria and Pope must have been familiar with them from another source, perhaps the more robust first edition of 1680.

15 Indeed, Ozell's translation of Boileau's third satire has the following note to line 20: 'Horace *gives a Description of a ridiculous Entertainment in the 8th* Satire *of the 11th Book; but there is hardly anything in his like this of* Mr. Despreaux'. *The Works of Monsieur Boileau.* Made *English* from the last PARIS *Edition;* By SEVERAL Hands (London, 1712).

16 This notwithstanding his apparently disparaging opinion of Rochester's versification in *An Allusion;* see *Observations,* I, 471.

17 See the description that Pope gives of *Epistle to Arbuthnot* in 'The Author to the Reader' at the beginning of the 1735 *Works* (vol. II): 'all I have to say of *Myself* will be found in my last Epistle'.

18 John Butt's assessment, *Twickenham Edition,* IV, vii.

19 In this poem, Horace is importuned while walking along the Sacred Way, by a would-be poet he knows only by name.

20 Peter Porter, 'The Professional Amateur' in *Spirit of Wit,* p. 72. As Porter suggests, this pose easily becomes that of 'the disinterested poet, the writer not above prejudice but free from faction'. See also Thormählen, pp. 334–5.

21 Rochester's 'I loath the Rabble' in *An Allusion* (c. 120) derives from Horace's *Odes,* III.i: 'odi profanum vulgus et arceo', 'I loath and shun the profane crowd'.

22 Rochester 1999, pp. 102–5. The volume contains the Scroope group of poems, and further references are to this edition.

23 Pope's note reads, 'It is but justice to own that the hint of *Eve* and the *Serpent* was taken from the *Verses on the Imitator of* Horace'. In that poem they compare Pope to '*the Snake of Eve*'.

24 Dustin Griffin suggests Rochester's attack on Mulgrave in *My Lord All-Pride* as a possible model for Sporus (Griffin, pp. 259–60).

25 Marianne Thormählen points out that in the 1670s Dryden's standing as a poet was as the writer of panegyrics, various occasional verses, particularly for the theatre, 'and some comedies and heroic plays' (Thormählen, p. 312).

26 *Imitation of Epistle II, i,* lines 305–6 (*Twickenham Edition,* IV, 221).

27 *Odes,* III.iii (lines 1–8).

28 See *Twickenham Edition,* IV, 101n. Pope had also ridiculed these lines of Addison's in the *Peri Bathous* (*The Prose Works of Alexander Pope,* vol. II, edited by Rosemary Cowler (Oxford, 1986), p. 218).

29 A note in the Twickenham edition suggests that Pope is following Boileau here (the conclusion of *Epistle* vii) as Boileau had followed Horace's *Satires,* I.x, without mentioning Rochester's *An Allusion.*

30 Pope's financial independence derived largely from his agreement with Lintot for the publication by subscription of the translation of the *Iliad.* For a full account of this venture, see D. Foxon, *Pope and the Early Eighteenth-century Book Trade,* revised and edited by James McLaverty (Oxford, 1991) pp. 51–63.

31 It is also worth noting that the terms by which Pope identifies Atterbury, that other 'Rochester', conjure up the earlier poet's name amongst those of his adversaries.

32 The list of lordly enthusiasts is, of course, also a politically significant one. Of the six, three – Granville, Sheffield and Atterbury ('mitred *Rochester*') – had been committed Jacobites, while two – Talbot and Somers – were Whigs. Although St John tips the balance firmly in favour of the Jacobite side, Pope is still able to suggest that he has

been encouraged from all political quarters, by those with power and influence and by those out of favour. See Howard Erskine-Hill, *The Augustan Idea in English Literature* (London, 1983), p. 311.

33 *Correspondence*, III, 502.

34 *Satires II, i* (lines 139–40). Here, the distinction between the 'unknown' enemies, be they 'Scribblers or Peers', and the (implicitly) 'famous' poet points to the particular status that lies behind Pope's self-presentation in the satires of the 1730s: he writes not simply as a 'proud professional' but as the (financially secure) foremost poet of his day.

11   *A Satyre against Reason and Mankind* from page to stage

1 That formative status is enhanced if we accept recently discovered evidence suggesting that the poem was composed in 1672 rather than 1674 as was previously supposed. See Harold Love and Stephen Parks, 'A Reasonable Satyr', *Times Literary Supplement*, 1 August 1997, p. 13.

2 The most comprehensive discussions of the context of *Against Reason and Mankind* are those in Griffin (pp. 156–96) and Thormählen (pp. 162–89); neither considers its impact upon the drama. For an account of verse responses see David M. Vieth, *Attribution in Restoration Poetry: A Study of Rochester's 'Poems' of 1680* (New Haven, 1963), pp. 178–80.

3 On Etherege's and Lee's portraits of Rochester see Robert D. Hume, 'Reading and Misreading *The Man of Mode*', *Criticism*, 14 (1972), 1–11, and his 'The Satiric Design of Nat. Lee's *The Princess of Cleve*', *Journal of English and German Philology*, 75 (1976), 117–38 respectively. Harold Weber discusses Rochester as a prototype of a Hobbesian libertine rake in the context of 1670s comedies in *The Restoration Rake-hero: Transformations in Sexual Understanding in Seventeenth-century England* (Madison, 1986), pp. 49–90.

4 For a discussion of late seventeenth-century *libertinage* in the context of both drama and poetry see Dale Underwood, *Etherege and the Seventeenth-century Comedy of Manners* (New Haven, 1957), pp. 10–40.

5 Thomas Hobbes, *Leviathan* (1651), edited by Richard Tuck (Cambridge, 1996), Part I, ch. 6, p. 39.

6 Chernaik, p. 24.

7 David Farley-Hills's contribution to the present volume reinforces the points we make in our introduction.

8 'The Effect of this [a particular Pique to *Dryden*] was discover'd by his Lordship's setting up *Crown* in Opposition to *Dryden*; he recommended him to the King, ordering him to make a Masque for the Court, when it was the Business of the Poet Laureat': 'The Memoiers [*sic*] of the Life of *John Wilmot*, Earl of *Rochester*. Written By Monsieur *St Evremont*, in a Letter to her Grace the Dutchess of *Mazarine*. Translated from the Original Manuscript', in *The Works of the Right Honourable the Late Earls of Rochester and Roscommon. With a Collection of Original Poems, Translations, Imitations, &c. by the most Eminent Hands* (2nd edition, London, 1707), sig. b7v. To be the recipient of that commission was both a great boon and a great honour, for the production of the masque was an important cultural and political event. See Andrew R. Walkling, 'Masque and Politics at the Restoration Court: John Crowne's *Calisto*', *Early Music* (February 1996), 27–62.

9 In his preface to *Don Carlos Prince of Spain* (London, 1676), Otway writes, 'I can never enough acknowledge the unspeakable Obligations I received from the *Earl* of *R*. who far above what I am ever able to deserve from him, seem'd almost to make it his business to establish it in the good opinion of the *King*, and his *Royal Highness*, from both of which I have since received Confirmations of their good liking of it, and Encouragement to proceed; and it is to him I must in all gratitude confess I owe the greatest part of my good success in this, and on whose Indulgency I extreamly build my hopes of a next' (sig. A3v).

10 Some time between the winter of 1671–2 and the spring of 1673, he supplied the prologue for a Court performance of Settle's *The Empress of Morocco*, and in the spring of 1677 the epilogue for Charles Davenant's *Circe*. He contributed an epilogue for an all-female production of a revived play in 1672 (see Edward L. Saslow, 'A "New" Epilogue by Rochester', *Restoration*, 23.1 (1999), 1–9) and may also have written the epilogue for Fane's *Love in the Dark* which opened in the spring of 1675.

11 Fane's *A Mask. Made at the Request of the late Earl of Rochester, for the Tragedy of Valentinian* was published in *Poems by Several Hands, and on Several Occasions* (London, 1685), a poetical miscellany edited by Nahum Tate.

12 Howard thanked Rochester for 'the sceen you are pleased to write' in a letter dated 7 April 1676. See *Letters*, p. 116.

13 See Robert D. Hume, 'Elizabeth Barry's First Roles and the Cast of *The Man of Mode*', *Theatre History Studies*, 5 (1985), 16–20.

14 *The Assignation or Love in a Nunnery*, in *The Works of John Dryden*, edited by Edward Niles Hooker *et al.*, 20 vols (Berkeley, 1956–), XI, 320–1. All further references to Dryden's works are to this edition and given parenthetically in the text.

15 John Sitter, *Arguments of Augustan Wit* (Cambridge, 1991), p. 95.

16 Thormählen, p. 195; David Trotter, 'Wanton Expressions' in *Spirit of Wit*, pp. 111–32.

17 Roger D. Lund, 'Irony as Subversion: Thomas Woolston and the Crime of Wit' in *The Margins of Orthodoxy: Heterodox Writing and Cultural Response, 1660–1750*, edited by Lund (Cambridge, 1995), pp. 170–94 (p. 171).

18 'An Answer to the Satyr *against* Mankind. By the Reverend Mr. *Griffith*', in *The Works of John Earl of Rochester* (London, 1714), pp. 59–65 (p. 64). On the authority of Anthony à Wood, Vieth ascribes this poem to Griffith (though he does not altogether reject its attribution to Edward Pococke made in some contemporary transcripts (Vieth, *Attribution in Restoration Poetry*, pp. 178–9)).

19 See his 'Ideology and Ideological State Apparatuses (Notes towards an Investigation)', first published in *La pensée* (1970), reprinted in Louis Althusser, *Essays on Ideology* (London, 1984), p. 29.

20 John Crowne, *The Countrey Wit* (London, 1675), sig. A4v and II, p. 22 respectively. This echo of lines 105–9 has been noted by Love and earlier critics and editors.

21 In *Aureng-Zebe* (whose dedication to the Earl of Mulgrave contains two verbal echoes of the poem: see Paul Hammond's 'Two Echoes of Rochester's *Satire* in Dryden', *Notes and Queries*, 233 (1988), 171), the eponymous hero resists what he perceives as an unreasonable suggestion of his beloved Indamora – that they should part now that his jealousy makes him unable to trust her – in a vein reminiscent of the defence of 'right reason' by the persona of *Against Reason and Mankind* (lines 99ff):

> Must I new bars to my own joy create?
> Refuse, my self, what I had forc'd from Fate?
> What though I am not lov'd?
> Reason's nice taste does our delights destroy:
> Brutes are more bless'd, who grosly feed on joy. (V.i.553–7)

In *Oedipus*, the blind prophet Tiresias condemns the insolence of Man's epistemological hankerings in words which recall the rebuttal of the 'formal band and beard' in *Against Reason and Mankind* (lines 76ff):

> But how can Finite measure Infinite?
> Reason! alas, it does not know it self!
> Yet Man, vain Man, wou'd with this short-lin'd Plummet,
> Fathom the vast Abysse of Heav'nly justice. (III.i.241ff)

And Dryden's unperformed opera *The State of Innocence* (*c.* 1673–4) based on Milton's *Paradise Lost* rewrites Satan's seduction of Eve so as to emphasise the 'rationality' of the woman's aspirations to the godhead (IV.ii) in a way which resonates with the diabolical presentation of human pursuit of (false) reason in Rochester's poem.

22 *Calisto: or, The Chaste Nimph. The Late Masque at Court, As it was frequently Presented there, By several Persons of Great Quality. With the Prologue, and the Songs betwixt the Acts. All Written by J. Crowne* (London, 1675), 'Epistle to the Reader', sig. a1v.

23 Jupiter's ultimate victory is wittily brought home in the Epilogue: in the final scene of the masque the audience have witnessed Jupiter bestow upon Calisto (and upon her equally chaste sister Nyphe) 'the small dominion of a Star' (V, p. 79); now he revokes his decree and decides to keep the two beauties in '*this inferiour World*' (p. 82).

24 See Louis Teeter, 'The Dramatic Use of Hobbes's Political Ideas' in *John Dryden*, edited by Earl Miner (London, 1972), pp. 27–57 (p. 36).

25 A manuscript cast list preserved in two scribal copies of *Lucina's Rape* (as Rochester called his revision of *Valentinian*) suggests that the play was produced, or intended to be produced, by the King's Company *c.* 1675–6. The first recorded performance of the play took place at Court on 11 February 1684. See John Downes, *Roscius Anglicanus*, edited by Judith Milhous and Robert D. Hume (London, 1987), p. 83n.

26 Harold Love, 'Was Lucina Betrayed at Whitehall?', pp. 179–90 above.

27 Raman Selden notes that '[t]he philosophy of the play's libertines has some general similarities to the views expressed in Rochester's *A Satyr against Reason and Mankind*', though he does not explore them. We believe that those similarities are both more specific and more pervasive than Selden allows. See his 'Rochester and Shadwell' in *Spirit of Wit*, pp. 177–87 (p. 189).

28 All references are to *The Complete Works of Thomas Shadwell*, edited by Montague Summers, 5 vols (London, 1927; repr. New York, 1968), vol. III, I, 25–6.

29 The attribution of this poem to Rochester has been disputed. For a convenient summary of the debate see Rochester 1999, 367–8.

30 Compare also Timon's exclamation against human-derived rules which bound and unnecessarily restrict pleasure with the passage in *Against Reason and Mankind* (lines 105–9) appropriated by Crowne in *The Countrey Wit*:

> Alas, by Nature we are too much confin'd,
> Our Libertie's so narrow, that we need not
> Find fetters for our selves: No, we should seize
> On pleasure wheresoever we can find it,
> Lest at another time we miss it there. (II, pp. 215–16)

31 Shadwell apportions to Apemantus and to Evandra many of the lines of Shakespeare's steward Flavius who, renamed Demetrius, in his version proves as dishonest and hypocritical as the rest of Timon's hangers-on.

32 See Robert D. Hume, *The Development of English Drama in the Late Seventeenth Century* (Oxford, 1976), pp. 312, 327.

33 *Roscius Anglicanus*, p. 78.

34 The entry for 25 July 1675, from *The Diary of Robert Hooke*, quoted in *The London Stage, 1600–1800, Part I: 1660–1700*, edited by William Van Lennep *et al.* (Carbondale, 1965), p. 234.

35 Charles Gildon, *Lives and Characters of the English Dramatick Poets* (London, [1699]), p. 124.

36 *The Vindication of The Duke of Guise*, in Dryden's *Works*, XIV, 319.

37 The latter, Charles Gildon noted in his *Lives and Characters* of 1699, was 'for a few Years past, as often acted at the Theatre Royal, as any Tragedy I know' (p. 129). For dates of eighteenth-century revivals of both of Shadwell's plays and Rochester's *Valentinian* see *The London Stage, 1660–1800. Part II: 1700–1729*, edited by Emmett L. Avery, 2 vols (Carbondale, 1960). Rochester's own *Valentinian*, though it commanded critical respect – John Dunton's *The Athenian Mercury* (vol. 5, no. 2, Saturday 5 December 1691) confidently pronounced that '*Valentinian* shall outlast, as it does outweigh whole Cartloads of theirs whose persons have survived him' – and though it was sometimes revived, was less a fixture of the repertory.

38 By contrast, the readers of Rochester's *Works* (London, 1707) were reminded, by St Evremond's 'Memoirs of the Earl of Rochester's Life', that 'Sir *George Etherege* wrote *Dorimant* in Sir *Fopling*, in Compliment to him, as drawing his Lordship's Character, and burnishing all the Foibles of it, to make them shine like Perfections' (sig. b8r).

39 Significantly, *Against Reason and Mankind* was accorded pride of place, being situated at the front of the volume, in the *Works* of 1707 published by Curll, and it was the one poem picked out for discussion in Rymer's preface to Rochester's *Works* of 1714 brought out by Tonson, which also prints Griffith's 'Answer'. Rymer's preface appeared with an edition of Rochester's poems published by Jacob Tonson in 1691 'with no editor's name and an unsigned preface', and was included in subsequent reprints of that edition in 1696, 1705, 1710, 1714 and 1732. It was only in the 1714 edition that the preface was attributed to Rymer. See *The Critical Works of Thomas Rymer*, edited by Curt A. Zimansky (New Haven, 1956), pp. 224–5.

40 See *The Art of English Poetry*, edited by Edward Bysshe, 2 vols (London, 1702), I, 223–5. Though he attributes these lines to Rochester, Bysshe does not specify the poem from which they derive. Gildon includes the very same extract from *Against Reason and Mankind* in his *The Complete Art of Poetry*, 2 vols (London, 1718), II, 227–9. Though there are minor differences of spelling and punctuation between his version and Bysshe's, it is clear that Gildon used the earlier compilation as his copy-text, for his version makes the same cuts to the original.

41 See *The British Parnassus: Or, A Compleat Common-Place-Book of English Poetry: Containing The most genuine, instructive, diverting and sublime Thoughts*, 2 vols (London, 1714), I, sig. A1v. Excerpts from *Valentinian*, too, appeared in contemporary anthologies: see Bysshe (ed.), *The Art of English Poetry* under headings 'FATE' and 'RAPE' respectively, I, 127, 296; and *Thesaurus Dramaticus. Containing all the Celebrated Passages, Soliloquies, Similies, Descriptions, and Other Poetical Beauties in the Body of English*

Plays, Antient and Modern, Digested under Proper Topics; with the Names of the Plays, and their Authors, referr'd to in the Margin, 2 vols (London, 1724), I, 20, 240.

42 *Gulliver's Travels*, Book IV, chs 1–4.

43 John Gay, *Fables* (London, 1727), XLIX.

44 John Gay, *The Beggar's Opera*, III.ii.4ff: 'Lions, Wolves, and Vulturs don't live together in Herds, Droves or Flocks. – Of all Animals of Prey, Man is the only sociable one. Every one of us preys upon his Neighbour, and yet we herd together' (*John Gay: Dramatic Works*, edited by John Fuller, 2 vols (Oxford, 1983), II, 46).

45 The influence is more pervasive than is suggested by Paul Baines in his detailed study 'From "nothing" to "silence": Rochester and Pope' in *Reading Rochester*, edited by Edward Burns (Liverpool, 1995), pp. 137–65. Julian Ferraro's contribution to the present volume is thus especially welcome in the attention it pays to the relationship between Rochester's *An Allusion to Horace* and *Satyr. [Timon]* and Pope's *Epistle to Arbuthnot*.

46 Joseph Spence, *Observations, Anecdotes, and Characters of Books and Men: Collected from Conversation*, edited by James M. Osborn, 2 vols (Oxford, 1966), no. 472, I, 202.

47 The latest of these is Ferraro, who explores some of the reasons behind Pope's ambivalence, in showing how Pope the professional writer has appropriated, but must also transform, the 'holiday writer's aristocratic self-presentation'.

48 Stephen Jeffreys, *The Libertine* (London, 1994), p. 3.

49 We are grateful to Professor Harold Love for sending us the text of *Against Reason and Mankind* from his Oxford English Texts edition of Rochester's *Works* before its publication, and to Professor Paul Hammond for his incisive comments on a draft of this essay.

12   Rochester and the theatre in the satires

1 *The Disabled Debauchee*, line 16, and *Against Reason and Mankind*, lines 94–7.

2 [*Song*] 'Leave this gawdy, guilded Stage', line 5.

3 *Letters*, p. 122.

4 Nicolas Boileau-Despréaux, *Épîtres, Art Poétique, Lutrin*, edited by C. H. Boudhors (Paris, 1925), 'L'art Poétique', lines 97–8. 'By all means, I agree, show your heroes as lovers, but don't turn them into simpering shepherds.'

5 Boileau, 'L'art Poétique', lines 111–12. 'Let Aeneas have a proper respect for the gods; reserve for each an appropriate character.'

6 Epilogue to *Love in the Dark*, lines 5–6.

7 See Rochester 1994, p. 371, notes to lines 16, 21, 30–1.

8 Rochester 1994, p. 371, note to line 16; note also Aaron Hill's description of actors' 'languid indolence' as 'fribbling laziness' (*The Prompter*, 7 November 1735).

9 Rochester 1994, p. 386. The references to Dryden are taken from *The Works of John Dryden*, edited by Sir Walter Scott and George Saintsbury, 18 vols (1882–93).

10 Rochester 1999, pp. 449–50 and Rochester 1994, p. 387.

11 Fribble and others are constantly commenting on Mrs Fribble's 'impertinence' (e.g., I.i.355, 370, 527; III.iii.424) which, of course, explains her name. See also Rochester 1994, p. 343, note to line 149.

12 References are to Thomas Shadwell, *Epsom Wells*, edited by D. M. Walmsley (Boston, London etc., 1930).

13 R. L. Root, 'Rochester's Debt to Shadwell in *Epsom Wells*', *Notes and Queries*, 221 (1976), 242–3.

14 *The Works of Thomas Shadwell*, edited by Montague Summers, 5 vols (London, 1927), II, 111.

15 Rochester 1994, p. 341.

16 *Rare Prologues and Epilogues, 1642–1700*, edited by A. N. Wiley (London, 1940), pp. xliii–xliv.

17 *Rare Prologues and Epilogues*, pp. xxvii, xxviii.

18 Jeremy Treglown, 'He knew my style, he swore' in *Spirit of Wit*, p. 84.

19 *The Dramatic Works of John Crowne* (Edinburgh, 1874; re-issued New York, 1967), I, 22, lines 12–18.

20 *The Diary of Samuel Pepys*, edited by Robert Latham and William Matthews, 11 vols (1970–83), 1 August 1668.

21 *The Works of Thomas Otway*, edited by J. C. Ghosh (Oxford, 1932; reprinted 1968), I, 99, lines 15–23.

13   Rochester, *The Man of Mode* and Mrs Barry

1 Samuel Johnson, *The Lives of the English Poets; and a Criticism of their Works*, 3 vols (Dublin, 1779), I, 427.

2 Jocelyn Powell, *Restoration Theatre Production* (London, 1984), p. 14.

3 *Restoration Theatre Production*, pp. 22–3. See also J. L. Styan, *Restoration Comedy in Performance* (Cambridge, 1986), p. 13.

4 See *The London Stage, 1660–1800, Part 1: 1660–1700*, edited by William van Lennep, Emmett L. Avery and Arthur H. Scouten (Carbondale, 1965), I, 325, and *The Prologues and Epilogues of the Restoration, 1660–1700: A Complete Edition*, edited by P. Danchin (Nancy, 1981–), II, iv, 511–18. Lyons notes that 'In their vivid and highly specific detail', the stage instructions, departing from usual practice at the time, 'indicate a closet drama, composed for reading rather than for performance', Rochester 1993, p. 314.

5 First published in 1935 by Vivian de Sola Pinto in *Enthusiast in Wit: A Portrait of John Wilmot Earl of Rochester 1647–1680* (London, 1962). The fragment appears in Rochester's handwriting in Nottingham MS Portland PwV.31. Vieth's opinion in 'hardly regret[ting] that Rochester did not finish his comedy, for it promises nothing better than mediocrity' (David M. Vieth, *Attribution in Restoration Poetry: A Study of Rochester's Poems of 1680* (New Haven and London, 1963), pp. 221–2) does less than full justice to an opening which, in structure and rhythm – its boisterous, sensible exchange between Dainty and the boy and the imminent arrival of Squabb – promises to say much about Dorimant's doppelgänger, Sir Fopling. As Dainty says, 'thus I'le raise my fortune which is all I want for I am an agreable Man and ev'ry Body Like's me' (Rochester 1999, p. 124).

6 Dryden, *All for Love: or, The World Well Lost*, 1678, sig. b4r.

7 See Greene, pp. 69, 75, 126, 143, and see also p. 173.

8 *Letters*, p. 98.

9 John Dennis, *The Critical Works of John Dennis*, edited by Edward Niles Hooker (Baltimore, 1939), 2 vols, II, 277.

10 *The London Stage*, I, clxiii.

11 Sir George Etherege, ed. W. B. Carnochan, *The Man of Mode*, Regents Restoration Drama Series (Whitstable, 1967), II.ii (p. 14). All quotations are from this edition.

12 See Rochester 1993, p. 55; it is not included in Rochester 1999. Vieth is prepared to favour Settle as the author, although he concludes that 'the question of authorship needs to be kept open' (*Attribution*, p. 312), a view supported by Keith Walker in his edition (Rochester 1984, p. 312).

13 See Pinto, *Enthusiast in Wit*, pp. 162–3. Pinto also cites the Hatton Correspondence, I, 133.

14 John Downes, *Roscius Anglicanus*, edited by Judith Milhous and Robert Hume (London, 1976), p. 57.

15 Montague Summers, *The Playhouse of Pepys* (London, 1935), p. 310. Later, Pepys recalls how cross Etherege himself was with the actors, 'that they were out of humour and had not their parts perfect' (*ibid.*).

16 *Ibid.*, p. 311.

17 *Ibid.*, p. 334. Summers names William Oldys as his principal source for this information. Ken Robinson has kindly pointed out that it is not generally known that Rochester was connected with Oldys's father, also William, who witnessed, as a lawyer, a letter of attorney for Rochester on 5 March 1679/80 (Bodleian MS. Montagu d.15 f. 240). For further reference to Oldys, see *Notes and Queries,* 3rd Series I (1862), 1–3, 21–3, 41–4, 61–4, 81–5. Rochester – or his manners, at least – provided Dryden with his inspiration for *Marriage-A-la-Mode*, and Greene claims that Summers's identification of the Earl with Duke Nemours in Nathanael Lee's *The Princess of Cleve* is strengthened by repetition in a speech by Nemours of a passage from Rochester's *Valentinian* (Graham Greene, 'Rochester and Lee', *Times Literary Supplement*, 1935, p. 697). In John Crowne's *City Politiques*, the figures of Artall and Florio, especially the latter, compare with Dorimant.

18 Greene, p. 119.

19 Jocelyn Powell, 'Restoration Theatre' in *Stratford-Upon-Avon Studies 6* (London, 1975), p. 69; Vieth, *Attribution*, pp. 137–8. Rochester was often referred to as Strephon, for example in Aphra Behn's poem *On the Death of the late Earl of Rochester*, 'Mourn, mourn, ye Muses, all your loss deplore, / The Young, the Noble Strephon is no more' (reprinted in *Critical Heritage*, pp. 101–4).

20 *The Critical Works of John Dennis*, II, 248.

21 Pinto, *Enthusiast in Wit*, p. 83. Pinto's source is *The Famous Pathologist or the Noble Mountebank*, a transcription by Thomas Alcock (Nottingham MS 1489).

22 *Letters*, p. 174.

23 Greene, p. 126.

24 According to Curll the two actresses were playing opposite each other in *Alexander the Great, or the Rival Queens* and acting with 'such vivacity' that 'Statira on hearing the King was nigh *begs the Gods to help her for that Moment*; on which *Roxana* [Barry] hastening the designed Blow, struck with such Force, that tho' the Point of the Dagger was blunted, it made way through Mrs. *Boutel's* Stayes, and entered about a Quarter Inch in the Flesh … some affirmed, Mrs. *Barry* was jealous of Mrs. *Boutel* and Lord *Rochester*, which made them suppose she did it with Design to destroy her', Curll, *The History of the English Stage* (1741), pp. 21–2. See also Johannes Prinz, *John Wilmot Earl of Rochester: His Life and Writings* (Leipzig, 1927), p. 53.

25 Hume argues that Rochester could have been at the performance on ?22 October (see Robert D. Hume, 'Elizabeth Barry's First Roles and the Cast of *The Man of Mode*',

Theatre History Studies (1985), 16–19) and see Colley Cibber, *An Apology for the Life of Mr. Colley Cibber, Comedian,* 2nd edition (London, 1740), p. 132.

26 *Letters,* pp. 129, 130.

27 J. H. Wilson, *All the King's Ladies* (Chicago, 1958), p. 111; Downes, *Roscius Anglicanus,* edited by Milhous and Hume, p. 76.

28 Dale Underwood, *Etherege and the Seventeenth-century Comedy of Manners* (New Haven and Oxford, 1957), p. 80.

29 Elizabeth Howe, *The First English Actresses* (Cambridge, 1992), p. 80.

30 Pinto, *Enthusiast in Wit,* p. 105. Pinto cites Cibber, II (1889), p. 302, as his source.

31 Aphra Behn, edited by Jane Spencer, *'The Rover' and Other Plays* (Oxford, 1995). It has often been noticed how similar are the names Willmore and Wilmot; see, for example, Maureen Duffy, *The Passionate Shepherdess* (London, 1977), p. 146.

32 Howe, *The First English Actresses,* p. 199.

33 Cibber, *Apology* (2nd edition), p. 132.

34 Curll, *History,* pp. 14–17.

35 Pinto, *Enthusiast in Wit,* p. 106.

36 Cibber, *Apology* (2nd edition), pp. 132–3.

37 *Revels History of Drama in English, VI, 1750–1880,* edited by Michael Booth *et al.* (London, 1975), p. 106.

38 *Bishop Burnet's History of His Own Time,* quoted in *The Letterbook of Sir George Etherege,* p. 206.

39 Both in Oxford CRO, MS Dil, xviii/f/3. I am grateful to Ken Robinson for drawing my attention to these references.

14   Was Lucina betrayed at Whitehall?

1 The relationship of the two versions to the sources is considered in my 'The Rapes of Lucina', to appear in *Print and the Other Media in Early Modern England,* edited by Michael Bristol and Arthur Marotti (Ohio State University Press; forthcoming).

2 Here I follow the argument of Philip Parsons, 'Restoration Tragedy as Total Theatre', in *Restoration Literature: Critical Approaches,* edited by Harold Love (London, 1972), pp. 27–68.

3 Text and numbering are those of my own Oxford English Texts edition (*see* Rochester 1999).

4 My principal source for information about the Palace buildings is *The Survey of London. Volume xiii: The parish of St. Margaret, Westminster – Part II* (London, 1930), pp. 41–115. References to PRO documents are given from this excellent source. There is a useful map of the palace in *The Diary of Samuel Pepys,* edited by Robert Latham and William Matthews (London, 1970–83), 10, 480–1. Two valuable sources by Simon Thurley, which became available only after the completion of this chapter, are *The Whitehall Palace Plan of 1670* (London, London Topographical Society, 1998) and *The Lost Palace of Whitehall* (London, Royal Institute of British Architects, 1998).

5 'Thence to White-hall and walked long in the galleries till (as they are commanded to all strange persons) one came to tell us, we not being known and being observed to walk there four or five hours (which was not true, unless they count my walking

there in the morning), he was commanded to ask who we were; which being told, he excused his Question and was satisfied. These things speak great fear and jealousys' (*Diary*, II, 239: 27 October 1662).

6 Pepys, 6, 85 and n., 10, 479; *Survey of London*, XII.51.

7 'Up and by coach to White-Hall; and there in the long matted-gallery I find Sir G. Carteret, Sir J. Mennes, and Sir W. Batten; and by and by comes the King to walk there, with three or four with him; and as soon as he saw us, "Oh," says he, "here is the Navy Office," and there walked twenty turns the length of the gallery – talking methought but ordinary talk. By and by came the Duke, and he walked and at last went into the Duke's lodgings. The King stayed so long that we could not discourse with the Duke, and so we parted' (4, 360: 2 November 1663).

8 The wording is that 'a building be erected for the Right honor^ble the Earle of Rochester in his Ma^ts Privy Garden at Whitehall betweene the Lord Keepers Lodgings and ye Lodgings his Lordpp now possesseth ... but soe that a light may be preserved into ye stone Gallery' (*Survey*, XIII.88, citing PRO LC 5/141, p. 95). The occupant of the building would be greeted from its main windows by a splendid view of the astronomical dials which were destroyed by Rochester, while drunk, in 1674. Perhaps his annoyance with them was long nourished.

9 Perhaps best described as 'anti-prelatical' in the sense given to that term in Mark Goldie, 'Danby, the Bishops and the Whigs' in *The Politics of Religion in Restoration England*, edited by Tim Harris, Paul Seaward and Mark Goldie (Oxford, 1990), pp. 75–105. The 'Addition' (lines 174–225) to *Against Reason and Mankind* amply establishes Rochester's adherence to this position.

10   *Emp*. The honesty of this Æcius
                    Who is indeed the Bull-worke of my Empire
                    Is to bee cherish't for the good it brings
                    Not vallu'd as a merit in the owner,
                    As Princes are Slaves bound up by Gratitude
                    And duty has noe claime beyond acknowledgement.

See also Ronald Hutton, *Charles II* (Oxford, 1989), pp. 251–3. Being a military figure, Æcius resembles Monck much more than Clarendon; but Charles never turned against Monck, whereas he destroyed Clarendon.

11 The poem, which also circulated independently without any indication of authorship, is found in both the 'Hartwell' (Yale MS Osborn b 334) and 'Harbin' manuscripts of verse by Rochester acquired from what seems to have been a family source. The Harbin text (that of my Oxford English Texts edition) is also used here; for the Yale text, see Harold Love and Stephen Parks, 'A Reasonable Satyr', *Times Literary Supplement*, 1 August 1997, p. 13.

12 'The Politics of Opera in Late Seventeenth-century London', *Cambridge Opera Journal*, 10 (1998), 35.

13 This is the version preserved by the 1685 quarto. Rochester's original *Lucina's Rape* survives in three manuscript sources.

15   Rochester's 'Death-bed repentance'

1 Longer studies by clergymen include, for example, Josiah Woodward, *Fair Warnings to a Careless World* (London, 1707); William Gilpin, *Moral Contrasts: Or, The Power of*

Religion (Lymington, 1798); George Gilfillan, *Specimens with Memoirs of the less known British Poets* (Edinburgh, 1860).

2 See, for example, *Letters*, p. 36, and Rochester 1993, p. xi.

3 Burnet, p. 13.

4 'Luke XXIII', lines 21–5 in *Jorge Luis Borges: Selected Poems 1923–1967*, edited by Norman Thomas DiGiovanni (London, 1972), p. 155.

5 Burnet, pp. 162–3, 51, 101, 100, 82.

6 Burnet, pp. 36, 72–3, 140–2.

7 Burnet, pp. 6–8, 12; see, for example, *Letters*, pp. 57, 73, 76–7, 228.

8 *Against the Heresies*, Book 4, chapter 20, section 7. For an accessible selection of the writings of St Irenaeus, see Robert M. Grant, *Irenaeus of Lyon* (London and New York), p. 153.

9 See, for example, the elegies on his death written by Aphra Behn and Anne Wharton, *Critical Heritage*, pp. 101–4, 107–8.

10 *The Lives of the English Poets*, 2 vols (Dublin, 1779), I, 426.

11 Burnet, pp. 38–9, 100–1.

12 *1680*, p. 13.

13 Burnet, pp. 120–1.

14 *Ibid.*, pp. 96–7.

15 *Ibid.*, pp. 141–2.

WHereas there is a Libel of leud ſcandalous **Poems**, lately Printed under the name of the **Earl of** *Rocheſter.* Whoever diſcovers the Printer to Mr. *Thomas Cary*, at the B *ew-Boar* in *Cheap-ſide*, or to *W.ll. Richards*, at his houſe in *Bow-ſtreet*, in *Covent-Garden* ſhall have **5 l. Reward.**

☞ Some Paſſages of the Life and Death of the Right Honourable *John* Earl of *Rocheſter*, who died the 26th of *July*, 1680. Writen by his own Direction on his Death-Bed, by *Gilbert Burnet*, D. D.

21 Advertisements from *The London Gazette*, 22–5 November 1680 and 3–7 February 1681

INDEX

Note: page numbers in *italic* refer to illustrations; 'n.' after a page reference indicates a note number on that page.